A HUNTER'S SAGA

A HUNTER'S SAGA

by

W. ROBERT FORAN

Foreword by
CAPTAIN C. R. S. PITMAN,
C.B.E., D.S.O., M.C.

THE ADVENTURERS CLUB

LONDON

THE ADVENTURERS CLUB
178–202 Great Portland Street, London, W.1

First published by Robert Hale Ltd 1961
This edition 1963

This book has been printed in Great Britain by
offset litho at Taylor Garnett Evans & Co. Ltd,
Watford, Herts, and bound by them

No game was ever yet worth a rap,
For a rational man to play,
Into which no accident, no mishap,
Could possibly find a way.

ADAM LINDSAY GORDON: *Weary Wayfarer*

CONTENTS

7

ILLUSTRATIONS

Between pp. 96–97

ACKNOWLEDGEMENTS

The copyright of the above illustrations is held as follows: nos. 8 and 12, A. F. Ayre, Nanyuki; 9, Rembrandt Studio, Nairobi; and 10. Arthur Firmin, Nairobi.

A*   9

ACKNOWLEDGEMENTS

My grateful thanks are expressed to those who so kindly gave me permission to reproduce some of their photographs to supplement those from my personal collection.

Some of the material in this book has previously been published in *The Field, Country Life, Chambers's Journal, Field Sports,* and *The Oxford Annual for Boys* (Britain); *The Adventure Magazine, The Argosy,* and *Boys' World* (U.S.A.); *The Outspan, Personality, The Farmer's Weekly,* and *Veld and Vlei* (South Africa); *The Illustrated Weekly of India,* and *Sinbad* (India); *Australian Outdoors and Fishing* (Sydney, N.S.W.); *New Zealand Outdoor* (Masterton, N.Z.); *East Africa Field and Farm,* and *The Kenya Weekly News* (Kenya Colony); and *The Uganda Argus* (Uganda).

W.R.F.

FOREWORD

MAJOR ROBERT FORAN is one of those persons to whom adventure is the breath of life, and in the course of a varied career he has been soldier, journalist and policeman. The lure of the wild has taken him to India, the Rockies, Mexico and Africa, and he is one of those fortunate old-timers who knew East Africa in its palmy days when wild life in bewildering variety swarmed everywhere. His readiness to share the unrivalled knowledge he has acquired during long years of big-game hunting is evinced by his numerous books, all of them classics. But he is not just a killer, and for long his able pen has been wielded more and more in the defence of what is left of Africa's splendid fauna, to safeguard for posterity a priceless heritage which rapacious man is so wantonly squandering. The tragedy of the seemingly once inexhaustible herds, but now alarmingly diminished, has become the urgent concern of mankind, and Major Foran's persistent warnings of impending doom should not be allowed to go unheeded.

As its title suggests, this is a story of adventure, in many strange lands, with a variety of wild beasts, most of which the author justifiably claims can be described as dangerous. The hazards of hunting such animals are faithfully portrayed; though disaster is so often associated with many of the outstanding incidents described, that one could be forgiven if one concluded that this type of sport is suicidal. It should serve as a valuable warning to those who might be inclined to undertake lightheartedly the pursuit of dangerous species, and Major Foran's experiences and experience provide a useful guide for others—as to what to do and what not to do. Above all he emphasizes and re-emphasizes the urgency for following up and putting out of its misery a wounded creature, not only from the humane aspect, but from the obvious necessity of avoiding leaving at large a would-be menace to human life.

Self-taught, his vast store of knowledge has been acquired in the hard way, by a process of trial and error, and in his own words there is "no better instructor than experience". Fearless and courageous, he is lucky to have emerged unscathed from some of his early encounters, when the impetuosity and rashness of youth could well have cost him his life. As others have done, he continued to learn throughout his hunting career. His hair-breadth escapes have been numerous, and his guardian angel or a kindly Providence has indeed looked after him well. The character of the man can best be judged by his unfailing solicitude for his staff, especially

11

in Africa, who served him long and faithfully, and who were equally solicitous for his welfare. The devotion so frequently shown by the untutored African is a priceless attribute. The success and survival of a big-game hunter is to a great extent dependent on the coolness and skill of his gun-bearer who has to do the right thing at the right moment, no matter what is taking place around him. It is an act of supreme faith, displaying the utmost confidence in the ability of the man with the gun of whom in fact the gun-bearer is an integral part. The untimely end of Major Foran's faithful gun-bearer, so swift and unexpected, brings a poignant note to the closing chapter. In the words of a famous epitaph, he was indeed "A very gallant gentleman".

Chelsea,   C. R. S. PITMAN

London.   (formerly Game Warden,

Uganda Protectorate).

PREFACE

As I have felt, so I have written.

A. W. KINGLAKE: *Eothen*

THIS DOES NOT represent the fruits of just one, or even two, brief big-game hunting experiences. I have selected episodes from the storehouse of memories which seem to me the outstanding incidents drawn from many shooting trips undertaken at different periods of my life in India, America, Mexico and Africa. They were highlights during many years devoted to hunting for game trophies or profit from ivory. My hunting career started in India at the close of 1902, but memories of many fascinating years devoted to this "royal sport" have remained undimmed in the twilight of my life.

In *A Breath of the Wilds* (1958) the shooting part of my hunting big-game was subordinated to recording observations, made in the field, of the habits and characteristics of the animals of Africa. I am now confining myself, for the most part, to those beasts commonly regarded as "dangerous" species. Inevitably, I experienced occasional tense moments when coming to grips with them. I would not have had it otherwise. If the shooting of a worthwhile trophy was rendered a simple process with an absence of danger, the majority of sportsmen would discover little genuine interest in its performance.

Here is related a truthful account of some adventures which provided me with lively and thrilling minutes. But it is not always like that, though there are some writers on the subject of big-game hunting who would like us to believe otherwise. If there are any who think that a hunter's days are packed with thrills and narrow escapes from serious injuries or sudden death, I would like to disabuse them. Such a conception is entirely fallacious. In actual fact, they know far more blank and tame days than fruitful or exciting ones. It is human nature that the latter experiences linger more vividly in one's recollections of the sport.

Like my contemporaries at the turn of this century, I did most of my big-game hunting in the hard way. Luxury conditions were eschewed and no experienced White Hunter served as an expert mentor. It was rare for me to have a companion, other than my native followers. I learned the correct technique by a process of trial and error, which is perhaps the best way.

13

No matter how proficient a hunter may become, he is always liable to commit occasional errors of judgement or behave with an unpardonable excess of recklessness when attacking one of the so-called "dangerous" species. But the blame for what results cannot fairly be attributed to the animal concerned in the episode. Not infrequently I was guilty of stupid or foolhardy actions. That I never suffered a bad mauling or worse was due more to good luck than sound technique. Often the penalties exacted for such unwise behaviour prove immeasurably severe and sometimes end in tragedy for the hunter or one of his companions.

Experience teaches a hunter the desirable policies to pursue and how to avoid foolhardy conduct when engaging any of the dangerous species of the fauna. There can be no better instructor than experience learned at first-hand. If conscious of bad craftsmanship, I was always at considerable pains to avoid any repetition of it. Lessons learned were never forgotten, else I should not be writing this book in my seventy-ninth year.

I hope that those who read these recollections of an extensive hunting career will derive as much pleasure as I have known in recalling them. Also that any who may intend to participate in this grand sport may find something in these pages which will be of service to them—what should be done and what avoided if the reader is desirous of emerging with a whole skin.

W. ROBERT FORAN

Nanyuki,
Kenya Colony,
May, 1960.

PART ONE

Shikar in India

Tyger, Tyger, burning bright
In the forests of the night.

WILLIAM BLAKE: *The Tyger*

I

Tiger! Tiger!

ONLY those who have experienced, in the heart of the Indian jungle, the thrill of hearing the insistent warning of a *shikari*, "*Bagh! Bagh, sahib!*", can appreciate to the full the intense degree of pleasure derived from those three words. It never seems to stale. Anyway, I did not know that reaction at any time during my all too brief hunting career in India.

The lucky sportsman who has killed his first tiger has every justification for self-pride; by the time he has shot a number of these striped cats he will entertain only a poor opinion of other forms of *shikar* in India, Burma, Thailand or Malaya. To my lasting regret opportunities for tiger hunting in those four countries were extremely limited. I write on the subject, therefore, with diffidence, realizing how little I know about it through actual experience.

A mere mention of this entrancing subject to a forest officer, or a man who has lived for many years on the fringe of the jungle in India, Burma, Thailand, Malaya and Sumatra, inevitably evokes stories of incidents, personal or otherwise, which might well daunt the most case-hardened hunters of lions in Africa. The conditions when hunting tiger are vastly different from those met while hunting the lion in Africa; in fact, there can be no basis for an equitable comparison between the quest for those two distinctive trophies.

The man who speaks truthfully of his first tiger hunt will nearly always admit to having experienced a sensation of genuine awe at sight of his quarry. Occasionally, he will also confess to having momentarily known a sickening and paralysing fear. I state candidly that this was my first reaction to a view of a tiger in its wild habitat. During the few subsequent meetings with this beast, when on military service in India, I was always conscious of acute discomfort until the issue had been joined and I became warmed up to the work in hand.

Although one's first impression of the tiger, when viewed in its natural state, may be recollected with a thrill of something approximating to dread, yet the fascination of hunting this animal soon becomes overmastering. One colonel in the Indian Army had a record of more than three hundred tigers to his credit at the time of his death. His name, of course, was famous amongst every sportsman and *shikari* in the East. After retiring from the army on pension he remained in the wild regions of India to continue big-game hunting, and there he died from natural causes.

It is a fallacy to think that the tiger is common in the East. Equally so is it for anyone to believe that a keen sportsman has only to desire a personal interview with the "King of the Jungle" in order to gratify that ambition and secure a number of grand trophies of the species. Exactly the reverse happens to be the case, as practically every sportsman has learned as soon as he had the opportunity of trying to add a tiger to his collection of big-game trophies.

The species is not particularly abundant, and since it normally preys upon other wild animals it follows that, if it becomes too plentiful in any particular region, those creatures upon which it subsists must soon be reduced in numbers almost to the verge of extinction. The tiger would then be compelled to move on elsewhere. Without doubt the ultimate result must be that the species would become extinct in course of time. Nature, however, rules the jungle and all life within it by an iron hand; and she has devised adequate safeguards aimed at obviating such a situation.

It is only when mankind upsets the meticulously planned balance of Nature that trouble is created, which may well have far-reaching results. Man himself is then called upon to pay the severe penalties exacted for his acts of folly. Although the final extinction of the tiger may become a probability in the future, there remain for the moment so many extensive areas rarely inhabited by mankind in India and other Eastern countries that the end of this species can be regarded as very remote.

But for the havoc wrought by mankind amongst those wild creatures upon which the tiger normally preys for sustenance, undoubtedly there would be sufficient food available for a great many more of this species to exist within easy range of human habitations. The increasing scarcity of its normal food supplies has compelled it to seek out haunts further removed from mankind's invasion of the wilderness regions and where game is still abundant solely because it is not subjected to senseless butchery. Thoughtless slaughter of the fauna in any country can only hasten the day when the fauna will have been wiped out of existence altogether.

If nowadays the tiger is less plentiful than Nature designed it to be, this fact is solely attributable to its normal diet having been exterminated, or nearly so, by legitimately licensed hunters or shameless poachers. All creatures must eat or die of starvation, and the tiger is no exception. Deprive it of its natural larder, and the species is forced to fall back upon human beings or the live-stock of villagers. None can blame it for doing that.

Run a finger over a map of the world from Baluchistan to Singapore, which is about an eighth of the globe. Between those two points lie Pakistan, India, Assam, Thailand, Burma and Malaya. There are towering ranges of mountains; broad and stately rivers —the Indus, Ganges, Jumna, Brahmaputra, Irrawaddy and Salween—all flowing to the ocean from the lofty and snow-covered Himalayan gable of the earth; and a vast region of jungles, deserts, dense forests, or tumbling hill-country. This was, and probably still is, one of the world's most rewarding regions for keen big-game hunters. And it can be extended even still further to Cambodia, Sumatra and other parts of Indonesia. Its only serious rivals are East and Central Africa. No tigers will be found in Africa, though in South Africa the name in Afrikaans for the leopard and cheetah is *tijger*. The species is also absent from Ceylon and Borneo.

It is the natural ambition of most sportsmen to test their nerves, skill and marksmanship upon a tiger, but the chance of doing so is not granted to all. I know of a number of ardent hunters in the East who lived there for many years but, having expended much time, money and hard work on the quest for a tiger, never suc-ceeded in shooting a single specimen.

Shortly after my arrival in India towards the close of 1902, after having served through the South African war, I was told the story of one such instance of sheer ill-luck. On the eve of returning to England on pension, a veteran colonel of the Indian Army decided to make one last effort to gratify his lifetime's ambition. Year after year he had failed to bag his tiger and, naturally enough, wanted badly to achieve this before bidding a permanent farewell to India. His *shikari* reported that a handsome tiger had been seen in the neighbourhood; and so, in company with three of his junior officers, he set out to hunt down this beast for a kill. It had been agreed amongst them that the colonel should have first shot if it was a practical possibility.

When the tiger emerged from the dense jungle into full view

of the four sportsmen, the colonel immediately fired at it. Most unfortunately, his bullet inflicted a severe wound but did not kill the beast. It was still capable of inflicting a great deal of damage; it nevertheless decided to get back into cover. In such cases it is usual (and always far wiser) to wait for an hour or two before following up the blood-spoor to deliver a merciful despatch to the wounded animal. Sufficient time is thus allowed for the wound to stiffen, which handicaps the beast's movements; while loss of blood also serves to weaken it. But the colonel, within sight of realizing his frustrated ambition, acted recklessly in his desire to clinch the matter.

After an exhausting and hazardous search, the beaters finally located the badly wounded beast which was then lying up in dense cover. But it retained too much hold on life to afford the colonel, or any of his companions, a fair shot at the beast for an outright kill. The tiger suddenly charged past the other members of the party, bowled over and killed the colonel, and then vanished before anyone had time to shoot. Instead of killing the tiger, the colonel lost his life and the Government saved his pension.

It is only the boldest and more experienced sportsmen who venture on foot into the dense jungle-wastes after a tiger. The more usual method employed is to sit on a *machan*—a roughly constructed platform or *charpoy* (bed)—erected securely in the fork of a tree overlooking either a dead or "live" bait. The tiger is shot when it arrives to enjoy a feast. I was told the story of a sportsman who was weak enough to accede to his wife's urgent pleadings to accompany him to the *machan* so as to watch the killing of a tiger over "live" bait. When the critical moment arrived, the lady doubted the security of her position, so offered up pious and loud appeals to the Almighty to keep the tiger away from them. The prayers were answered. Her voice alarmed the tiger, which bolted at once and before the husband could fire a shot. Ever afterwards his advice to friends was: "If you want a tiger, for God's sake don't take along a prayerful woman to the *machan!*"

A second method—far more exciting, costly and picturesque— is to go after the tiger with the assistance of trained *shikar* elephants and an army of beaters. This is what I would describe as hunting in a crowd, and personally think a crowd when out hunting is an abomination. The sportsmen ride in the howdahs on the backs of elephants. Their giant mounts crash through the high grass, bushes and undergrowth while the search is on for a lurking tiger. When one is driven out into the open by the beaters or advancing line of elephants, the sportsman nearest to it shoots. Should the tiger not be killed by the first bullet fired, there is always likely to ensue plenty of excitement for all concerned with the affair. The wounded tiger will attack ferociously and can cause a considerable amount of damage before being shot dead.

A third device is a "beat". This is probably the most popular of all methods among the majority of sportsmen who have not much in the way of financial resources at their command. It can be a fairly elaborate business, demanding expert knowledge and most careful organization beforehand. The object of a "beat" is to induce the tiger to *walk* quietly and unsuspiciously up to a sportsman's tree.

At various times I tested all three of these methods of hunting the tiger; but I much preferred hunting the species on foot because I considered this was the most exciting way as well as more sporting. Shooting a tiger from the howdah of a trained *shikar* elephant never made any strong appeal to me; doing so at night from a *machan* still less so, though to destroy a man-eater or a persistent cattle-killer the last method is often a necessity. Shooting tiger from a *machan* during a beat was even less favoured, though I had only one experience of it. Those who have read and greatly enjoyed that fascinating book (1) of the late Colonel Jim Corbett, an acknowledged expert and authority without a peer, will appreciate readily enough that many of his notorious man-eating tigers were destroyed when he was hunting them on foot in the hard way.

The Bengal tiger can become such a terrible scourge to the Indian peasants dwelling close to the jungles that it is little less than the task of a Good Samaritan to destroy this type of brute whenever an opportunity is offered. A sportsman who succeeds in putting paid to the account of a man-eater or cattle-killer is a public benefactor. He will be acclaimed by the Indian villagers as a hero after delivering them from a deadly menace. He is moreover, fully entitled to their gratitude, since his task will not be accomplished normally without the grave personal danger that he may be either severely mauled or killed.

Tigers are great travellers. Each individual wanders about over an extensive tract of countryside and it hunts, more or less, to a set plan of operations. A beast may prey upon as many as twenty or more villages, visiting one today and another tomorrow; and not infrequently its "kills" occur at places situated long distances apart. Sometimes a man-eater, however, will make its headquarters near a cluster of villages for a week or so, while exacting a regular toll from either human beings or their livestock. Such a type of menace becomes well-known to the *ryots* (peasants), who generally bestow upon it a special nickname as a

(1) *The Man-Eaters of Kumaon* (India 1911 and London 1946)

mark of distinction. Local people will often encounter that particular tiger on pathways through the jungle, when it is crossing
over cultivated lands, or gliding soundlessly through the shadows
in the forest.

The species has a most uncanny ability to move, even in the
thickest type of cover, with a complete absence of noise. It possesses a keen sense of sight and hearing, but it is debatable if it uses
its powers of scent to any noticeable extent. I believe it rarely
depends upon smell to locate its prey or avoid danger. Tigers
have a musk-like odour, which is easily discerned from a distance
by other animals. When a tiger is in an area, therefore, the game
moves out and so the predatory beast does not remain in that
locality for more than a few days at most.

Occasionally, tigers develop into confirmed and persistent man-
eaters. When this happens, of course, intense terror overwhelms
the simple-minded peasants. They become so stricken that
nothing is capable of inducing them to leave their villages even to
work in the fields until the brute has been destroyed. And the
death of this beast may well be drawn out. Until it is finally
killed, many victims will have been taken and their bodies
devoured. It is surprising how little effort is made by the villagers
to deal suitably with this dreadful menace.

Man-eating tigers are not uncommon in India, but less so in
Malaya. They do not exist as plentifully as similar depraved
lions in Africa, though the latter appear to enjoy a larger measure
of publicity than is accorded to the tiger in the East. In the
official statistics of one year in India it was recorded that tigers
had been responsible for the loss of 809 human beings; while the
total mortality caused by wild beasts (crocodiles excluded, but
poisonous snakes included) amounted to 18,471 people of both
sexes and all ages. Those officially sponsored statistics are
staggering to contemplate. During that same year under review
it was stated that at least 48,400 livestock had fallen as victims to
marauding beasts.

Nevertheless, the destruction of life is not all one-sided. In that
identical year no less than 27,000 "dangerous" beasts had been
destroyed; and, in addition, 116,500 poisonous or non-poisonous
snakes killed. How many more could have been added to either
side of the ledger in this eternal war waged in the jungles is anyone's guess. Many instances, no doubt, were not brought to
official notice and thus escaped inclusion in the statistics.

Could such a state of affairs exist elsewhere? I am inclined to
doubt it. If similar official records were compiled in, for example,
East or Central Africa covering a period of twelve months, I think
they might disclose much smaller totals on both sides of the ledger.

The indifference of the peasants in India to such a grave situation is almost incredible. It is not possible to fathom their attitude to what may be happening in their midst almost daily and which must be in the nature of a dreadful nightmare. Life of any kind, human or animal, seems to be reckoned as of little account in their conception of a normal state of existence. Perhaps this can be attributed to the fact that they have been called upon for untold ages to pay heavily in losses of people and livestock—both being the victims of wild beasts. In consequence of long familiarity they have become as supinely passive to such a grievous menace as their own meek cattle. A forest officer assured me cynically that the life of an average Indian peasant was so miserable in any event that he made no real effort, or only a very minor one, to preserve it. Such a view may seem far-fetched, but it does approximate to the truth of the matter.

A man-eating tiger (like a man-eating lion) goes about its ghastly work in a devastating silence. To my way of thinking there can be nothing that so chills the blood with horror than a mental picture of such a sinister brute stealthily entering a forest village in India during the night, pausing momentarily at each miserable habitation, and moving onwards as silently as a cloud's shadow passing over the face of the moon. It is in quest of an easy means of entrance to a hut to claim a human victim upon which to gorge. The occupants of every habitation lie awake, staring blankly and fearfully at a frail doorway, utterly benumbed and paralysed with terror, and listening intently for the slightest hint of the brute's attack upon their humble home. A ghastly period of horrible expectancy of a cruel ending to their lives must be experienced, while for them it is a night of crushing terror. Mentally, they review every single detail of their crude and ineffectual defences, while regretting, now that it is far too late, the weak spots not strengthened because of sheer sloth.

The sharp crackling of a twig trodden upon startles a man. He strains his eyes through the darkness, clutches a knife (the sole weapon he possesses), listens intently, and his body trembles with an acute state of apprehension. Then he hears the soft tread of the marauding tiger pause at the doorway of his own abode. A moment later, the ferocious brute launches its heavy body at the flimsy door and crashes inwards. As if born out of the stillness of the night, the terror-stricken man perceives the dim shape of the man-eater standing inside the hut and silhouetted against the moonlight. He knows full well that this is no apparition created by a terrified mind, but is genuine and a deadly menace.

Before he has time to yell for help, the tiger has felled him with a hefty blow from a fore-paw and seized his body in its powerful jaws. The man-eater bounds away into the depths of the encompassing jungle with its human prey, carrying the victim by the neck much as a cat with a mouse. At dawn, the other badly frightened villagers crowd around the empty hut. The writing is plain upon the earth for all to read. There arises a shrill wail of mourning throughout the small cluster of crude huts—mourning for a neighbour whom they will never see again.

Such a fearsome incident is of almost daily occurrence in one or another portion of India where the tiger still roams at large. Entire tracts of countryside and clusters of villages may well become depopulated through the depredations of the striped "King of the Jungle", so that the advent upon the scene of a sportsman actuated with a desire to destroy the brute will, naturally enough, always be welcomed joyfully by the *ryots*. They hail him as a public benefactor. To them he spells deliverance from a fearful scourge, relief from hourly and daily terrors, and a defender of their right to live. The combined rôle of big-game hunter and "Good Samaritan" is not at all unpleasing.

The local population, almost invariably, will keep sportsmen well posted about the movements of any tigers in their district. They are also eager to serve as beaters on a hunt, but for a financial consideration. You may not even attempt to preserve their miserable lives without being expected to pay handsomely for this privilege! They believe firmly that a labourer is worthy of his hire.

But it can be next to impossible for a sportsman to prove successful in destroying a man-eating tiger unless assisted by a corps of beaters, so he pays readily enough for their services. Also, if employing a *machan*, it is essential to purchase from the sorely afflicted villagers, either a bullock or domesticated buffalo for use as a live bait over which to sit for a killing.

2

Tiger Hunting de luxe

MY FIRST tiger hunt was staged beside the Nerbudda river, near Jubbalpur in the northern area of the Central Province of India. It happened nearly 58 years ago. Yet my recollections of that remarkable experience still remain vividly green in every detail. Indeed, the occasion provided a memorable incident in a somewhat adventurous career.

Shortly after arrival from South Africa towards the close of 1902 I was attached for a year to a British battalion of infantry while learning the language to qualify for transfer to the Bengal Lancers of the Indian Army. That this ambition came to nothing is neither here nor there. Suffice is it to say that I went off as a Special Service Officer to Somaliland for the campaign then in progress against the Mad Mullah after spending only eight months in India.

A brother officer informed me gleefully that he had just been invited to participate in tiger hunting, the *shikar* having been arranged by the wealthy Maharaja of a State. It was to be performed in a most luxurious manner, the shooting being done from howdahs on trained riding elephants. That type of tiger hunting is, more or less, the prerogative of princes, viceroys and other V.I.Ps. Quite naturally, he was feeling extremely flattered at receiving this unexpected invitation; and, indeed, a signal honour had been conferred upon him.

I experienced an acute envy of his good fortune, so I pleaded with him to try and get me included in the invitation. Somehow he managed to wangle this. Through his kindness and the generosity of this princely host, the path was rendered smooth for me to gratify a consuming ambition—to shoot a tiger. I took with me a Holland and Holland .450/.500 rifle, a .350 Rigby Mauser, and a 12-bore shotgun by Daniel Fraser of Edinburgh. Up to then I had only a very limited experience of shooting big-game in Southern Africa, because opportunities for indulging in the sport were extremely scarce during the South African war.

On our arrival at the site of the hunting camp, near Jubbalpur, we found everything fully prepared, the other guns assembled, and all in readiness to begin hunting. The camp was run on a most costly and luxurious style. We were given a cordial welcome. Our host and fellow-guests made up a very happy party and not a discordant note was struck. We were the tyros, for all other members of the *shikar* had enjoyed much experience of hunting tigers and some of them were renowned all over India. Our host, the Maharaja, had a reputation for being a first-class shot and a very skilled sportsman; and he had a hundred or more tigers to his credit, so I was told by a distinguished member of the party. It was our hope that we should not disgrace ourselves by a poor performance when in such august company.

The elephants were ridden up to us by their mahouts early on the first morning, commanded to kneel, ladders placed against the howdahs, and we climbed up to take our places in the strong wicker-basket contraptions. As soon as all the sportsmen were aboard, the signal was given to move off in the direction of the

selected hunting terrain. Each elephant unhinged itself into altitudes, the movement conveying to my mind a sensation of being
on the summit of a hillock in the throes of a mild earthquake.
Then off we ambled in single file towards the bank of the
Nerbudda river.

That particular area had for long enjoyed a notable reputation
for furnishing good bags of tiger. The flow of the years since then
may well have shattered that renown. A favourite habitat of the
species is likely to be shot out quickly by sportsmen, for it is
their Mecca until all tigers therein are either killed or have been
forced to withdraw to pastures new. I have been told that nowadays a shooting block of ten square miles with only one known
tiger in it is not to be despised.

It occurred to me as we advanced that a tiger would not have
much chance against this formidable party, all armed with heavy
cordite rifles. The first experience of this method of hunting tigers,
or any other dangerous species, did not make a strong appeal to
me. Later, that reaction was confirmed. The elephants ridden
were expertly trained for the work. They were supposed to stand
up boldly to a charging tiger and not to flinch when a heavy rifle
was discharged from their backs. I say "supposed" advisedly,
because I think it is improbable that many elephants are wholly
devoid of fear where the tiger is concerned.

In addition to the riding elephants, there were also a largish
number of trained *shikar* elephants, ridden by their regular
mahouts, which would be employed in beating the jungle for
tigers and then to drive them up to our rifles. We resembled an
elephant-mounted army on the line of march. So far, at any rate,
it all looked extremely simple and struck me as lacking in real
danger; and, for that reason, the method seemed none too sporting, though many true sportsmen have employed it when out after
tiger in India.

After a brief consultation, the head *shikari* turned off into a
section of the jungle where a kill had been contrived by a tiger on
the previous night—a domesticated buffalo sacrificed when stray-
ing too far from the others while out grazing. Normally, the killer
would hang about the spot after its first meal to drive off jackals,
vultures and other carrion-feeders which might attempt to pilfer
its larder. As the tiger is nocturnal in habit, it generally sleeps
during the daytime in some shady and secluded spot near the
banquet to be enjoyed again at night. Naturally and instinctively,
the tiger shuns all dens.

We hoped to kill this particular beast. It had been reported as
an exceptionally large and handsome male about 10 feet in length,
which can be considered good in India, for even a 9-foot one is

worth getting. If the information was correct, then the beast might well prove a worthy prize.

This outing being my first tiger shoot, the excitement I experienced was intense. The entire proceedings were novel to me and to the brother officer who shared the howdah with me. Very few details of what was afoot could have escaped our keen observation.

Approaching closer to the site of the kill, the head *shikari* directed our attention to a flock of scraggy-necked vultures perched lethargically upon nearby trees. The signs were auspicious, indicating that the tiger was lurking near at hand and exercising its undoubted rights over the carcase of the buffalo it had killed. Some of the elephants were now twitching their ears, swaying trunks from side to side, and treading the ground uneasily. Evidently, they had got a whiff of the tiger's musk-like odour on the air-currents.

The corps of beaters and *shikar* elephants now made a detour of about half a mile to get in rear of the tiger, while all the sportsmen took up their allotted positions on the fringe of an open glade at the edge of a belt of thick jungle. We had been instructed to remain immobile there until the tiger was driven up to our rifles and had actually broken cover.

As elephants walk at the approximate rate of six miles an hour, it was not too long before the din created by the beating of drums and loud shouts of the beaters reverberated through the jungle in front of us. The terrific noise scared monkeys, peacocks, smaller birds, and other inhabitants of the jungle-lands into rapid flight. Sambur, swamp deer, barking deer, and other species of game broke past us singly, in pairs, or in threes. A diminutive mouse deer, not more than 12 inches high at shoulder, plunged wildly between the legs of the elephant upon which my friend and I were perched. That small creature started a positive riot.

With a loud snort of fear, our elephant agilely swung around and tried to bolt back to the camp. Had it not been for the mahout's vigorously applied *ankus* (steel-goad) treatment, we might have been carried off at speed from the scene and possibly brained against a large bough of a tree. This display of acute nervousness on the part of a trained riding elephant rather rocked my confidence in its courage in the face of a tiger's merciless attack. As a matter of fact, however, I had grossly misjudged our big mount.

The din created by the beaters momentarily became louder and louder. We could distinctly hear, too, the peculiar drumming sound made by the elephants to signal that a dangerous beast was close at hand. This brought us all erect in our howdahs, rifles held ready for instant action, and eyes eagerly searching the edge of the jungle for a glimpse of the tiger now resolutely being driven in our direction. Just at that moment a deer in panic-stricken flight sped past us. It was moving too swiftly and we were too intent on looking for the tiger to see what kind it was. Our *shikari* pointed to the left-front, whispering tensely the magic words: "*Bagh! Bagh, sahib!*"

And then I spotted the beast. This was the first tiger I had seen outside a cage. Indeed, a red-letter day for me! I have never forgotten that moment in spite of the passage of more than half a century. Before us was a large tiger, jaws almost touching the ground as it sneaked, half-crouching and half-crawling on its white belly, through the vegetation on the fringe of the jungle. It halted for an instant in suspense, apparently indecisive as to whether to make a bolt to safety from the advancing half-circle of noisy beaters in rear or attack us boldly.

There will nearly always come a moment when hunting big-game can become gravely hazardous. With a shattering roar—a kind of coughing vibration of great power—a tiger will generally advance in a series of mighty bounds straight at its foe. The speed of the attack is astounding. When at springing distance it hurls its heavy body through the air upon the nearest elephant. That is the moment when a sportsman's steady nerves and accuracy in aiming can severely be tested. There is no margin for error. Unless the tiger is then killed outright, it will land on the head or trunk of the elephant, biting with its fangs and clawing with the talons of all four feet. Such a savage and lightning attack is devastating in its effect.

Other members of the party had warned us just what to expect and what to do. The sights of my rifle came on the tiger, aiming downwards at the spine between the withers; and that is the most telling spot when looking down at a beast. As I aimed, the brute's eyes were blazing at me like green emeralds, its cruel fangs bared and glittering like polished ivory. Just as I was about to squeeze the trigger of the right barrel, our elephant suddenly went berserk and charged all out at the oncoming tiger while emitting a shrill scream of mingled hate and anger. This happened so unexpectedly that I was caught napping, shaken out of the howdah before I could clutch at the side of the basket, and landed with considerable force on my back in a clump of thick bushes. Luckily, the latter broke my fall. I suffered no worse than shock and fright at my predicament.

As I landed on my back both barrels of the .450/.500 rifle were discharged simultaneously. This may have been caused by the violence of my fall or because a finger was on the trigger when I was thrown out unceremoniously from the howdah. Where the bullets sped I know not, but they caused no casualties. The terrific kick of the double discharge shook me severely and badly bruised the right shoulder, as could only be expected. It required a few moments to collect my wits.

Then I heard my friend's rifle speak sharply, but he only succeeded in wounding the tiger. There was now plenty of excitement all around. The noise of his shot, the trumpeting of elephants, the tiger's coughing roars, and the shouting and drumming of our beaters combined to create a cacophony of nerve-shattering sounds which almost deafened me. It achieved nothing in soothing my badly rocked nervous system but, if anything, served to accentuate the acute sense of discomfiture being experienced.

Hastily scrambling erect, I stood spellbound to watch the fearsome spectacle being enacted. It benumbed me into inactivity. The tiger was undaunted and met the elephant's onslaught without flinching. With a lithe spring upwards it landed upon the elephant's head to sink claws and fangs deep into the neck and trunk; and I saw the mahout beating vigorously at the tiger with his *ankus*, while the elephant valiantly strove to throw off its vicious assailant.

As I watched this amazing animal fight, it was impossible not to experience an immense measure of relief at having been spilled incontinently out of the howdah. My friend's position there looked unenviable. Although not in the slightest degree relishing my present situation on ground-level in the wings of the stage, yet it did seem to me safer than being so unpleasantly close as in the howdah to an enraged, wounded tiger bent on mischief.

Recovering control of my wits, I carefully tested the mechanism of the rifle and found it still in perfect working order. Hastily reloading, I glanced rapidly around. The other sportsmen's elephants were now manœuvring about the combatants, seeking an opening to fire an effective shot at the tiger. I also stood ready to shoot at the first favourable opportunity and, in the meantime, watched the Homeric battle being waged with the keenest possible interest.

It was utterly impracticable for any rifle to come into action, for the tiger and elephant were too mixed up for risking a shot. My friend in the howdah was equally powerless to intervene. A bullet from his rifle would probably have hit the mahout or elephant instead of the tiger. Wisely, he refrained from shooting.

Resenting the hefty blows from the mahout's *ankus,* the tiger sank its wicked claws into the man's thigh and endeavoured to jerk him down bodily from his seat astride the neck of the elephant. This spurred me into action. Moving quickly to one side, I risked a chancy shot and emptied the right barrel into the tiger's shoulder from a stance almost broadside on to the brute. I fired well up behind the shoulder but raised the aiming point appreciably because firing upwards. With a mighty roar of pain the tiger fell backwards to the ground. Thereupon the greatly angered elephant, bleeding profusely from a number of terrible gashes, was upon it instantly. The injured tiger was not granted a moment to recover. The elephant tusked and trampled the striped cat into a pulp before it was possible for the mahout to drive the beast off its hated foe.

I have always thought the most fascinating part of big-game hunting is that so often the totally unexpected seems to happen. In this particular incident I had been quite unprepared to see a large *shikar* elephant attempt to bolt from a harmless and diminutive mouse deer, and then charge boldly at an attacking tiger. Yet both of those things had occurred. As a matter of fact, I am almost positive that the elephant had started to charge the tiger before my companion in the howdah wounded the latter beast.

It is highly improbable that I shall ever forget that first experience with a tiger in its natural environment.

The mahout and elephant richly deserved the fullest credit for their share in that day's events; and later, when back at camp, the Maharaja suitably rewarded man and beast on a generous scale. The mahout received a handsome cash bonus, while his mount was given a bountiful ration of its favourite food.

Now I had seen my first tiger in the wild state and managed to deliver the killing shot at it. But the trophy was not mine. My friend had drawn first blood and, by the rules of the sport, the tiger was his trophy. In any case, I wasted no vain regrets over losing it. The pelt had been rendered valueless through the enraged attack by the elephant.

That was tough luck on my friend. It so happened that this was the first tiger he had ever seen or shot at. At least, he could now claim to have bagged a tiger in the wild heart of the Indian jungle, and that is more than many other sportsmen can say truthfully.

I still had to accomplish the feat.

3

The Next Tiger Hunt

OF AN entirely different character was my next attempt to bag a tiger. It was done from a *machan,* which had been expertly prepared by my Indian *shikari* in a suitable tree over a live bait. The latter was a village buffalo of ancient vintage, which had been bought for the purpose from a *ryot* in a nearby cluster of miserable huts and went unprotestingly to the sacrificial altar. My companion on this occasion was a captain in the Indian Cavalry (Central India Horse) and a very fine sportsman who already had killed several tigers.

Many will wholeheartedly disagree with my opinion, that big-game hunting in India is not generally so dangerous as in Africa. Perhaps I am unduly biased because the majority of my hunting with a rifle or camera was performed in the erstwhile "Dark Continent". Naturally, my knowledge of big-game hunting in Africa far exceeds that in India or the Far East. Every sportsman is fully entitled, of course, to voice his own individual opinion; but always provided, that he is able to speak with knowledge of the hunting conditions in both lands. It is most unwise to appear dogmatic. So very often the attendant circumstances are widely different. No man could possibly know *all* the answers.

I would say that in India no genuine hardships have to be endured when hunting the tiger, unless doing so on foot as in the case of the lion or elephant in Africa. Most of the shooting is done in comparative comfort, if not in what almost amounts to the height of luxury. You are either carried to your quarry in a howdah on the back of a *shikar* elephant in order to have the tiger driven up to the muzzle of your rifle, or you sit and wait on a *machan* at night over a "live" or dead bait until the tiger arrives for a gorge.

On the other hand, certainly in olden times the hunter in Africa spoored and faced his dangerous beasts on foot. He had to work hard to come to terms with the trophy sought, and often was forced to accept grave risks of suffering a mauling or even worse. Frequently, too, he only got a shot at some coveted specimen after days of strenuous spooring and hunting his quarry. In much earlier years in Africa one normally hunted solo and only accompanied by a few African followers. In modern times, however, the sportsman is generally shepherded by a thoroughly expert and reliable White Hunter, whose profession calls upon him to make certain that his client comes back with a whole skin.

In India, only too often, a crowd turns out. I infinitely prefer to shoot on my lonesome, and have generally contrived it that way. It was indeed rare for me to accept a companion on a shooting *safari* in Africa. Apart from disliking a crowd when hunting, I have always maintained that by shooting solo the risks of a tragic ending are reduced and another hunter is not unwittingly placed in danger by a personal lapse in hunting technique; equally so, you are not liable to become involved in any gross mistakes committed by others hunting with you.

The professional White Hunter is in duty bound to cover up all errors committed by his client (or clients); and not a few of these experts have suffered severe injuries or lost their lives when covering up stupid mistakes perpetrated by a novice in their charge. The White Hunter is entitled to demand a high fee for taking out a shooting *safari*, and may even earn it at the cost of his life. It is tragic enough to die because of your own errors in hunting, but far worse if that fate results from foolish conduct or bad marksmanship on the part of a sportsman in your company.

My second tiger hunt was contrived because the headman of a distant village had informed my friend in the Central India Horse that a large tiger was persistently killing the cattle of his village. It had become almost a nightly marauding. The headman begged my friend to come to his village and deliver them from this costly menace to their livestock. The invitation was accepted at once. He kindly asked me to accompany him.

Our applications for the necessary period of leave were granted by our respective Commanding Officers. Both Colonels were fine sportsmen, each had shot many tigers, and they always encouraged their junior officers to become efficient big-game hunters. Having completed the essential preparations, we made our way to the village concerned.

In order to entice our quarry to the near vicinity of our respective *machans*, we bought two buffalo at the village and had them tethered securely under each tree as live bait. This may sound an abominably cruel business. But a few aged buffalo sacrificed to a tiger as a means of saving the lives of the many, under all the circumstances, can be justified. The few must die so that the many may live. They were old beasts, long past their prime and utility in the service of mankind, and the owners' compensation fully satisfied them for their loss. If the tiger appeared upon the scene that night, the deaths of these animals would be quick and almost painless.

Candidly, I have never liked the idea of using live bait to lure even a dangerous beast to its ultimate destruction. I only resorted to it when no dead bait was available, or in the case of confirmed man-killers and cattle-raiders which normally can only be tackled in the night-time. As a device to secure trophies, it strikes me as an unsporting method. I know it has sometimes been done by sportsmen in Africa to get lion trophies; but a zebra or antelope can be shot to provide dead bait and, if the carcase is dragged well over the area before being pegged down, this is just as effective in producing results. There is no necessity to secure a live bullock, donkey or goat to attract a lion to within easy range of your "blind".

The headman assured us that this tiger was an old and case-hardened offender, a most cunning type of brute, and well-known to all the inhabitants of the district. Although many strenuous efforts had been made to destroy so persistent a marauder, all of them had failed signally in achieving this purpose. The villagers conveyed an impression to us that they regarded this tiger as endowed with supernatural powers and, therefore, it was immune to being killed by any human agency. They are simple-minded folk with strong beliefs in the supernatural. Notwithstanding, we were keen to test our luck in contriving the destruction of this village scourge, earnestly trusting that Dame Fortune would smile kindly upon us. Although the cavalry officer had shot a number of tigers, I still had to get my first one.

Our places on the respective *machans* were occupied at a little over an hour before sunset. I made myself as comfortable as the circumstances permitted and arranged everything handy which might be required during the night's vigil, so disposed that it could be possible to pick them up without any noise or only a slight show of movement. As time dragged on, I found it was atrociously unpleasant to sit in a cramped position as immobile as a graven image upon an unsteady and smallish platform in a tree which creaked and swayed in the night-wind. My slightest movement caused the *machan* to creak noisily, and the sound must inevitably alarm the tiger if it was lurking anywhere in the vicinity.

I know of far more pleasurable occupations than sitting all night on a *machan* for a chance to put paid to the account of a malignant destroyer. It is no sinecure to sit in a cramped position hour after hour, perfectly motionless, smoking prohibited, and with eyes and ears straining for a shot at a dark smudge that will be moving stealthily towards the bait through the black pall of darkness. Every faculty must be alerted. No vestige of a false move is permissible, or the night's vigil becomes just so much wasted effort.

Fireflies waved their minute lamps in my face. Every conceivable kind of insect pest buzzed around my head or bit savagely at each atom of exposed flesh. For full measure a few venturesome lizards playfully dropped down my neck and wriggled slimily on chest or back. And I abominate all soft and clammy creatures! During that long night's vigil I suffered the tortures of the damned, and a number of times regretted having embarked upon it. The tiger's life did not seem worth all these ghastly experiences. On the morrow, of course, I viewed the affair from an entirely different perspective and the night's discomforts struck me as having been more amusing than repulsive.

To be perched on a *machan* firmly fixed in a tree over bait for a tiger, panther, lion, leopard or other beast is, generally speaking, either an exciting or intensely boring, tedious and uncomfortable experience. Which it happens to be, I think, depends chiefly upon the prevailing temperature, the prevalence or otherwise of viciously biting insects, or one's particular mood at the time. But I have no recollection of ever finding any particle of pleasure in it, only atrocious discomforts always to be endured stoically. Yet some sportsmen have assured me emphatically that they revelled in every minute of such a night's vigil and, moreover, had no cause for complaint about being cramped or uncomfortable. What may be one man's fancy is not necessarily another's pet pigeon.

I found the hours of waiting dragged by with a maddening sluggishness. Nearing dawn, I suddenly heard the buffalo tethered beneath my tree tugging at the rope in order to gain its freedom. Straining my eyes for a glimpse of the expected visitor, I made out dimly a largish black shape moving stealthily and noiselessly across a small open space directly in front of my perch. A dull thud followed shortly afterwards. Immediately there sounded a terrified bellow from the buffalo, and then the noise of a violent but mercifully brief struggle. A few moments later all was again quiet. For a time I waited impatiently for the light to strengthen so that it would become possible to take good aim at the target; and during this interval my ears were assailed by the sloppy and tearing noises always made by a member of the carnivora when busy gorging upon an unbled carcase.

It was still scarcely light enough to sight the rifle for a killing shot. But I aimed with the aid of luminous sights at a dark mass below the *machan*, shooting full into the centre of it with the right barrel of the .450/.500 Holland and Holland. I distinctly heard the thud of the heavy bullet striking the target. A savage growl and a number of angry snarls echoed from the spot, assuring me that the killer of the live bait had been hit good and hearty.

The report of my shot had scarcely ebbed when I heard two more from the right, which indicated that something of importance was occurring near my companion's *machan*. With the stupidity and foolhardiness of a young novice, I jumped down from the *machan* and landed on all fours upon the ground. Quickly rising, I went forward slowly and cautiously to where had been the black object at which I had fired. My rifle kept the spot covered in case the tiger had only been wounded and now would charge home at me.

It was an asinine thing to have done. After that night's adventure, I learned far more sense and never again was guilty of repeating such folly. My conduct shrieked aloud for disaster. For any hunter to approach too close to a wounded beast of the dangerous species must be rated as an act of supreme folly. To his sudden dismay he discovers that there remains a considerable kick in the animal erroneously credited with being almost dead—if not already so. Before he has either time to shoot or sidestep the danger, the beast puts forth its last ounce of strength to be avenged by mauling or killing the aggressor. Thus are the lives of rash sportsmen forfeited. One cannot blame the animal for what transpires, as the fault must rest squarely upon the shoulders of the man.

Wisdom in the hunting of big-game dictates that not a single thing should be taken for granted, especially when following up an animal which has been wounded and in order to deliver a merciful despatch. Not even when one's quarry happens to be a harmless member of the antelope or gazelle species can this safely be done. For example, a wounded and "bayed" sable, roan, oryx or gemsbok antelope of Africa has often been known to wound a hunter when approached too close in a foolhardy manner. Many a good hunting dog, too, has lost its life through being too venturesome.

As I neared the carcase of the buffalo bait, I heard my companion shout loudly: "I've hit the blighter, old chap!" I yelled back what I believed to be the truth: "And so have I!"

I fired another bullet into the black mass on the ground ahead of me, but saw no signs of any movement. In order to make quite positive that the tiger was dead, I gathered and ignited a bunch of dry grass to illuminate the spot; and then, to my amazement, saw that a large male panther had been killed instead of the tiger. Once again the totally unexpected had happened!

While examining the trophy with the aid of this makeshift torch, I heard two more shots from my companion; and then, in rapid succession, six revolver shots. I realized instantly that he must be in some kind of serious trouble. I ran at best speed in his direction, reloading my rifle while stumbling over the rough ground in the bad light of a dawning.

When I gained his side he told me breathlessly that, just as my first shot was fired, the tiger had distinctly been seen by him and he shot at it. The beast went down to the bullet. But it came erect again almost instantly, so he let it have the second barrel. As the tiger now remained motionless on the ground he felt sure of having killed it, so climbed down from the *machan* to inspect the trophy. When about twenty yards away, the tiger suddenly rose and charged straight at him. He fired both barrels into it. The beast rolled over with a ferocious growl of mingled pain and anger, but

B

promptly came erect once more and resumed the charge. He emptied the chamber of his Webley revolver into it. One lucky bullet hit the tiger in the centre of the neck between head and shoulders, which killed it instantly. This shot will either kill or stop a charging tiger, but there is allowed no margin for any error.

The trophy was skinned after sunrise. Nine bullets were extracted from its body, so only one of my companion's shots had failed to register on the target. That tiger had died hard. It is often astounding how much lead this species can take before finally being killed.

On our triumphant return to the village with the two fine trophies of a tiger and panther, the headman staggered us by insisting that the wrong tiger had been shot. Only that night, he stated emphatically, the persistent marauder had taken a bullock from the village. Not only had it been seen but also recognized by a night-watchman when the beast was killing the bullock.

Although tired after the all-night affair, yet we accompanied a guide to where the "kill" of this tiger had been dragged into cover. I could know no peace of mind until having killed my first tiger, while every rebuff merely served to render me the more determined to gratify this ambition. My companion was equally keen to complete the task which we had undertaken and see the final drop of the curtain.

We concealed ourselves and waited on the bank of a shallow nala (dry watercourse), where the partially consumed carcase of the bullock had been parked by the tiger. This was, of course, a sheer waste of time. We learned that later. Until dusk, when we finally abandoned our futile wait, the cattle-raiding tiger had not put in an appearance at the kill to feed again upon it. This was a bitter disappointment. Both badly needed a good night's sleep, so we felt disinclined to sit up for this elusive beast on two nights in succession. It was mutually agreed to resume operations next day.

On the following morning, soon after daybreak, we left camp to ascertain if the tiger had returned to its kill during the night. Indubitably, it had. The remains of the bullock had been dragged for some distance from the spot where it had been located on the previous morning. Now the tiger had cached its larder in a dense and thorny patch of jungle. This was unsuitable from our point of view, so some of the villagers were co-opted to serve as scene-shifters; and, under our supervision, the stage was reset to conform with what we considered was the most effective arrangement of the properties. We had two machans constructed in nearby trees to overlook the bullock's remains, which the ryots dragged out into the open from a canopy of junglegrowth. The stage now set as it ought to be, we returned to camp for lunch. It was intended to occupy the *machans* a full hour before sunset and have all in readiness for a return visit from the tiger.

Not long before the waning light restricted visibility I perceived the tiger advancing slowly and noiselessly through the thicket where the remains of its kill had originally rested. It appeared to be puzzled at not finding its meal where this should be. The tiger glanced back over a shoulder once, and then came straight on to the kill without any show of hesitation. I was afraid that it might see me on the *machan* and bolt off in alarm, should I raise myself or the rifle to shoot before its head was hidden under the tree. Later, I was told that a tiger rarely is known to glance upwards and normally keeps its eyes on the ground; so I need not have bothered. It was only by the exercise of the utmost self-control that I remained patient before gradually raising myself to aim and shoot. The beast presented me with a fairly good target. I fired well up behind the shoulder but raising somewhat the aiming point as the tiger was below me. The bullet struck true with a heavy thud.

With obvious pain and difficulty, it dragged itself into cover. It was moving slowly. I let it have the second barrel, but missed badly through over-excitement and because of too hasty shooting. After a longish wait, we both climbed down from our trees. I felt almost certain that the first bullet had wounded the beast severely and it could not have retreated for any great distance. We discussed the problem with which we were confronted; finally, it was decided that the best plan was to wait longer before attempting to follow up the blood-spoor. It was wiser to allow sufficient time for the wound to stiffen and thus reduce the tiger's capacity for doing damage.

Now it was almost dark. Neither of us, though both Irish, was quite so mad as to try spooring a wounded tiger at night through thickish jungle. Tomorrow morning, good enough; but tonight most decidedly we would *not* go after the beast. We walked back to camp, contacted the village headman and told him our news, and also arranged for a body of beaters to be ready at dawn to assist us in giving the *coup de grâce* to the wounded tiger. A merciful despatch must be given, and with the least possible delay but with due regard to personal security. That rule must be honoured.

As soon as it was sufficiently light we returned to the spot where the tiger had been wounded. The blood-spoor was followed up through terribly "thick stuff", in which there existed a constant and real danger. Naturally, our advance was slow and cautious. Every possible precaution had to be taken in order to obviate being caught napping.

Presently I heard the tiger groaning somewhere ahead of our line of advance, though we could see nothing of it. The blood-spoor now led us into a densely jungled and narow *nala*, where it was far from easy to spot the tiger. The consistent blood drops near the pug of a front paw indicated that the tiger had suffered a wound in the shoulder; while an occasional frothy blood spoor told us that the bullet must have got the lungs. It should not prove, therefore, too difficult to end its sufferings once the beast had been located.

I was moving onward slightly ahead of my companion, the *shikaris* and beaters. It was my tiger by right of having first wounded it and, therefore, the point of most danger fell to my lot. But my heart was in my mouth. The beaters had been instruc-ted sternly to move along both banks of the *nala* and throw in stones to bring out the beast for a shot at it; but under no circum-stances whatsoever must they enter this nasty *nala*. Possibly, the latter injunction was unnecessary. They must have known how foolish it would be to do so and what were the likely consequences.

The beat got on its way. Before long I saw the big head of the tiger in the *nala*, near the bank on which I was moving and about 20 to 30 yards distant. Only the head was visible. It seemed likely that the tiger would break out on my side of the *nala*, but one can never predict with certainty what a wild beast may do under any set of circumstances. At that moment a beater threw a stone at the spot where the tiger's head showed, and this brought it erect to stand broadside on to me. Angrily growling, the beast charged. I let it have the right barrel, dropping it in its tracks with a bullet just below the centre of the chin and striking the chest squarely; and hit it again with a bullet from the left barrel in the head. The latter shot is not always satisfactory because it often fails to kill instantly but makes the beast more savage. This shot halted the tiger and afforded me sufficient respite to reload the rifle.

Having done so, I stood immobile and waited for what might happen next. But the prostrate beast made no movement. I could distinctly hear it, however, making a sort of smothered groaning noise at short intervals. At last, even this weird sound ceased. Believing that the tiger must now be dead, I advanced cautiously and slowly to investigate; but suddenly it struggled violently, raised its head, and strove to stand erect. This was too much for my liking. I shot at the back of the neck in hope of fracturing the spine. Once more the tiger collapsed and remained still. Thinking that now it must surely be dead, I cast all caution to the four winds, kept my eyes glued on the body with rifle held ready for instant use, and went in close. With the rankest possible stupidity,

I grabbed hold of the tail to straighten it out for a measurement of my first tiger trophy.

I dropped that tail as if it had been a red-hot lump of coal. Immediately on touching it, the tiger began to gasp, open and shut its massive jaws, and evince signs of life. I fired a bullet into the head from close range, which killed it instantly. Later, when skinning the carcase we found no less than five bullets in the body and each having struck a vital spot. So that tiger, too, had died hard and taken a lot of lead. How it managed to survive the first four wounds inflicted by a .450/.500 rifle puzzled us.

The incident furnished a remarkably good illustration of the extreme degree of care which should *always* be exercised when approaching any dangerous species of wild beast which may be thought to have been killed. Lack of caution may well entail the hunter's own death or a severe mauling. Too much care cannot be taken. It was a lesson which thereafter was never forgotten; and in later years the knowledge gained that day often stood me in good stead.

My companion was very irate because I had been so stupid as to go up close to a presumed dead tiger and pull its tail straight without first making positive of its death. Indeed, he said some scathing things all of which I knew to be deserved.

4

Some Other Tigers

A BEAT for a tiger is probably one of the most popular of all methods adopted by sportsmen, but I was not especially enamoured by it. In order to be successful it is essential to make elaborate preparations and it demands expert knowledge. Meticulous planning must be carried out before embarking upon a beat. Only once did I participate in one of these affairs; but my luck was dead out on that occasion, though the proceedings were certainly interesting.

My colonel was a very keen *shikari* and had done a great deal of tiger hunting. Most of his periods of leave were devoted to big-game *shikar* and he had already collected a notable number of fine trophies. I remember that his score of tigers then stood at twenty-three. His junior officers treated him with the utmost respect, almost amounting to reverence.

He was kind enough to invite me to join him on a beat for

tigers, which had been organized with meticulous attention to the necessary details. I accepted with alacrity. But my knowledge of what this entailed was microscopical. Having no intention of sailing under false colours, I confessed this truth to him; but already he was aware of the fact.

As matters transpired it was his day, not mine. He killed the only tiger which came into the beat, while I never had the slightest opportunity even to fire my rifle. Notwithstanding, the day did afford me an interesting experience of this method of hunting the species, though I thought it lacked much of the excitement derived from stalking a quarry on foot.

The first essential for a beat, of course, is to locate a tiger's whereabouts. For many years certain areas of India's jungles have been a traditional habitat of this species, and my colonel had selected one of them for his "Operation Tiger". The local villagers had informed him that a good male beast was quite frequently to be seen in the region chosen for the beat. After we had settled into camp, a village headman reported to us that the tiger was still roaming about in the neighbourhood. The first requisite for success, therefore, had been fulfilled.

A tiger may disclose its presence in a particular area by killing the livestock of the *ryots,* if the normal food supply happens to have become scarce. And this is almost a certainty if a tiger is roaming about. Being a heavy animal it leaves a clear-cut pug mark; and especially is this the case when a tiger has traversed wet, muddy or sandy paths during the course of its peregrinations.

The shape of the pug's impression clearly indicates to the knowledgeable whether the spoor was made by a tiger or tigress. For example, the male leaves a broad pug mark, roughly about the size of a dessert plate; whereas that of the tigress is smaller and more oval in shape. One soon learns to interpret at once whether the spoor is that of a male or female.

The sportsman engaged upon a tiger beat is perched on a *machan* erected in a carefully selected tree, under which a live bait has been tethered by a stout rope from a leg to a firm peg. The rope is strong enough to hold the buffalo or bullock, but does not prevent the immense strength of a tiger from breaking it to drag the carcase into dense cover for a meal.

A beat is always performed during the hours of daylight. Its chief object is to induce the tiger to walk up quietly to the *machan,* or several of them, for a member of the party to make his kill. No difficulty is experienced in enlisting the necessary number of villagers to serve as beaters. As a matter of fact, they rather enjoy the fun and even more appreciate the payments made to them for their services.

Normally, tigers are extremely suspicious creatures. They are easily scared if all does not seem as it should be in their immediate vicinity. They become ferociously enraged once they realize that their lives are seriously being threatened; and, if alarmed during a beat, it is likely that they will turn back upon the beaters. Then almost anything may happen. Not improbably there will be casualties among the gang of beaters, while the quarry is definitely lost. A really well planned and organized beat, such as this one undoubtedly was, keeps the tiger walking from cover to cover in the general direction of the sportsmen on their *machans*. Gradually and surely, it will be driven towards a spot where a sportsman is afforded a reasonable chance to shoot it dead.

That was what happened on this occasion. All panned out as my colonel had desired. The beat was astonishingly well devised, though quite a longish time was required to drive the tiger up to the *machan* occupied by him. He killed it expertly with the first bullet. As there was only this one tiger in the beat, and it was not driven in the direction of myself, I was completely out of luck. But this outcome was just as it should have been, for it was the colonel's beat, he was footing the bill, and I was only there as his guest. Although I might envy his trophy—9 feet 10 inches between pegs—I had no cause for complaint. If there had been another tiger around, it would have been driven up skilfully to me instead of to the colonel.

In so far as able to judge, I think the area of the beat extended approximately for a quarter of a mile in length and was shaped somewhat like a large funnel. Our respective *machans* were positioned at the neck of this funnel through which the tiger was being driven towards us. The outer fringe of the area was hedged by men up trees, who are styled "stops". Their exact positions had been carefully selected by the colonel and his experienced *shikari*, so that they could cover efficiently any *nalas* along which the tiger might elect to walk out of the "beat".

If one of the "stops" either sees or hears the tiger advancing in the direction of the tree occupied by him, he promptly turns it by tapping loudly upon the bole or by making some other type of noise to scare the beast into turning away though without unduly alarming it. The tiger thinks that some wood-cutters are at work nearby, so at once gives the spot a wide berth—unless, of course, he chances to be a persistent man-eater.

The chief secret of success rests upon the maintenance of absolute silence until such time as the beaters have taken up their allotted positions. Thus, the tiger is not disturbed until all is in perfect readiness for the driving operations to start. A system of signals is prearranged. The head *shikari*, I noted, was at considerable pains to make sure that every man thoroughly under-stood them and their exact significance. After a shot was fired, the "stops" and beaters would be advised about what had happened by a shrill blast from a police-whistle. A long and sustained whistle would notify them that the tiger was dead; and, therefore, it would be safe for the "stops" to descend from their trees and converge upon the mouth of the funnel. Two short whistles told them that the tiger had only been wounded, its exact position was still unknown, and all must remain in their trees until in receipt of further orders. A succession of short whistles would warn the "stops" and beaters that the tiger had turned back, so all beaters must scramble up the nearest tree to a safe height without any delay. The ascent needed only a few seconds to accomplish, for the Indian *ryot* is as agile as a monkey where tree-climbing is con-cerned—even more so when a tiger is in the offing. And, probably, this beast was a wounded one at large!

As soon as the head *shikari* became satisfied that all was as it should be, he gave the prearranged signal for the beat to get under way. He took charge of the gang of beaters and directed them from the centre of the half-circle. The entire organization was perfection. Not a single hitch occurred and everything went like clockwork.

When on the move I think it is seldom that a tiger keeps to a straight course. When in a beat it will often endeavour to make its way to a flank of the funnel, but is at once turned back by an alert "stop". All kinds of species of other game animals, of course, may come out of a beat, but these are allowed to pass unhurt by the sportsmen on *machans*. They are after a tiger, not lesser game. A shot fired would instantly ruin a beat, and all the work done in preparation for it would be so much wasted effort.

If no animals come out of the beat, this fact furnishes positive evidence that the tiger is within the area and other creatures departed therefrom in the cause of self-preservation. As none came out of this particular beat, our belief was strong that the tiger was present and our chances good for putting paid to its account. One less cattle-killer in the district would be welcomed joyfully by the villagers.

Should a beat contain a tiger within it, this is styled a live beat; but if there happens to be none, it is known as a dead beat. We were lucky enough to experience the former.

If a tiger is shot with a heavy rifle in a vital spot of its anatomy, generally it will crumple up and die quickly with a twitch of its tail. But if one is hit in a non-vital spot, even with two or more bullets, the vitality of the beast can be positively astounding. It may then travel for a long distance and cause a great deal of havoc before finally succumbing in some patch of thick cover. Many sportsmen dislike shooting a tiger in the head because this is not always successful in killing the animal and might well ruin the mask of a trophy. The beast will eventually die from the wound because it is unable to lick the injury to keep it clean and so get rid of the maggots, allowing the wound to heal up.

On this occasion my colonel's shot killed the tiger instantly. He enjoyed a reputation for being a first-class marksman with either a rifle or shotgun, and was rarely known to need more than one bullet to kill a beast.

There are various different shots, of course, advocated by sportsmen as being the best to take. I have insufficient practical experience of hunting the tiger to express an opinion on this somewhat controversial subject. Suffice for me to say, if given a fair chance I would much prefer to take a three-quarter shot at the neck well up behind the shoulder as the bullet will then sever an artery and travel onwards into the heart, even if not fracturing the spine. Except when the beast is really close to you, the head shot can prove a tricky one because the brain of a tiger is relatively small; while even an inch or less off the fatal mark can make all the difference between an outright kill or having left on your hands a very angry and wounded tiger still to be dealt with. This task is never a sinecure and one not to be envied. It can always prove a dangerous and unpleasant business up to the final drop of the curtain.

There have been recorded a number of instances when a tiger shot in the head has charged the hunter with immense ferocity, either badly mauling or killing the man before itself going down for keeps. If a tiger is immediately below a sportsman on a *machan*, a shot generally proving effective is a bullet through the nape of the neck. It should fracture the spinal vertebra and kill the beast. With such a shot had the colonel dropped the tiger on this beat.

An evergreen subject for controversy is whether or not a tiger possesses strong powers of smell or whether it employs its nose when hunting for prey.

Recently this subject was revived in correspondence to *The Field*. A number of interesting letters from sportsmen were published, both for and against; and it was astonishing how widely divergent were opinions expressed by those who had hunted the species in India, Burma, Malaya and elsewhere in the Far East. The three greatest authorities on the tiger were Colonel Jim Corbett, A. A. Dunbar Brander and F. W. Champion—in so far as India is concerned. They had spent a lifetime in the jungles of India, hunting and closely observing the tiger's habits. They are more likely to know the correct answers than sportsmen who make only occasional hunting trips after tiger. A sportsman is not always a sound naturalist or reliable observer, being far more interested in the actual hunting activities than in studying animals' ways.

All three of those acknowledged authorities maintained that the tiger does not rely upon its nose but its eyes and ears; though it can scent, the beast rarely uses its nose. For what it may be worth, my personal experience tallied with the opinions of these accepted experts. A tiger-hunter has never to bother his head about the wind-direction. I am inclined to think that this animal's powers of scent are negligible, else seldom utilized. If you are able to smell a tiger in the area over which you are hunting, and you most certainly can, then it is unlikely that the beast can smell you; but it would be safe to wager that the animal has seen or heard you long before you smell it.

There have been occasions when an individual tiger has been observed to be employing its nose, and such incidents were duly recorded; but in general practice I do not believe this animal relies to any extent upon its powers of smell. Quite likely, the keen sight and hearing of the tiger have dulled its scenting capacities through disuse. This is equally applicable to the panther of Asia or leopard in Africa. But the lion will quite often, and normally does, employ its nose to lead it up to a kill left out for bait. That is why a carcase is dragged about over an extensive area of ground around where it will eventually be deposited to attract a lion (or lions) to the spot for a free feed, and then shot over it by a sportsman.

The ambition to increase my score of this species was not destined to remain long ungratified. I was out on my own, sitting on a *machan* over the partially consumed remains of a village buffalo which a large tiger was believed to have killed. There was a full moon and visibility around my perch in the tree none too bad. That night I did not have to wait any length of time for the killer to put in an appearance. I heard a tiger calling in the jungle at intervals and the sound of its loud voice gradually coming nearer; and the fact that it was moving in my direction became abundantly evident by the general degree of disturbance created amongst the monkey population of the area. They were scurrying past my tree to make themselves scarce, and using a lot of bad language. After about a quarter of an hour the monkey exodus ceased.

Shortly afterwards I heard a low and mournful moaning from the tiger. Then a grand old male stalked majestically into full view: a magnificent specimen of its kind and a worthy prize to acquire. This animal was soon joined by two others, both females.

This occasioned surprise, because the village headman had mentioned that only a tiger was involved in the cattle-killing raids on their livestock. And I believed, from what had been told me by others, that the two sexes of the species did not usually keep company except during the mating time; generally they hunted on their own.

For an appreciable time the trio stood in a group fairly close to the kill, each alerted and listening intently before advancing to gorge upon the carcase of the buffalo. The large tiger was the more distant from the tree and on my right hand, while the two tigresses were together and 20 yards from it. Before I could take aim at a vital spot to be sure of making an outright kill, the tiger stepped back into the shadows and now offered only a chancy target at which to shoot. So I covered the bigger of the two tigresses with my rifle, fired and dropped her dead where she was standing. The tiger and other tigress immediately scattered and bolted into cover, giving me no opportunity for a shot at either of them with the second barrel.

There followed a dead silence for about half an hour. I strongly suspected both animals must have departed for good and would not again return to the spot during that night. About this, as it transpired, I was grossly mistaken. Suddenly I heard a tiger moving on my left front and then another on my right, though neither beast was visible. This action on their part greatly puzzled me, because it did not seem to be "according to Cocker". As they came across my front in the bright moonlight when approaching the kill, I shot at the tigress before she entered a darkened patch on my right. I felt positive that she had been wounded, though how severely I did not know. She succeeded in gaining cover before I could fire again.

Once more absolute silence reigned all around my tree. A little later, however, I heard a tiger on my right walking heavily away from the spot; and next also another moving on my left towards the kill from rear of the *machan*. Soon the tiger began to call, shattering the stillness of the night with a suddenness that was unnerving. Its calls continued at intervals of roughly half a minute, and were maintained for close upon an hour. Then I saw the large male beast come up to the dead tigress and begin to lick her body with its tongue.

I was sorely tempted to shoot at it immediately. But its position was none too favourable for a killing aim, so my impatience had to be curbed. The tiger wandered off again, calling at short intervals and each time from a greater distance as it came round on its circling detour. The movements of the other animal were no longer heard. About three-quarters of an hour later the tiger returned towards the kill, making the air quiver with the immense volume of its voice reverberating through the encompassing jungle. It halted abruptly and listened intently for a few minutes, then advanced boldly to the buffalo's carcase and started to eat with the noises so typical of both tiger and lion when enjoying a hearty meal.

Peering through the moonlight I could make out the tiger's form stretched at full length at the tail end of the carcase but lying at right angles to it. Momentarily it raised its head, and my bullet found its mark well up behind the shoulder. It roared savagely and rolled on the ground, but must have been mortally wounded. Before I had time to let it have the second barrel, the tiger had vanished and could now be heard crashing its way through the jungle. I estimated that it had covered fifty yards from the kill to gain cover. There followed a cessation of all sounds, which was extremely weird after all the recent commotion. There was not a breath of night-wind and even the insect life of the jungle seemed to be muted.

Dawn brought with it all the usual awakening noises of the wilderness regions. The kill and dead tigress were still in the same position; and not much more of the former had been consumed by the tiger. There were no signs of it or of the second tigress. I had no means of knowing whether the tiger and tigress had died of their wounds during the night or if now it had become incumbent upon me to finish them off as soon as possible. I suspected the probability was that I had some real dirty work ahead of me as soon as the morning became light enough to search for the two beasts. One wounded individual of the species to kill was not in the nature of an enviable task, but a brace of them even far less so. Wisely, I remained on the *machan* until the *shikari* and beaters were heard approaching the tree. Then I climbed down to join them. I explained what had been occurring during the night, and they appeared to take as grim a view of what must now be done as I did.

We picked up the blood-spoor and started to follow it. I took the lead, the *shikari* close upon my heels, and the beaters lagging behind well in our rear. It was soon evident that both beasts had followed the same path through the thickish jungle, for often their pug marks overlapped and at other times were quite distinct from each other. The blood splashes were plentiful, many being of a frothy character which indicated that the lungs of one or both had been hit. It was difficult to determine which was the case. We had progressed rather less than a quarter of a mile when we found the tigress lying dead about five yards off the track. About sixty yards further on was the corpse of the tiger. This came as an immense relief to my mind, and no less so to that of those accompanying me, for now I was relieved of continuing with what promised to be a hazardous undertaking.

Three of the species falling to my rifle on a single night was an occasion for rejoicing. I felt well pleased with myself. The *shikari* was sent back to the village to recruit some more men to help us carry back to camp the three heavy carcases. The return procession was certainly imposing.

On arrival at the camp the trophies were measured carefully with a steel-tape between two upright pegs—one driven into the ground at tip of nose and the other at tip of tail. They were not taped over the curves, as the difference registered between the two kinds of measurement may well be as much as 8 inches or even a trifle more. The tiger was 9 feet 4 inches, while the females taped 8 feet 3 inches and 7 feet 6 inches respectively. Any 9-foot tiger may be regarded as a worthy prize, and an 8-foot and over tigress likewise.

Now my score was four of the species, the two males being really good specimens and the larger of the tigresses none too bad. That particular night's vigil had proved definitely rewarding. The villagers voiced their intense pleasure at having been relieved of the presence in their vicinity of these cattle-killers.

5

The Affair of a Man-eater

ALTHOUGH I had now brought down four tigers I was not satisfied with my score. Say what you will, tiger hunting grows upon a sportsman and his ambitions refuse to be ignored. A hope is always cherished that an even more magnificent trophy may fall to your rifle one day in the future.

A notorious man-eater was the subject of my next tiger experience in India. This particular brute preyed almost exclusively upon mankind. In the process it had succeeded in striking acute terror into the hearts of every man, woman and child in the district over which it marauded with such a ruthless ferocity. The District Officer had done his utmost to destroy this pest, but all his efforts had proved in vain. Rewards offered to the local inhabitants for the destruction of this grave menace to human life had been equally unproductive. The man-eating tiger was far too cunning to be caught napping.

Having heard much about what was happening, I wrote to the District Officer and asked if he would allow me to assist him in his determined efforts to slay the brute. He cordially invited me to join him at a named village and share in another resolute hunt for the marauder to put paid to its long overdue account. I was granted two weeks' shooting leave by my colonel, and hastened to the rendezvous arranged with the District Officer.

My host was already in camp there. Everything had been arranged for the attack on this beast. The man-eater had been reported to him as having been viewed near this particular village on the previous evening, and so our chances of proving successful appeared to be bright. Yet it is never possible to predict with any degree of certainty the outcome of a tiger hunt.

The stage had been set expertly before we set out from camp in the middle of the afternoon for the selected site of operations. Two *machans* had been prepared in trees overlooking the man-eater's favourite place for drinking, and an aged bullock tethered close to each tree. We hoped that the brute might fancy a change of diet from human flesh. As no human beings were reported as having been taken during the past three days, the beast was probably hungry. If so, it would not spurn the meal provided by us and requiring so little effort.

We were settled on our *machans* a full hour before the sun went down to its night's rest. Once I heard the grand organ-like call of a tiger from a distant spot—*Ar-r-o-ungh*; and much trusted that this was the brute which we wanted to destroy. The call was repeated shortly afterwards, and this followed by *Ar-r, Ar-r*. But the sounds still came from a considerable distance away from us. For a long time afterwards there ensued a chilling silence. My hopes that the man-eater would approach the two tethered bullocks sank to zero. Hour after hour passed without any incident to relieve the monotony of our vigil, and it looked as if all the carefully laid plans must fail in their purpose. Then once more, and now from much nearer, sounded that mighty voice—*Ar-r-o-ungh*; and this was succeeded by a brief *Ar-r, Ar-r*, followed by the first call repeated. But the tiger still seemed too far away. For a long time afterwards nothing more was heard.

It was nearing dawn, and I must have been dozing after a long night's fruitless and uncomfortable wait on the *machan*, when I was startled into alertness in a split-second by the reports of two shots fired in rapid succession by the District Officer. Instantly, every faculty was alert. A moment or two later I saw the tiger at a distance of about forty yards from my tree. I shot at it but too hastily for good aiming and, though hearing the bullet strike home, evidently no serious damage to the brute had been caused.

I swore angrily when the beast vanished swiftly into the dense and matted jungle.

My companion called out that he was positive of having wounded the tiger severely and now was about to climb down from the *machan*. Although not in any way fancying this idea, yet I felt it was incumbent upon me to do likewise. With a wounded tiger, most probably the notorious man-eater, in the vicinity and whose exact whereabouts was unknown to us, I would have preferred to remain on my *machan* until daylight. Having joined my companion on the ground, I regretted doing so; but took heart when noting how little perturbed he appeared to be about our dangerous situation.

We did not have to wait long before the sky became flecked with dullish grey lights. Soon faint streaks of pink, blue and yellow showed here and there on the eastern horizon. A new day was being born. We consulted in whispers about what was best to be done. Both appreciated that to follow up a wounded tiger, probably a confirmed man-eater, was a difficult and highly dangerous proposition.

Finally, it was mutually agreed between us that wisdom dictated that we should wait until the light strengthened and the gang of beaters arrived from the village. They had been ordered to join us at daylight if they heard any shots fired during the night. Their anxiously expectant ears must have heard the shooting. Our *shikaris* would collect the beaters at dawn and also see that there was no undue delay in joining us; and then could be organized the quest for the wounded tiger.

As soon as they arrived on the scene, we explained to them what it was proposed to do and what must not be done by the beaters. The latter did not appear to be enthusiastic, though not one of them raised any objections. Judging by their grim faces, I suspected that they considered us mad. Possibly, they were correct.

The blood-trail was quickly picked up by one of our *shikari* who, after following it cautiously for a short distance, suddenly halted to stoop down and pick up a large leaf. After examining this closely, he about-turned and commented: "*Kuhn, sahib. Kuhn!*" He indicated a large smear of blood on the leaf held out towards us, then pointed to the pug mark of a forefoot where also could be seen blood. The District Officer assured me that the latter evidence showed that the tiger had received a shoulder wound and blood was dripping down its foreleg as it moved onwards.

This was a heartening sign. But it also demanded the utmost caution during our further advance through the thick stuff. A wounded man-eating tiger can be just about the nastiest of wild beasts to tackle in thick cover, even more deadly than a man-eating lion under similar conditions. Both of us realized this fact.

There was a possibility that this wounded brute might get clear away from us, and then innocents would be made to suffer for what we had started but failed to finish. At all costs to ourselves such an eventuality had to be obviated. Though neither of us had the foggiest idea as to where the tiger might have hidden, both agreed that the blood-spoor must be followed up relentlessly.

It was obvious to me that neither our *shikaris* nor the beaters liked the idea one least little particle. Indeed, the headman of the beaters sullenly protested against them being expected to participate in such foolishness. They knew the local man-eater far too intimately to have any desire to play with it at close quarters. Frankly, my sympathies were entirely with them.

The District Officer spoke to them earnestly in their own language, but what he said had little effect in relieving their state of acute depression and nervousness. Finally, he told them that, if they were feeling so terrified, they could keep in rear of us when we went forward along the blood-spoor. To this suggestion they raised no objections, because it relieved them from accepting any major risks. And it was *their* man-eater which we were striving to destroy for them! I speculated as to what use the beaters would be. It seemed to me that it might have been wiser to dispense with their unwilling services and send them home. But the District Officer thought that they might be needed before long, so he kept them with us.

When we started forward, the *shikaris* walked close behind us but the beaters trailed along at some distance in rear. Their expressions were sullen. I heartily dislike having in my company unwilling comrades on an adventure, and thought it would have been wiser to send them back to their village to prevent their becoming more of an embarrassment than a use to us. However, the District Officer had decided otherwise, and it was not for me to protest.

The blood trail was simple enough to spoor and was ever becoming more profuse. Presently it led us down the centre of a fairly wide *nala*. The District Officer ordered the beaters to walk along the summits of both banks, and they complied with a marked show of reluctance; while our two *shikari* elected to keep with them rather than with us. In this formation we advanced cautiously and with every faculty keenly alerted. Eventually, we gained a point where the *nala* took an abrupt turn around a small thicket of tamarisk bushes. We halted just short of this spot for a whispered consultation. It was agreed to separate; the District Officer going round one flank of the thicket, while I went round the other.

As I gained the far extremity of the bushes, a water-hole came into full view. And there was the tiger, lying down in the water with only its head visible above the surface. I took careful aim and fired at the head but, though the bullet sped true to its mark, it failed to kill the beast. I suspect that it only inflicted a glancing wound, or perhaps the tiger was endowed with an exceptionally tough skull. With a loud roar of anger, the man-eater sprang out of the water with an amazing show of agility and bolted off round the far side of the thicket. I shouted a warning to my companion. Later, he ited that, though hearing my shot distinctly, he did not hear the shouted warning to be on his guard. I had yelled out to him at the full force of my lungs' power. In any case, the sound of my shot ought to have told him that the tiger was located and made him fully prepared to deal with any eventualities.

A moment or two later I heard two shots fired on the other flank of the thicket, so knew that my companion must have seen the wounded tiger. The reports were followed instantly by an angry roar and shrill human cry for help. Running at top speed round the end of the thicket, my eyes beheld a scene that made the blood run cold and brought me to an abrupt halt. The District Officer was down on the ground and the tiger, its jaws dripping blood, stood over his prostrate body.

The two *shikaris*, carrying our second rifles and followed by some of the beaters, must have heard the three shots and loud yells. They now came running towards the spot, breaking through the vegetation at a point quite close to the tiger standing over the District Officer. Instantly, the brute abandoned its victim and charged straight at the two running *shikaris*. Both men fired at it, but failed to stop or turn the infuriated beast. One of them dropped his weapon and foolishly turned about to run away; but the other stood his ground and shot again at the tiger as it rushed in upon him. A faulty cartridge misfired. He ejected it and reloaded from the magazine, but was afforded insufficient time to shoot again. The huge bulk of the tiger sailed through the air and bore the unlucky *shikari* to the ground. While all this was rapidly taking place, I had no chance of shooting at the tiger and feared hitting the man instead of the beast over him. Afterwards I blamed myself bitterly for not having accepted that desperate risk. But it is easy to be wise after the event.

I saw that the tiger was using its claws upon the prostrate *shikari*. Once it paused to wipe its face with a forepaw, much in the manner of a cat after lapping up a saucer of milk. For a few moments I was frozen into immobility by the horror of what my eyes beheld, the swift course of events having prevented brain and body from functioning normally. Then I ran forward in the hope of being able to get in a safe shot at the tiger as it mauled the man on the ground. When about ten yards distant my sights came on, and I sent a bullet into the heart of the beast. It sank in a limp heap upon the prone *shikari* and did not move again.

Certain that the tiger was dead, I shouted to the beaters to hurry to the aid of the mauled man and then ran towards the District Officer. He was sitting up, busy wiping blood from his face and clothes with bunches of dry grass. Miraculously, he had suffered no more than bad shock and a few minor gashes from the brute's talons. The blood was that of the tiger which had dripped upon him as it stood over his body.

He told me that as he was shooting at the tiger it had sprung and knocked him down by sheer weight of the impact. For a short time he was stunned. Upon recovering, he found the heavy body of the man-eater astride him; and its hot blood was flowing freely over his face and chest. To his amazement, the beast had not mauled him. When the two *shikari* came running up, the tiger left him to charge straight for them. Although sore, bruised, badly shaken, and suffering from several gashes from claws, nothing worse had happened to him. The District Officer had been extremely fortunate to come off so lightly from this terrifying experience. Having done all possible to attend to his minor injuries, I went back to the mauled *shikari*, who was in the service of my companion.

The beaters and my *shikari* had done everything feasible for him with the limited means available. But I could see that he was in a real bad way. We improvised a stretcher and some of the beaters carried him back to the camp. I much doubted if he would survive the journey. My *shikari* and the other beaters were left to skin the dead man-eater and bring back the trophy to us. I followed the stretcher-party with the District Officer.

When the mauled man arrived at the camp he was scarcely breathing and his case seemed to be definitely hopeless. He died a couple of hours later without regaining consciousness. His skull had been terribly fractured by a hefty blow from the tiger's fore-paw, and his body was a mass of terrible gashes from the claws. Why neither my companion nor the *shikari* had been bitten was difficult to explain; but later the reason was made plain to us.

The dead tiger was emphatically identified by the villagers as the man-eater. They knew it far too well by sight for there to be any possibility of being mistaken about it. We found ourselves acclaimed by the village as popular heroes. The exuberance of the gratitude displayed by these simple peasants can readily be understood, for, at long last, all would be able to sleep at night without the nightmare of a constant fear of being taken by this man-eating tiger. I am sure that they must have revelled in their first night of real freedom from such a deadly scourge, and all slept like logs during the hours of darkness.

When we went back to examine the skinned carcase of this tiger, it was seen that my shot at its head (easily identified because I alone was using soft-nosed bullets) had passed through the bridge of the beast's nose and shattered both jaws. Because of this serious injury it had been unable to use its long and strong canine teeth to bite my companion or the dead *shikari*. That fact saved the former's life. To be knocked down by a wounded man-eating tiger and escape without suffering other than minor scratches from the claws must indeed be a rare occurrence.

The relatives of the killed *shikari* were adequately compensated for their loss by the District Officer, and to this he added all the wages due to the man. As the *shikari* had been running to his help when meeting death, he thought the amount of compensation should be higher than customary. The relatives appeared greatly pleased with his generosity.

The trophy belonged to my companion and there could be no argument about this, for he had drawn first blood. In any case, he richly deserved the spoils. Yet it seemed to me that I was getting rather into a habit of being in at the death of tigers and not acquiring the desired trophies. I still had only four to show, and was hankering to add to them. Something had to be done about it.

6

Drama of the Indian Jungle

MY NEXT outing after tiger, unaccompanied by another sportsman, proved an especially epic experience. It so happened that this was the last chance I was to have, and the final curtain could not have been excelled. The episode will forever be treasured in my memories of big-game hunting.

It was my good fortune to be a silent and passive eye-witness of an unrehearsed comedy and next of a real drama in the wild heart of the Indian jungle. Both incidents were staged and produced by Mother Nature—always an expert in show craftsmanship. Yet it is the drama which stands out more clear-cut in my recollections of that memorable night. The comedy was merely a light-heartedly acted curtain-raiser, but deliciously played, to the enthralling drama that followed shortly afterwards. Literally, I sat in the gallery as the audience of a terrific and spectacular duel to the death between two mighty creatures. I gazed down at Nature in the raw and watched a scene that surely must have stirred even a blasé Nero into displaying enthusiasm. I would wager that Nero never witnessed a greater combat staged in an amphitheatre in ancient Rome.

That fiercely fought battle for life brought home to me the savage nature of wild beasts in their relations with each other; and also how it is that every hour must be filled with constant threats to their lives. One moment they know and are enjoying a carefree existence, killing and eating their fill, and experiencing a sense of contentment; and the next they are fighting a mortal duel against some unexpected foe. Bluff, cunning, strength, trickery, agility, ferocity and sureness in attack or defence—those are the only suits of armour worn by the animal gladiators in the amphitheatres of the jungle. But no man could ever teach one of them a single trick in the game of life or death. They know *all* the answers.

I had occupied the *machan* prepared for me at the chosen site earlier in the late afternoon than needs be. It would be three hours before the sun sank, after which I hoped to be able to dispose of a notorious cattle-killing tiger of the district. The *machan* over-looked the carcase of a buffalo taken by this brute from a nearby village on the previous night. Very little of it had been eaten by the marauder, and the likelihood was that the tiger would return to it and feast during darkness.

My *shikari* and six villagers had seen me settled on my post. Then they returned to the village but had been ordered to rejoin me shortly after sunrise. I was left to my own devices during that lonely night's vigil. The early occupation of the *machan* was dictated by two considerations: to make certain that all possible arrangements had been perfected; and to study wild life at sunset. Several other advantages, not to be despised, were offered. It lessened the possibilities of alarming the tiger, which would be lying up near its "kill"; gave ample time to carry out any minor adjustments thought necessary; and I should be rested before the beast showed up to resume its feasting on the carcase of the buffalo.

A *charpoy* (bed) had been secured for me in the fork of the tree at a height of about six feet above the ground. The tree stood solitary and almost at the fringe of dense jungle, but overlooked a comparatively large open space. There was also a swampy patch in the centre of the open space, beyond it being a grim belt of tangled undergrowth fringing a forest area. It had a forbidding aspect—cruel and sinister and savagely wild.

The tiger had dragged its "kill" less than fifty yards from my tree and, strangely enough, not bothered to conceal it from vultures or other carrion-feeders. The villagers thought the killer was the identical beast being sought by me, and until its advent, I could revel in a peep at Nature and not become too bored with my vigil on the *charpoy*.

Before the sun set I saw a jackal emerge from cover, advance cautiously across the open ground, and loaf around the "kill". It behaved in an aimless sort of manner, but kept at some distance from the carcase. To read through its pretence was simple. Patently, the jackal's intention was to deceive the world into believing that it had no designs upon the feast available. I found it amusing to watch its antics. The meat must have proved a tremendous temptation to this jackal, but it was strong-minded enough to resist being too precipitate in pilfering the tiger's supper.

After a time it disappeared into the jungle. I was sorry to see it go, for its clownish behaviour had pleasantly relieved the tedium of waiting for the tiger to put in an appearance. The latter was nearly due to arrive for a meal, and the jackal was quite obviously not minded to risk being caught while eating the rightful owner's food. Presently, much to my surprise the jackal stepped out once more before the footlights to give an unsolicited encore. It must have made a complete, or almost complete, circuit of the spot because it now reappeared from the opposite direction to that where it vanished. Now it walked boldly up to within a few paces of the carcase, moving forward steadily and evincing no particle of fear. No sooner was it within reach than the jackal hastily jumped backwards, as if suddenly alarmed by some suspicious sound. Yet I had heard nothing.

For a few minutes it stood immobile, listening intently and poised ready for instant flight. It repeated this performance several times, always approaching a little closer to the coveted meat. Then it craned forward its head, gradually and cautiously touched the carcase with its nose, and immediately all its fears seemed to evaporate. The jackal dropped the mask of coy shyness and suspicion. Evidently, it had decided that the tiger was not nearby. As these preliminary acrobatic performances had not elicited even a warning growl that this was a private larder and must not be pillaged, it indicated that the tiger was not thereabouts. The coast seemingly being clear, the jackal set to work in a very businesslike manner to pilfer some of the buffalo meat.

First, it tore open the extended stomach. The stench was so nauseating that I squirmed slightly on the *machan*, in acute revolt at the abominable smell. While getting a handkerchief from a pocket to clamp over nose and mouth, I must have made a slight noise and alarmed the jackal. Instantly it glanced up at me for a split-second and then vanished from the stage like a wisp of smoke. No more was seen of this amusing creature. The entire incident had been first-rate entertainment, but I wished that it had been possible to watch what happened if the tiger had caught the jackal stealing from its larder.

For a long time afterwards I was completely absorbed in observing the actors of the jungle pass across the stage. There was scarcely a dull moment. The scraggy trees surrounding the open space were silhouetted against a setting sun that blazed in the west like a huge ball of incandescent copper. The day insects gradually ceased their irritating biting and humming. The fairy life of the night, whose dawn is sunset, now came buzzing in myriads from their places of concealment like the ballet of an elfin chorus. A stately crane stepped daintily through the grass and reeds edging the swamp. Fat-breasted little birds of brilliant plumage settled themselves upon twigs or boughs, twittered cheer-fully and kissed each other good-night, ruffled their gorgeous feathers, and then tucked heads under wings to sleep until the dawn. Nature was now retiring to rest. Only the predatory slayers were on the prowl, seeking out victims to be devoured.

I inhaled the evening breeze, deeply stirred and delighted by everything around me. The swamp air, sweet to the nostrils, almost intoxicated; fitful puffs of breeze increased in strength to a night-wind force, which soothed my sun-baked body; and all my senses revelled in this fascinatingly picturesque unveiling of Nature's own bedchamber. Surely, none could have remained insensible to the charms of that perfect picture of the wilderness.

I became alert suddenly. A heavy body was forcing a way through the tangled masses of vegetation directly in front of my *machan*. It was far too noisy to be a tiger. I speculated as to what kind of actor was now about to occupy the centre of the stage.

The grass swayed and was crushed down. A few moments later a magnificent cow buffalo breasted her way out of that thick mat of high grass and undergrowth to stand out boldly on the open space directly in front of my tree. She carried a massive and inspiring sweep of horns: one of the best I ever saw on a female of the species in India or Africa. With her powerful bulk, terrifically strong shoulders, big head and thick bosses, she pre-sented a grand picture to gladden the eyes. Not having yet shot an Asiatic buffalo (*Bos bubalus*), the temptation to fire was difficult to resist. Momentarily, I hesitated and held the rifle ready for use, but I was after the cattle-killing tiger, and so did nothing. Looking back I have always felt immensely glad that the tiger was foremost in my thoughts, and this grand cow buffalo was spared a bullet from the rifle.

Suspiciously, she sniffed the air with widened nostrils; and then threw up her head to bellow like a thunderclap. The tree seemed to quiver to the vibrations of that majestic challenge to all living creatures in the jungle. A few moments later I heard an answering bellow from a considerable distance back in the forest, sounding faint after the great volume of the cow's powerful voice. She replied joyously to her mate, shook her great head vigorously, and then drove the sharp points of her curved horns into the earth with a vicious stab. Evidently she was feeling good and wished all the world to know it. Then, leisurely and evincing no signs of trepidation, she advanced towards the tiger's "kill"; sniffed at the carcase thoughtfully; and once again shattered the stillness of the dying day with the thunder of her mighty voice. It was a sound of challenging defiance; arresting, menacing and provocative to all hearing that bellow. She may have scented the tiger at the "kill" and was now warning it off.

Suddenly, however, the cow displayed signs of palpable unease, swiftly about-turned to confront the suspected point of danger with the head lowered and eyes peering intently at the fringe of the forest. I followed the direction of her steadfast gaze and almost immediately perceived what she had seen. My heart began to thump with the intensity of excitement aroused, for the tiger was there and just clear of the edge of the jungle. It was skulking along furtively and soundlessly, white belly almost sweeping the ground.

The tiger must have seen the buffalo and sensed there was likely to be a spot of trouble for it. The beast halted abruptly in its stealthy approach. It stood motionless, save for the twitching of its tail from side to side. The cow scattered the earth with a swift stroke of a forefoot, but her steady eyes never wavered from that intent stare at an ancient foe. Both remained alert and on guard. Eyes held eyes, savagely and unflinchingly, and there was perceptible a deadly hatred in the entire attitude of each formidable beast which foretold an imminent battle royal between them.

Shoot that tiger I would not, for the final act of the jungle drama promised to be a remarkably spectacular experience.

The tiger crept onward stealthily farther into the open. Not once did it straighten out its elastic body; its ferocious eyes were glaring fixedly at the buffalo, and its long tail swished the grass angrily. It conveyed to me an impression of a monster striped cat stalking a bird with the utmost intentness. The massive jaws were half-open, held low to the ground, and dripped saliva. The buffalo moved only to keep facing the tiger, neither advancing nor retreating; and there was noticeable a deadly menace in her entire rigid stance. If the tiger was so ill-advised as to launch an attack upon her, I thought she would prove a most formidable antagonist.

Patiently, the tiger was going to attack. Round and round it went in ever narrowing circles, always striving to get in position to rear of the buffalo for a sudden spring upon her back. But she was too quick for this manœuvre. Obviously she could not be taught much in the matter of ring tactics. Her footwork was superbly perfect; she knew every trick, and used them as circumstances dictated.

The jungle-cat paused momentarily in its circling movement, drew itself into a ball, tail lashing the ground with furious blows, and then without sound or warning its huge body sprang at the quarry with the speed of a rocket. At the same instant, with a thunderous bellow and great sweep of horns lowered, the buffalo charged home at her adversary. She met the latter's body in mid-air. The shock occasioned by the terrific impact hurled both backwards to the ground. In a split-second, however, they had struggled erect again and regained a firm stance facing each other. With a roar and bellow once more they charged resolutely. The tiger missed. But its leap landed it in rear of the buffalo; and, with an almost incredible agility, it had about-turned to spring full upon her back. But before the long and sharp canines could sink deep into her neck, she threw herself over backwards and rolled upon the tiger. Her move was astute and effective. In order to save itself from being crushed to death under the immense weight of that massive body, the tiger loosened its hold on her. As she regained her feet, it was ready and fastened itself upon her right shoulder. The buffalo shook the tiger clear and, with an angry bellow, charged full tilt at her foe. She bowled over the tiger as if it had been a ninepin, and then rammed its body against the stout bole of a nearby tree—I think it was a large tamarind.

Blood was now flowing freely from her bellowing mouth and from deep gashes torn in her neck, shoulder and haunches. She withdrew a short distance to gain charging space to finish off this deadly foe. But the tiger was still fit and game enough to fight on, though badly gored and crushed from the buffalo's onslaught. Once again it sprang in to the attack, this time succeeding in landing fair and square between the huge bosses of the horns. The striped body completely covered her face. Fangs and claws sank deep into the cow's body; blood filled the tiger's mouth, coursing in red rivers down her face; and her own ran down the flanks from many wounds inflicted. She bellowed loudly in pain.

Lowering the head almost to touch the ground with her nose, she charged at full speed against the large tree, her burden still festooned over head and face. I heard a loud and sickening thud as they crashed up against the solid bole and saw the cow stagger backwards until almost squatting on her rump. With amazing rapidity she recovered her poise. A feeble roar from the tiger told me that its distress must be great. That terrific impact had completed its undoing. In a limp heap, it collapsed upon the ground and lay still. The buffalo had delivered a mighty upper-cut and knocked out her adversary for a full count.

I watched her draw back a short distance, carefully measuring the mark. A short and swift rush forward, a sharp twist of the cruel horns, and she had gored the tiger's prostrate body again and again. It tried desperately to crawl away into cover and escape this pitiless onslaught, but now it was only too patent that the beast had had enough. Rather more than enough, too! But there are no referees at a fight in the wilds between two mighty beasts and none to call "time". Only the death of one, or of both, combatants could end that merciless battle. That now seemed near at hand.

A triumphant bellow shook the open space and caused my *machan* to quiver. The buffalo charged home in a final effort to conclude the fight, lifted the mangled and crushed body of the tiger upon the formidable horns, gave a sharp twist to the massive head, and flung its adversary some distance away as if it was no more than a bale of hay. The tiger probably died as its body hit the ground with a resounding thud. The buffalo did not even trouble herself to follow up and make certain that the beast was dead. She *knew* her foe to be destroyed.

I found it impossible to resist shouting "Bravo!" All throughout that titanic fight my sympathies had been with the cow buffalo, even though she had robbed me of a good tiger trophy. Yet no tiger's skin could have been a substitute for the sight of that stupendous battle to the death waged in the heart of the Indian jungle.

Such an opportunity comes normally but once to a man in a lifetime of big-game hunting—even if then. But some years later in Kenya Colony I was extraordinarily fortunate to witness the final stages of another fight to a finish between a black-maned lion and a bull buffalo. Should others feel sceptical that a hunter could possibly watch two battles royal between great beasts of the animal kingdom, it may be mentioned that the late Jim Sutherland, during his long and noteworthy career as a professional elephant-hunter in Africa, actually witnessed three such unusual episodes; and the late Colonel J. Stevenson-Hamilton, who was for close on half a century the Warden of the Kruger National Park in South Africa, recorded seeing at least two (I am not positive it was not three) similar spectacles. Say what you may, it is just a matter of luck.

The black pall of night shortly cloaked the land and shut out any further sight of the arena. Later, a young and tranquil moon shed its ethereal light upon the stage; and twinkling stars began to wink down at me from the dark canopy of sky overhead. I heard the cow buffalo bellow triumphantly. She was answered almost immediately from close at hand in the forest, and then I heard the crashing of a rapid departure to rejoin her mate in the wings of the stage. The curtain was then lowered soundlessly.

Frankly, I was delighted that the buffalo had won the fight; glad, too, that the tiger had gone down to such a magnificent creature. She had asked for no mercy, and given none.

There was no option but to continue an uncomfortable night on the *machan,* and wait there until the *shikari* and beaters arrived on the scene at dawn from the village. When they joined me, we all went to stare at the mangled corpse of the tiger which could no longer prey upon the livestock of the villagers. I related to them the story of the evening's events, and all expressed envy of what I had been privileged to witness.

The tiger's carcase was left where it rested. The trophy was not mine, but the cow buffalo's.

7

An Elephant Rodeo in the Himalayas

AT VARIOUS times and in different countries it has been my privilege to be an eyewitness of most systems employed in the capture of wild elephants for subsequent domestication and service of mankind. The most common one is that of a *keddah* (stockade). It varies little in its essential details whether staged in India, Burma, Ceylon, Thailand, Malaya or Indo-China. At all times it is a really interesting spectacle.

The wild African elephant is also captured for domestication in the former Belgian Congo, but nowhere else on the continent. The elephant-farms there are kept supplied with pupils by roping the smaller animals after they have been rounded up first by fully trained elephants, mounted horsemen, and members of the Azande tribe on foot. Nowhere else in the world, in so far as I know, is this operation carried out on similar lines. I would say that the process must be unique. It is amazing how successful can be the capture of wild elephants in the Belgian Congo, also the ease with which they are then tamed and taught all that is required of them.

An elephant rodeo staged in the foothills of the Himalayas in India is, I think, the nearest approach to the Belgian system. There the wild animals are rounded up and roped in the style of cowboys with steers on large American or Canadian cattle ranches. It is a most exciting performance. I much doubt if many Europeans have witnessed it or even know anything much about how it is done. By and large, it can be rated as real man's work. But I question if it could be accomplished with any measure of success without being helped by trained elephants which have been domesticated for a number of years.

I had returned to India in 1932 on a political and journalistic mission, with Calcutta as my headquarters; and had no intention of engaging in any big-game hunting with either rifle or camera. I had the good fortune to be invited as a guest to watch one of these elephant rodeos being carried out. The experience I then enjoyed can never be forgotten. Whenever the memory of it becomes vividly alive, I am always reminded of the lines in Wordsworth's *Intimations of Immortality:*

> It is not now as it hath been of yore;
> > Turn whereso'er I may,
> > By night or day,
> The things which I have seen I now can see no more.

At a dinner party in Calcutta I chanced to be seated next to a Raja, a noted *shikari* in India. Our conversation mostly concerned big-game hunting in Africa, and I told him about the method of capturing elephants in the Belgian Congo. He was very interested and cordially invited me to be his guest at a round-up of wild Asiatic elephants in his State. They would be caught and trained for his future service.

I travelled to his capital and was hospitably entertained at the palace. The selected stage for this elephant rodeo was in the neighbourhood of a jungle village tucked away in the foothills of the Himalayas. Two days later my princely host drove me in his large car to the camp prepared for us, but the last half of the journey, perforce, was covered in a howdah on riding elephants and which waited for our arrival at the point of change-over in transport. His Rolls-Royce could not tackle the rough track through the jungle to the camp-site. Seventy trained *keddah* elephants had lumbered into the well-appointed camp a day ahead of us. On the following morning the proceedings would be started on their way shortly after daybreak. The Raja told me that it might require a week or more to complete the task.

The huge camp and encompassing jungle were astir at the first chill greyness of the false dawn. Through the mist and clouds of

dust I could dimly perceive a foraging squad of elephants bringing in huge loads of bamboo-shoots and other favourite food of
the animals forming a part of the Raja's retinue. From the plain
below the camp's perimeter there faintly sounded in my ears the
monotonous throb of innumerable tom-toms. Vapoury columns
of bluish-grey smoke curled upwards lazily into the cold and
invigorating air from many small fires scattered about the encamp-
ment. Harsh cries and occasional weird chanting shattered the
stillness of the partially awakened jungle life. In my nostrils was
the pungent odour of the elephant-lines. There can be no mistak-
ing that strong and somewhat offensive smell; and when hunting
for ivory in Africa I have often detected the recent passage of a
herd of elephants by this odour before even picking up their spoor.

Presently the mahouts—those past-masters of elephant training
and management—clambered on to a foreleg and were hoisted
by the animal's trunk to a seat upon the neck of the kneeling
elephant. One by one, the animals rose erect. The *keddah* moved
off in the direction of the area selected for our thrilling adventure.
Shambling noiselessly in single file over the rough, narrow and
tortuously winding track, the elephants stretched out far ahead
until the leaders were lost to view upon entering the outskirts of
the dense jungle wastes.

The Raja gave a sharp command. The elephant ridden by him
and the one assigned to me at once padded forward in the wake
of the procession. Only our two animals were equipped with
howdahs. My picturesquely attired host maintained a short distance in front of me. I had noted that all the *keddah* elephants
were stripped for the serious business upon which they were
engaged, each being furnished solely with a thick pad such as
commonly is used when out on *shikar*. Some stout ropes of hemp
were slung about them, at which the *mugli-walas* clutched when-
evèr in imminent danger of losing their balance and near to slipping off the rump of the animal ridden.

A *mugli-wala* is an almost nude man, adorned only with a
dhoti (loincloth), who stands perilously upon either the back or
rump of the elephant in rear of its mahout. Armed with a stout
bludgeon, the business end of which bristles with sharp iron spikes,
it is his duty to belabour the beast, hard and fast, with this weapon
whenever a sudden spurt of speed or some decisive action is
needed. Experiencing a resounding blow and pin-pricks on its
posterior, the elephant promptly responds to this scurvy treatment
in the desired manner. The mahout, armed with a hooked *ankus*
(steel goad), normally controls the movements of the beast ridden
by him; but the *mugli-wala's* shrewd blows to the stern supply
the incentive for a greater show of activity.

Most of the heavy work of a *mugli-wala* is performed when standing erect upon the elephant's back or rump. The trick of balancing is learned only after much practice and suffering many painful falls from aloft. After seeing these men in action, I had no hankering to become a *mugli-wala*. Indeed, it must prove a hazardous form of employment and not improbably also a poorly paid one; but I was assured that there never was any shortage of recruits for this special type of work. This greatly surprised me.

A large army of beaters on foot had left the jungle village before the *keddah* elephants moved out of the camp for the day's operations. Long since they had climbed out of sight into the timbered foothills of the Himalayas. Garbed only in a *dhoti* and turban they bore a heterogeneous collection of noise-producing instruments—ancient flintlocks, tom-toms, tin pans, quaintly fashioned horn trumpets, and other miscellanea of that type. Watching them set forth, it was abundantly patent to me that every man of this jovial and highly important section of the *keddah* regarded his day's work in the light of an enjoyable frolic. For the time being, at any rate, they had to cork up their exuberance.

Having heard the terrific din created by the beaters during a tiger hunt in India on previous occasions, I thought that these men seemed strangely muted. But their share in this elephant rodeo was merely to form a silent cordon upon three sides of a *nala* in a deep valley, whereabouts the herd of wild elephants had been located by *shikaris* who had been despatched for this purpose on the previous day. They had skilfully reconnoitred this area for us. The moment for the beaters to become noiseful had not arrived and, in the meantime, they must continue to be patient.

In order to gain their appointed stations, these men must work their way up the steep slopes of the hillsides and through dense junglegrowth. Making any sort of noise was strictly prohibited. The accidental snapping of a twig carelessly trodden underfoot, a stone sent rolling down the hillside, or a thoughtlessly raised voice would inevitably send the herd off in panic-stricken flight to the next *nala* or even a distant valley. Once having thoroughly been alarmed, the likelihood was that they would be contacted no more that day or even possibly for many more days to come. That would necessitate a repetition of all the preliminary arrangements. The desire was to capture wild elephants, not drive them in terrified flight from the neighbourhood. Stealth, silence and cunning were the watchwords therefore until such time as the issue became joined. It must be conceded that the corps of beaters honourably played their part by faithfully respecting every taboo.

The throat of the canyon was situated high up in the foothills

and fully a mile in width. During the seasons of monsoon a flood
of water rushed through it in half a dozen channels separated by
low and thickly timbered ridges. In the winter months, however,
these watercourses were practically dry. As it was now the cold
season of the year, the *nalas* were entirely waterless and formed
open rock-strewn thoroughfares along which slow travel was a
possibility either on foot or on an elephant. I much doubt if a
horse could have safely been ridden there. Not unlikely, it would
have ended in a bad spill for its rider and a fractured leg for the
animal.

As soon as the *keddah* arrived at this outlet in the valley, it
split up noiselessly into a number of small bands. Each one com-
prised from eight to ten elephants. All the men and animals knew
exactly what to do and what was expected of them. These groups
took up their stations about the wide *nala*, and positioned themselves in such a manner as to block all natural avenues of escape
for the herd of wild elephants about to be rounded up. The plan
was to capture the animals one at a time, which was about as much
as could be achieved in the circumstances. On the main watershed
at the head of the valley, and on the surrounding ridges on either
flank of it, the impatient army of beaters were still silently on
guard, awaiting the signal to begin driving the herd of wild
elephants towards the expectant groups of trained animals.

In this manner was the stage suitably set and the net cunningly
spread. Soon all was in readiness. There was plainly perceptible
an atmosphere of tenseness pervading every man and beast around
us; only the Raja appeared to be displaying no reactions. All of
the preliminaries were carried out noiselessly and no commands
given, for all taking part in this round-up had been trained to
perfection. *Keddahs* are always noteworthy for the astute strategy,
efficiency and perfect organization displayed by all taking part in
them. Even the trained elephants know their job backwards. They
furnish an astonishing example of what competent training and
good organization can accomplish.

Satisfied that everything was now in readiness, the Raja
beckoned me to accompany him to the summit of a knoll dividing
the two main dry watercourses. I followed silently in the wake
of his mount and ranged up alongside him as he halted. From this
vantage point the entire scene was clearly visible to both of us. We
could watch the proceedings perfectly from this natural grandstand.

The countryside displayed winding and irregular ridges, their
slopes breaking away steeply into rocky and narrow gorges. In a
few of the lesser *nalas* could be seen a very few small, stagnant
and widely separated pools of water; and the undergrowth was as

dry as tinder, crackling sharply underfoot. A carelessly dropped match or cigarette butt would have set ablaze the countryside for many miles around. The order of the day was no smoking. Eastwards in the far distant horizon could be viewed the immense, forbidding and snow-crowned ranges of the Himalayas, tracing their clear-cut, jagged and desiccated outlines against an azure canopy of sky. Some of the peaks looked positive giants. The spectacle was beautiful and magnificent: Nature's artistically contrived frieze against a distant background of blue sky.

No breath of wind relieved the stifling heat of a dry and oppressive morning after the sun had risen high in the heavens. The jungle below and all around us was remarkably still and silent; no sound, however faint, came out of it to our intently listening ears. If the herd of wild elephants did happen to be in this carefully cast net, then they were being astonishingly quiet and not disclosing their presence to us. Far below the knoll, also on our immediate right, could distinctly be picked out one or two small bands of *keddah* elephants. They were lazily curling and uncurling their trunks, ears flapping rhythmically, and tails flicking the flanks; while the mahouts sat immobile on their necks like bronze statues of the Buddha. The *mugli-walas* seemed tense with suppressed excitement, every faculty keenly alerted, and eyes straining upwards to the rugged slopes of the timbered hillsides. The beaters, silent and watchful, were concealed from our sight in the dense matted junglegrowth. Not even a slight movement betrayed their whereabouts.

Suddenly I was startled by a parakeet shrieking shrilly in acute alarm. Instantly bedlam broke loose. From the ridges towering high above the knoll now burst forth a cacophony of noise—gunshots, tom-toms beaten furiously, high-pitched human voices yelling at full force of their lungs, the hearty banging of tin pans, and harsh-noted blasts on crude horns. All combined to create a terrific discord of sounds, such as must inevitably have stricken abject terror deep into the heart of the most valiant wild elephant.

The beaters were now uncorked. They were at liberty to let loose their bottled-up exuberance. They did so with an obvious relish and keen spirit of rivalry to be the most noiseful. The appalling din echoed loudly over the hillsides and through the valley, being cast back and forth from range to range like a shuttlecock in a game of badminton. The volume of sound and reverberating echoes swelled enormously as the army of beaters began to force their way downwards through the dense jungle and then close in upon the herd of wild elephants. It was not long before the latter had been enveloped on three sides and driven relentlessly towards the *keddah* groups dotted along the fourth flank. They were given no option but to take to flight from the encircling wall of advancing beaters.

By now absolutely terrified, with the instinct to escape uppermost, the herd broke down the slopes of the hillside in top-gear. Seventeen utterly panic-stricken beasts ploughed a wide path through the bush and timber, breaking down the smaller saplings with sharp reports like revolver shots, and causing the jungle to groan under that maddened stampede of giant bodies.

A few minutes later they had cleared the timber. We could plainly view the members of the herd, and I counted one large bull, four smaller ones, six mature cows, three immature cows, and three calves of varying ages and size. I was disappointed at the smallness of the herd trapped within that painstakingly cast net, because I had been accustomed to encountering herds in Africa which numbered from 40 to 800 or more animals. But a swift glance at the face of the Raja at once reassured me. He was beaming with pleasure. Obviously he was content with the size of the herd and the number of them likely to accrue to him. All was grist that came to his mill.

From then onwards thrills and excitements piled up so fast that no time was granted for clear thinking or even much chance to follow closely the successive stages of this elephant rodeo. I quite forgot to bring into action the camera, which had been the chief object of my presence, and thus stupidly forfeited a rare opportunity for securing a unique series of photographs.

Rumbling down the hillside like an avalanche towards one of the *nalas*, the herd found itself confronted by a group of immobile *keddah* elephants. The wild animals came to an abrupt halt in their headlong flight and trumpeted shrilly in mingled rage and terror, plainly at a loss what next to do for the best. The three calves, perceiving this strange array of man-ridden members of their own kind blocking the way to escape, made short and frenzied rushes into the jungle while squealing pitifully. But they soon returned to the protection of their mothers.

For a few minutes the large herd-bull and its companions stood their ground steadfastly, obviously striving to reason out this unusual situation in which they had become involved and utterly bewildered by the swift course of events. Then they also made frantic plunges into the jungle, but at once discovered themselves to be surrounded by a ring of *keddah* elephants. What must have proved even more terrifying was the realization that this grim barrier of their enemies was resolutely narrowing its circle and ever drawing in closer to them. Not a single line of retreat had been left open.

The nearest group of the *keddah* elephants was already in hot pursuit of the scattering herd, being quickly reinforced by 30 or more spike-driven giants from an adjacent *nala*. The fight was on. Things had to be done with a rush and on the spur of the moment. Each group acted upon its own initiative, just guided by the rapidly changing tactics of the hunted herd and nature of the terrain over which it was moving. Events were far too lively and rapid for the issue of any orders. But all automatically knew exactly what had to be done.

It appeared to me that the various groups were endeavouring to corner each individual member of the herd in turn, and then close in upon it for final capture by roping. I could now hear the mahouts shouting crisp commands to their mounts, while plying the *ankus* vigorously to the head of the *hathi* (elephant); and now the *mugli-walas* had become frenziedly dancing dervishes, solely concerned with delivering the maximum number of stimulating blows to the stern of the beast upon whose rump they were precariously perched. How they managed to sustain their balance there was beyond my comprehension. They were putting hearts and brawn into their jobs, leaving absolutely nothing to chance; and, moreover, they appeared to be enjoying themselves hugely.

The big herd bull seemed to be the chief prize sought. The fight for its capture was staged, for the most part, in full view of the eminence upon which the Raja and I were posted. It was possible for us to witness a perfect picture of all that happened within the shadows cast by the snow-capped peaks of the Himalayas. I would not have foregone that thrilling spectacle for anything which might be offered in exchange.

In their efforts to corral the herd-bull, the *keddah* elephants were now crashing around in a haphazard fashion and in all directions through the jungle. They were making heavy seas of their passage. Thick clouds of suffocating dust shrouded their movements; while the din created on every hand, to which I was contributing my mite, sounded deafening and awe-inspiring.

Realizing instinctively that it was about to be cornered effectually, the large beast made short and infuriated dashes up and down the hillside's steep slopes and across the dry *nala*. I reckoned that it must have crossed the latter many times. But the bull was never able to travel far without finding further progress blocked by one or more groups of *keddah* elephants. In the meantime the trained animals slowly but surely worked the herd-bull down the hillside and out of the dense junglegrowth, all the time resolutely closing in upon the quarry. Every manoeuvre was carried out magnificently and timed with absolute perfection. The masterly strategy was superb in both its conception and execution.

C

Finally, the entire turbulent herd came crashing down the hillside through a thicket of bamboo, and shortly afterwards thundered out on to the open watercourse. Several groups of *keddah* elephants were already positioned in ambush for just such an eventuality. I was impressed by the patent enjoyment evinced by the trained animals in hunting down and capturing some of their own wild kind. Quite obviously, they were putting their hearts into this formidable task and deriving immense pleasure in its accomplishment.

Rushing pellmell into the trap laid ahead and persistently hustled from the rear, it was clear to me that the herd-bull must be forced to surrender to the inevitable. I think it appreciated this truth, too. The bull was telling the world as much in loud trumpet blasts of anger, terror and mortification. The jungle and hills resounded to that mighty, strident and enraged series of vocal protestations. The other members of the herd and the tamed animals were also contributing to this elephantine chorus echoing over the valley. The noise all about us was deafening.

A *mugli-wala's* crowning effort was to spike his *hathi* on its stern so effectively that its mahout was enabled to achieve the profitable honour of being the first man to slip a noose of stout rope over the head of the herd-bull. It is a feat which only a genuine expert could hope to accomplish. And thus the giant animal was competently lassoed and brought to a firm anchorage from which it could not hope to escape. The rivalry for this distinction was markedly keen, for the pecuniary rewards were not to be despised; and the jubilant shouts of the successful mahout proclaimed his pride in the achievement. His *mugli-wala* was no less vociferous in expressing triumph, no doubt later receiving a minor share of the mahout's well-earned bonus for effecting the capture of a wild elephant.

Immediately the herd-bull had securely been moored by the head, the other *keddah* elephants swarmed around the furiously resisting captive. They butted the enraged bull with their heads from all angles and before long had rendered any further resistance a futile expenditure of energy. Surrender to the inevitable was conceded with ill-grace. Agilely sliding down the sterns of their *hathis,* the indomitable *mugli-walas* bored their way fearlessly through a forest of giant legs and waving trunks. In a remarkably brief time they had hobbled the prize with ropes, fore and aft; and it was only then that the herd-bull ceased to fight to regain its freedom.

The other members of the herd were left for another day. One or two at a time would be captured and dragged back to camp; and when all had been collected the elephant rodeo would pack up until such time as more beasts were needed for training in the service of the State's Raja.

For the journey to camp strong ropes were lashed about the big prisoner's head and shoulders to serve as towing-lines for three *keddah* elephants, which now went to the head of the procession being formed up. A stout hawser was also stretched from the hind-legs of the captive to a couple of restraining animals at the rear. Thus harnessed, the herd-bull proceeded on its way reluctantly and with many shrill trumpeted protests at this ignoble treatment meted out to it by mankind and its own kin.

It was a slow march back to the camp, where the bull would begin its service for the Raja throughout the rest of its long life. Occasionally, on the homeward trail the large prisoner baulked with a grim determination; but a few rough and viciously delivered butts from the heads of the rearguard elephants quickly induced the recalcitrant beast to proceed on its way. On other occasions the towing-lines snapped taut under the strain imposed by the three animals in the vanguard. If this failed to convince the captive of the advisability of stepping along lively and without pausing to argue about it, a couple of elephants, holding a watching brief on either flank, promptly charged and viciously rammed their heads into the anatomy of the herd-bull. This always jarred it loose from any obstinate stance and called forth shrilly trumpeted vituperation of these heartless assailants. The rough treatment invariably proved effective and the procession moved onwards to the camp.

The "big policemen" thoroughly knew their jobs. They could handle this large, truculent and resisting prisoner with the utmost competence. If it attempted to rush the three animals in the lead, the ropes at the stern at once brought it up standing; wild dashes to right or left signally failed in relieving its plight; and just hanging fire on the track always brought in its wake painful retribution from the freelance *hathis* stationed on either flank. All its efforts to escape proving futile, the captive eventually submitted with the best grace possible under the unpleasant circumstances. That frame of mind, however, was not simply induced.

As time passed, our journey over the rough track proceeded with fewer interruptions; already the herd-bull was absorbing the first lesson in a prolonged curriculum of education; also appreciating that its former relished state of independence had become a memory of the past, knowledge that must have proved a bitter pill. Although the journey back to camp had been tempestuous and very different from our tranquil advance at dawn, it concluded in the manner most desired. On arrival at the camp the large captive was moored securely to four *Semul* (*bombax Malabaricum*) —giant silk cotton trees; and thus held prisoner.

The course of training started almost immediately. It is an intricate and astounding business. The feat demands an immense stock of patience, unwavering kindness in treatment, and expert understanding of the character of an elephant. The mahouts of India are superlative masters of their ancient and hereditary craft. The systems followed meticulously by them have remained unchanged for many centuries: from the era of Hannibal, and even long before then.

Once captured, the wild elephant is allowed to work off an excess of spleen by struggling strenuously to regain its freedom. This struggle is permitted to run its course until the beast's spirit has been broken. Only then can the next stages of the training process safely be taken in hand. Domestication is achieved in slow and patient steps until the big "pupil" becomes absolutely docile and will instantly obey every order issued by its regular mahout. The latter is held solely responsible for taming and training the beast. His job is no sinecure.

This particular elephant rodeo did not break up until every member of the herd had been captured and dragged back to the camp. The subsequent captures and return journeys, however, were nothing like so stormy or difficult as that experienced in the case of the herd-bull; and they were also far less punctuated by obstructive tactics on the part of unwilling prisoners. It looked as if the constant harassing suffered for a week or more must have taken most of the fight out of the four bulls, nine cows and three calves.

In a few years these captured wild elephants would have been perfectly tamed and trained to serve as invaluable allies of mankind. As likely as not, too, some would eventually be employed on a similar rodeo organized to capture more of their wild free-roaming kind. Throughout their lives in captivity they would know only kindness of treatment and consideration for their welfare, which alone can convert them into valuable animals in a domesticated state.

PART TWO

The Rockies and Mexico Desert

The mountain sheep are sweeter,
But the valley sheep are fatter.
                    Thomas Love Peacock.

8

Big-Horn, Elk, Wapiti and Moose

EARLY in February, 1909, I went off to the United States with John E—— to do some hunting in the Rockies. Both of us were on leave from the army and had become bored with London. We intended to spend four months on a shooting trip after Big-Horn, Elk, Wapiti, Moose and Bear. At New York we concluded all the essential arrangements, and we were ready early in March to make a start for the agreed rendezvous with our trapper-guide. Then I was suddenly invited to accompany ex-President Theodore Roosevelt's *safari* through Africa in the capacity of a special correspondent for *The Associated Press.* This upset our plans. With no objections raised by John to my defection, I accepted the assignment with intense joy. I sailed with Colonel Roosevelt's party for East Africa, and was with them for the entire eighteen months through Kenya, Uganda, Lado Enclave, the Sudan and Egypt, Europe and back to New York.

John had decided to resign his commission and remain in the United States. It was agreed that our postponed hunting trip in the Rockies should be carried out on my return from Africa. I rejoined him at Chicago in July of the following year, and at once we started the ball rolling. Through the kindness of a sportsman friend there, adequate arrangements had been completed for us in advance. He had engaged the services of a famous guide and trapper, a Delaware Indian named Little Beaver, to look after us and our material comforts; and the guide would be awaiting our advent at the agreed rendezvous with the outfit essential for the hunting trip. Little Beaver had taken out this friend on a number of occasions and was highly recommended by him.

But it was not until March of 1911 that I could manage to get away from the journalistic work upon which I was engaged. Then we headed for the base-camp which had been established by Little Beaver on the Arkansas River. On arrival there we found everything in readiness for us. The guide was eager to begin hunting with the least possible delay, which coincided with our own wishes. It was mid-March and the severity of the winter was now relaxing; and Little Beaver stated that the ice on the river had moved for the first time on the previous day. In about seven days we could take the trail towards Pike's Peak in the Rockies, where he proposed we should do our hunting, without experiencing too much discomfort from the weather conditions. We were jubilant when hearing his news. After big-game hunting in India and Africa this adventure promised to be a novel one for both of us. It certainly was.

Little Beaver's reputation as a guide and trapper stood high. We appreciated that our hunting would be performed under the guidance of a real expert. It was soon apparent to us that he possessed an uncanny gift for interpreting correctly all the signs of Nature and the ways of the denizens of the wild regions. Our riding and pack-animals were in charge of two experienced mountainmen, Jim and Billy, and they could not have been bettered. Both were capable hunters and trappers. Moreover, they proved cheerful companions in camp and on the trail. Those attributes mean much for the success of any hunting-party.

Exactly as Little Beaver predicted, we had a spell of fine weather shortly after our arrival at the base-camp, and the ice on the river now began to move steadily away. In a couple of days the Arkansas was rid of its winter coat except only near the banks, where the water froze over at night but melted again next morning under the heat of the sun's rays. Geese and innumerable varieties of wildfowl began to make their appearance. John and I enjoyed some first-rate sport with our shotguns, keeping the party well-supplied with birds for the table—an agreeable change of diet. Little Beaver instructed us how to shoot down the wildfowl on the wing with a .22 rifle and, in the course of a few days, we became reasonably efficient.

The blue bird followed close upon the geese and wildfowl. When the first robin was observed near the camp, Little Beaver announced that the winter was at an end; and he proposed that we should now take the trail and head up into the Rockies. John and I promptly agreed. Jim and Billy collected our animals from the poor pasturage near the camp; and shortly all was in readiness to break camp and advance towards our selected hunting terrain.

It was on the last day of March that we took the trail and headed for the mountainous areas in the foothills of the Rockies.

The grass there was more abundant and of a far better quality than had been available near the base-camp. Beside the Arkansas and in its neighbourhood no sign of spring vegetation had yet made its appearance. But, as we moved onwards into the mountains, we saw that the new grass was starting to shoot up; and the higher we climbed the more forward was the vegetation, though it was still only in its early stages of renewed growth. Little Beaver pointed out to us all the signs of spring: the bunch-grass becoming green at its roots, absinthe and greasewood throwing out their buds. But the cotton-woods and larger trees at low altitudes as yet displayed no signs of leaf. The cherry and currant bushes continued to appear dry and sapless, but this would not be for much longer—until the weather conditions warmed up.

Every thicket was now crowded with bird-life and resounded with their joyous songs. The open plains were alive with prairie-dogs, all busily occupied in repairing their homes and barking lustily as we rode near their large towns. Turkeys, too, were calling insistently from amongst the timber. At dawn and dusk the booming of the prairie-fowl could be heard on all sides of us. Of a truth, spring was here!

The carpet of snow had now disappeared entirely from the plains and valleys, but Pike's Peak and the surrounding ranges were still wrapped in their winter mantles. The Peak itself, some-times appearing whitely crowned and at others darkly sombre, was often concealed from our sight for an hour or more by a massed curtain of white vapoury clouds; but when these shrouds lifted, the mountains, which had appeared previously to be black and furrowed, were displayed white and smooth. For some periods in the daytime they could be seen clearly and then were greatly admired for their beautiful scenic effects.

We travelled leisurely up the Arkansas and made camp at the first fork on this river—about fifty miles from our original base. Hereabouts were found an abundance of deer. There need never be experienced by us any shortage of fresh meat. We remained at this camp for a week, while allowing our animals to fatten up on the plentiful and luxuriant buffalo-grass.

Then we moved on to the main fork of the Arkansas, from there following the course of Boiling Springs Creek. Soon we were shut in by high mountain ranges and elevated ridges, which rose up from both banks of the river. Through this narrow valley Boiling Springs Creek had become a rapid and turbulent torrent, foaming and tumbling over rocks and boulders, and its banks fringed with oak or a shrubbery of brushwood.

Not many miles further on the canyon opened out into a small and shelving glade. This was a delightful paradise for hunters.

Little Beaver assured us that this spot was visited only on rare occasions by mountainmen, and suggested that our permanent camp should be located there. To this we agreed at once, for no more ideal spot could possibly have been chosen for the purpose. This glade was entirely encompassed by rugged mountains and offered excellent pasturage for our animals. Immediately above us, and high up into the drifting clouds, towered Pike's Peak (14,109 feet altitude). From the camp we could see, in this gigantic amphitheatre, ridge after ridge clothed profusely with pine and cedar trees rising up to meet the stupendous mass of the Rockies. The latter stretched far away to the north and south, their immensely high peaks clearly visible to us above the strata of cumulus clouds which concealed the rugged bases and furrowed flanks from our eyes. The panorama offered a magnificent spectacle, one which never failed to delight us. Like Mount Kenya in East Africa, the Rockies can never stale, for the rapid changes in their aspect are seldom constant for any length of time but always create new wonders at which to marvel.

Soon after dawn on the first morning at this camp I set out alone to reconnoitre our environments. Presently I stretched myself out on a flat-surfaced rock, rifle ready to hand, and surveyed the countryside through field-glasses. The sun was now mounting steadily above the eastern horizon and the morning becoming warmer. Beautifully plumaged birds were twittering noisily in the trees and shrubs all around me. Ravens and magpies chattered overhead. And I was suddenly startled by the noise of a rock tumbling down the mountainside with a clatter. It made me glance upwards in that direction. There I spotted six big-horns, the Rocky Mountain wild sheep, perched precariously upon a pinnacle of rock, gazing below them speculatively rather than with an acute suspicion that all was not well in the vicinity. The enormous horns seemed disproportionately heavy for their bodies. At any moment I fully expected to see them lose their balance and topple over the edge of the rock upon which they perched.

Slowly and stealthily, I raised the rifle to my shoulder, twisted around cautiously, and took aim at the largest ram. These slight movements, however, did not escape the notice of the sheep which instantly sought safety in rapid flight—before it was possible for me to fire. They leaped agilely from rock to rock, and swiftly vanished out of sight up the steepest portion of the mountainside. Once only was there a brief chance of a shot at the ram I had picked but the range seemed to me overlong. Having no wish merely to wound the animal, I refrained from shooting and let them all go unharmed. I contented myself with watching their flight, immensely interested and thrilled by the agile performance.

The big-horn partakes of the nature of the deer and goat, resembling the latter animal more particularly in its habits and characteristic preference for high and inaccessible parts of mountain ranges. Little Beaver had told me that the big-horn seldom descends into the upland valleys, other than during exceptionally severe winter seasons. Sportsmen regard them as trophies *par excellence* in the Rockies. As a matter of fact, in size the big-horns come between that attained by our domestic sheep and the common red deer, but it is more strongly built than the latter animal.

By using my field-glasses I had been able to note that the colouring of these big-horns was a brownish-dun and the hair tipped with a darker tinge in the old rams. I could see a whitish streak showing on the hindquarters, and the tail was shorter than that of a red deer but tipped with black hairs. Horns carried by rams are enormous and curve backwards over the withers. I estimated that some horns on these rams were fully three feet long, while the circumference close to the head must have been about twenty inches. Watching their speedy flight up the mountainside, once I saw these sheep leap from a height of approximately twenty to thirty feet, alighting on the spread of horns and thereby saving themselves from a possible fractured or dislocated bone (or bones). It was an astonishing performance; one at which I greatly marvelled.

Shortly after the six big-horns had disappeared from sight, a small herd of black-tail deer leisurely traversed a corner of the glade and within easy range of me. I was on the point of shooting at the largest ram when I observed John stalking up to the herd from another angle. Until then I did not know that he also had left camp after me for some hunting. I thought that he was exposing himself far too freely to the black-tails for any hope of proving successful in securing a trophy. And the herd took instant fright, bolting off at speed out of range of both our rifles. Any hope of killing one was lost inevitably. I felt bitterly chagrined, because the ram I was about to shoot when John obtruded himself upon the scene was a really grand specimen of the species. However, it had to be accepted with good grace.

I retraced my way to the camp and related the events of the morning to a sympathetic Little Beaver. He consoled me with a promise that next day I should be taken out after a grizzly bear; and with this prospect I forgot the loss of a black-tail ram. Never having seen a grizzly outside a menagerie or zoological garden, I was, naturally enough, intensely eager to try conclusions with one in its wild state on the mountains.

That night, after a delectable dinner, we squatted around a

C*

fragantly smelling pine-log fire while Little Beaver discoursed long and learnedly about the subject of grizzly bears. He assured us that it was the fiercest and most to be feared animal on the mountains; its strength and tenacious hold upon life made an encounter with one anything but a desirable experience; and it was considered by the majority of hunters unwise to tackle a grizzly unless accompanied by a supporting rifle in experienced hands. He also said that, like most other wild beasts, the grizzly usually tries to sidestep a man; but, at certain seasons of the year when maddened by hunger or a compelling urge to mate, this animal will not infrequently charge home at first sight of a human being. A hug at close quarters could be anything but a loving embrace and could soon crush the life out of a man. The bear's sharp talons are capable of causing ghastly wounds.

Little Beaver, Jim and Billy regaled us with some grim stories of sanguinary encounters with grizzly bears. These were not at all pleasant hearing. No doubt their intention was to induce us to exercise the utmost caution when trailing one of these animals. We were warned sternly against foolhardy behaviour, and John and I promised to conduct ourselves circumspectly at all times.

Later we told our mentor and his two companions something about our big-game hunting experiences in Eastern Africa—with elephant, lion, buffalo and rhinoceros, and also of my own brief hunts after tiger in India. I suspected that they thought we were romancing. When I assured them of my belief that hunting elephants in Africa for their valuable ivory had convinced me that the species was the most dangerous of all, they expressed disbelief. After all, I do not suppose that one of them had ever seen an elephant except in a travelling circus, and this an Asiatic one, so their scepticism was pardonable. It might also have caused them to think that we were liable to accept grave risks and invite serious trouble.

I slept like a log that night, wholly undisturbed by the blood-thirsty adventures with grizzly which had been narrated over the camp-fire. Next morning, however, John admitted to having had rather a nightmarish dream closely associated with a bear. I suppose that was natural enough.

The loud chattering of a magpie overhead awakened me at dawn. Scrambling out of my blankets, I went outside the tent in pyjamas and a dressing-gown to watch a new day being born; and I was rewarded with a remarkable spectacle. The massive bulk of Pike's Peak was soon tinged with the most brilliant colour-effects. Daybreak in this wild and desolate spot was marvellously beautiful, while a peaceful serenity brooded over the countryside. My sole regret was that it ended far too soon.

Although the deep gorge in which we were camped was still shrouded in gloom, yet the tops of the mountains showed up grey and indistinct through the early morning mists. A faint glow of light broke over the ridge which shut out the valley from the east and, spreading gradually over the sky, disclosed to my eyes the snow-capped heights of Pike's Peak. A wreath of mist encircled it. Then the mist began to lift and evaporate until, suddenly, the hitherto dull white of the summit glowed like burnished silver; and, almost at the same moment, the entire eastern sky blazed with golden lights. Pike's Peak and the lower ridges, catching the reflections of this glorious brightness, glittered in the beams thrown out by the rising sun. Next, peeping boldly over the crest of the mountains, the sun flooded the valley with its dazzling light. A new day had been born in all its glory.

The others had now risen and were busily occupied with preparations for the day's hunting. Jim and Billy cooked our breakfast. They were remaining behind in charge of the camp and animals during our absence. Little Beaver, supremely confident in his skill, was accompanying his clients; and he made clear to us his fixed resolve to see that neither behaved otherwise than "according to Cocker".

Presently we followed silently in the wake of the guide as he climbed steadily and effortlessly up the face of the steep mountainside. It soon became evident to him that there were plenty of bears about. But he still had to learn whether or not these animals had vacated their winter hibernating quarters this early in the season. A few of the tracks encountered, however, warned him that they were of recent making. We followed one of them for several miles through the wildest part of the mountainous region, but never even glimpsed the bear.

While we were intent upon this quest, a clattering in our rear like a cavalry regiment at the gallop made me hold my rifle in readiness for immediate action. Looking back over our trail I saw a herd of a hundred or more elk dashing past us like a bunch of driven horses. In their passage down the mountainside they carried with them a small avalanche of rocks, stone and earth. The elk were rapidly gone from sight. We were given no chance to shoot, and a snap-shot was more likely to wound than kill. It was a great disappointment.

Later on that day, however, John and I each killed a fine ram of this grand species which provided ample compensations for our earlier frustration. We had agreed to shoot no more than one specimen of any species, rather than be a party to sacrificing animal life heedlessly. The latter would have been a deplorable thing to have done. The antlers of my trophy were not quite as

good as those obtained by John, but there was little enough really
to choose between the two heads.

Although we devoted nearly all of the daylight hours to an
intensive search for a bear of any variety, yet success eluded us.
Towards sunset we decided to call it a day. Little Beaver led us
back to camp, which we reached long after darkness had fallen
upon the countryside. Not once did he put a foot wrong. He
seemed to know instinctively the right paths to follow, even though
it was too dark to see the way.

Such disappointing days when out big-game hunting are all
in the luck of this "royal sport". If the truth be told, a sportsman
experiences far more blank days than rewarding ones; but if
inspired by a genuine hunter's spirit, he will accept the bad days
uncomplainingly. There is always a tomorrow. But even a sportsman's blank days will have furnished him with experiences which
are fascinating and vastly interesting, which compensate for
failure to collect a coveted trophy.

John was keen to secure good specimens of a wapiti and a
moose; whereas I only desired to photograph these two species in
their natural environment. For a number of days in succession
Little Beaver took us out to satisfy our respective ambitions, but
success eluded us in so far as the wapiti was concerned, though
eventually I did photograph a bull moose; and having done so,
John killed this beast cleanly with his first bullet.

It is a curious fact that a number of these two species were imported into New Zealand some years ago and liberated there in a
suitable area of country. The wapiti thrived exceedingly well in
that alien land and multiplied to such a great and unexpected
extent that the New Zealand Government has now to employ a
band of professional hunters to keep the herds down to reasonable numbers. Some near world record heads of wapiti have been
shot in New Zealand during fairly recent years.

On the other hand, the imported moose failed to establish itself
though why this should have proved the case does not seem to be
understood in New Zealand. Though a few of the species may still
survive, their actual numbers seem to be doubtful. One of the last
specimens of the moose known to have been shot in New Zealand
was a bull killed in the Fiordland district, and it is believed that
before long the species will have been exterminated in New
Zealand. The same lamentable situation can be found in the
United States, where this animal is reported to be on the verge
of total extirpation. In Canada, however, the moose is protected
so rigidly by law that it still provides sportsmen with some good
hunting where this is legally permissible.

The moose is the largest and heaviest species of the deer genus, and commonly known as an elk in Europe or Asia. By no stretch of the imagination can it be called a graceful animal. Its neck and body are short and bulky, legs overlong, and it has no tail worthy of notice. Nevertheless a bull moose, weighing in the neighbourhood of 1,400 pounds and with well-developed, symmetrical and broadly palmated antlers, undoubtedly does present an imposing picture. It affords a grand sight which can only be viewed in the wilds. When taken from its natural habitat and kept in captivity, this creature never attains a ripe old age. Not unlikely, this fact partially explains failure of the species to establish itself in New Zealand.

The moose inhabits the forests of America from Maine northwards, and from Alaska to Nova Scotia. The Alaskan type is rated the largest of the species, standing from six to seven feet at withers; carries the largest antlers with spreads of about seventy inches. But there are records of bull moose shot in the Yukon and Northern Quebec to indicate that specimens existing there are as big and have antlers which give a spread measurement not put to shame by that of the Alaskan type. I believe that the record for North America is $74\frac{1}{4}$ inches; and this prize was shot in the Yukon.

The cow moose is even less attractive in its appearance because of its mule-like head. Lacking antlers, the cow's elongated and almost grotesquely shaped nose becomes particularly emphasized. Of all members of the deer genus, the female moose is alone styled a cow instead of a doe. The bull is said to be in its prime when aged from six to eight years; when four years old it will be found that bulls carry a long "bell" (the hirsute appendage hanging down from the throat but dissimilar to the dewlap of the eland in Africa). It seems to be credited popularly that no cow moose is endowed with a "bell", but some hunters claimed to have encountered several cows thus adorned. I am unable to contribute anything on the subject.

Little Beaver informed me that the antlers of the bull of this species diminish with each annual renewal, becoming like two gnarled and knotted spikes when reaching old age. He believed that, in the wild state, this animal will live for twenty years. He also declared that aged bull moose display no evidence of waning physical powers, but there can be discerned unmistakable signs of mental decline into a state of mild dotage or senile decay.

Judging by my sole contact with this species, I should be inclined to think the hunting of a moose must demand an appreciation of the fact that this creature has a far keener nose than eyesight, while their hearing is remarkably good. When encountering this one individual of the species Little Beaver cautioned us to make the stalk up-wind, move forward slowly and cautiously, and avoid stepping upon any dry sticks. He also declared that a suspicious bull moose, when hearing or scenting a hunter, could vanish noiselessly and almost on tip-toe. It was soon miles away from the danger zone. The beast never lopes or gallops, but its jog-trot is much faster than generally credited. They can also swim with remarkable ease and speed.

Our guide stated that a wounded bull moose could be highly dangerous. Large animals as they are, this creature has little vitality after being hit by a bullet fired from a modern high-velocity rifle. Little Beaver stated that it will nearly always drop dead within a short distance of the place where it had been hit in a vital spot; and that is what happened in the case of the bull moose killed by John.

9

Grizzly Bear

DAY after day we were driven hard by Little Beaver. He took us out at crack of dawn to comb all the canyons and valleys in the mountains which seemed likely to offer possibilities of locating a shootable bear. We made one expedition away from camp which lasted for three days, going high up into the rugged flanks of Pike's Peak and well above the snow-line. The climb took us to an altitude of about 10,000 feet. But still no bears showed themselves as a target, and we began to despair of achieving our ambition.

John and I felt increasingly frustrated and depressed in spirit. Little Beaver, however, begged us not to be discouraged by this apparent scarcity of our chief quarry, claiming that he had seen a number of clear signs that bears were beginning to vacate their winter hibernating quarters. Indeed, their tracks became more frequent almost daily. But not a bear was glimpsed. He promised that soon we should be given a chance to test our skill and courage by tackling a grizzly. Both of us fervently trusted that our guide was not being too optimistic, but this was rather an unjust attitude on our part.

Then, one day when hunting around the base of Pike's Peak, we did encounter a large she-bear. The animal came out hurriedly and grunting menacingly from a patch of cedars, where she had been lying up. As we approached she headed at speed up the slopes of the mountainside. Dodging among rocks and boulders as she climbed it was impracticable for either of us to risk a shot at her. Little Beaver stated that she was a very old beast and quite the grizzliest of grizzly bears which he had ever seen.

Although the bear was only a short distance away from us when disturbed, she was soon lost to sight. As it was then beginning to become dark, our guide refused to consider following up the animal. Though he agreed that it might be possible to get up close enough to her for making a clean kill, as grizzly bears seldom run far—especially in early spring when weak and lank after a prolonged period of hibernation—he rated this specimen unworthy of the risks involved in pursuit of her when the light was fading fast.

We were disgusted at being compelled to return to camp without a shot at the first grizzly we had seen in its wild state. I consoled myself with the reflection that one of these creatures had been seen at close range, while this brief encounter with a formidable animal had not caused me any nervousness. All that had been told to us about this species had given us the impression that it might prove even more dangerous to hunt than elephant, lion, leopard or buffalo.

Throughout our hunting time Little Beaver had industriously been setting traps. He made a point of visiting them when out with us in quest of bears but, so far, every trap had been found unsprung.

On the following morning we left camp as soon as it was light in order to search for grizzly bears. When we looked for the first trap, which had been set close to a mountain tarn, it had gone from where it had been placed by Little Beaver two days earlier. He was greatly puzzled about this. But there were seen quite fresh bear "signs" on the bank of the stream, so we walked beside the water in search of the missing trap. Suddenly we heard the distinct sounds of some large and heavy animal forcing its way through a thicket of wild plum bushes which belted the creek.

Concealing ourselves behind a large rock we expectantly awaited developments. Presently a huge grizzly emerged from the bushes and, limping on three legs, made its way towards a flat-surfaced rock fairly close to our hiding-place. The bear mounted this rock and then seated itself upon it. One of its forepaws was raised to a level with the face and then, to our amazement, we perceived that this paw had been caught in the missing trap. Part of the broken chain, which had anchored the trap to the ground, was dangling down from the paw.

As we watched, the grizzly lifted the iron-gloved paw close to its eyes and proceeded to examine this novel appendage. It did so gravely and with a display of lively curiosity, turning the paw this way and that, quaintly lowering its head from side to side, and then staring at the trap out of a corner of an eye with obvious bewilderment. Patently, it was unable to solve the mystery of this strange object which firmly gripped and pained its fore-paw. Every now and again, the bear would sniff suspiciously at the trap or tap it upon the rock. As the last action only hurt the paw still worse, it did not repeat this many times. The animal next began to lick the steel trap with a pink tongue, as if deprecating any anger caused to a queer contraption fixed on its paw and anxious to conciliate this strange enemy which was hurting it badly.

Having closely observed these curious antics for some time, and as the bear seemed to be disinclined to resume its meanderings, Little Beaver whispered to me that I should shoot to kill. My position afforded the easiest shot at the target. Nothing loth, I took steady aim, gently squeezed the trigger, and killed the grizzly outright where sitting on the rock. It was, in every sense of the word, a "sitter" and nothing could have been easier than making the kill. But I experienced no pride in the accomplishment. Little Beaver released the trapped paw, deftly skinned the trophy, and concealed the pelt in the fork of a nearby tree. It was weighed down by the trap. Then we resumed our quest for other grizzly bears that might be roaming about the mountainside.

Little Beaver had told us that all bears are exceedingly partial to wild plums and cherries. Consequently, a thicket of these bushes after the fruit had ripened was the most likely spot in which to find them. Whenever they can get wild fruits, he said, they much preferred them to edible roots. But as yet the spring was insufficiently advanced for the fruit to have ripened, and he wisely decided to search elsewhere for our quarry. Luck did not favour us again that day. Late in the afternoon we made our way back to the tree where my trophy had been deposited, retrieved it, and continued silently on our way to the camp in that lovely open glade.

Two days later Little Beaver again led us into the mountains after grizzly. He left us to rest on the bank of a small creek running down the hillside while going off to examine some of the traps which had been set by him a few days earlier. Because we had not come upon any freshly made bear marks, he considered it was safe enough to leave his clients and no possible harm was likely to befall them during a short absence.

It was not long before John became bored with inactivity, scrambled up, and wandered off through a cherry thicket skirting the creek. He left me on guard over our packs and to my own devices. Suddenly he saw a large grizzly he-bear turning over the turf with its nose, quietly and industriously, in search of pig-nuts and yampa roots, both of which were abundant hereabouts. He whistled softly to attract my attention. I heard his signal and interpreted it correctly, and hurried to join him. John pointed to the bear, whispering that he intended to kill it before Little Beaver returned. I agreed to this proposal. I had already secured my trophy, but John still lacked one; and this seemed far too good a chance to let slip.

We began to creep forward as noiselessly as possible. The bear had not yet been alarmed and seemed ignorant of our nearby presence, for it went on digging. We gained the edge of the thicket without disturbing the beast; and now saw that it was standing broadside on to us and fairly well exposed at a range of approximately fifty yards. While I covered him with my rifle, John fired at this tempting target but his bullet failed to inflict a mortal wound. Growling savagely, the grizzly leaped clean into the air and then, seeing us at the fringe of the thicket, charged instantly in our direction. It was now maddened by pain and anger, fully intending to be revenged upon those who had injured it severely.

I was just about to shoot into its chest when John shouted that we had better run for it; and, at the same moment, he left the tree behind which he was standing to bolt back through the thicket. It struck me that there was no option but to follow his example, so I refrained from shooting and ran after him. Yet I much doubted the wisdom of our behaviour, and disliked doing it. Never before, or since, had I run from any wild beast I was hunting with a rifle or camera, because I always considered such an action more likely to result in a fatality than would standing your ground. I know of a number of instances where hunters have lost their lives because they did what we did on this occasion.

Once committed to running from this grizzly, I struck out a line for myself hoping this would make the bear confused about which man to follow. The thicket was far too dense for either of us to make any speed, but the weight and strength of the grizzly forced a way through every obstruction with comparative ease. It kept close on our heels, and even gaining ground upon us. About a hundred yards from the thicket was a steepish bluff and, between the two points, a small stretch of level plateau. We made for the open ground as fast as we could run, as it seemed to offer the best chance of escaping from the murderous pursuit of the grizzly. Having gained the bluff, we could about-face and shoot to kill.

We both sped across the plateau. When little more than half-way to the bluff, the bear had closed up to within about thirty yards of us. John was running about fifty yards to my right when I saw him trip over a concealed root or stone, and fall prone on his face. The bear made straight for him. As he regained his feet, the animal rose up on its hind-legs only three yards away. As the bear closed, John yelled out to me to shoot it but this looked too risky as the chances were I would hit him instead of the animal. I saw him fire a bullet into the chest of the beast, but the next instant the rifle was knocked out of his hands by a savage blow from a fore-paw. The grizzly embraced John in a terrific hug, with claws ripping at his body mercilessly. Then it rolled over with its victim on to the ground, with John underneath.

His situation was perilous, and John struggled desperately to get free. Although he must have been suffering terrible punishment from the fiendishly sharp talons, he did not lose his presence of mind. Drawing a hunting-knife from its sheath on the belt, he plunged the keen blade again and again into the body of the grizzly. The latter, made still more savage and enraged by these vicious stabs, continued to tear John with talons and fangs; and the knife slipped from his nerveless hands. Mercifully, he must have lost consciousness.

All this had taken only a few minutes in reality, though it seemed more like many hours to me. I was powerless to do a single thing to help John, not daring to shoot; I had been compelled to watch this ghastly disaster with a quaking heart and terror-stricken eyes. I thought that John had been killed. So I fired a shot at the bear and hit it in a vital spot. Down it went on top of my friend, killed stone dead.

I ran at topmost speed to find Little Beaver and get his help. My lusty and frenzied shouts were quickly answered by the guide, who had heard the shooting and was now hurrying towards the spot. A few moments later he and I were running back to where lay John and the grizzly. As we ran side by side, I told Little Beaver as best I could what had happened.

On gaining the spot, now a bloody shambles, we were immensely relieved to find that John was still alive and breathing faintly. The grizzly was dead, its huge bulk sprawled over my stricken friend; but with our combined efforts, we dragged the heavy carcase to one side. It was only too obvious to us that John's condition was grievous. He was only just alive. We did all we could but Little Beaver entertained little hope of preserving his life. As we attended to the ghastly injuries inflicted by the grizzly, the guide gave me rapid orders.

I must hasten back to the camp, tell Jim and Billy what had occurred, and get them to make a stretcher of some kind. All three of us must then hurry back to the spot bringing the stretcher, all available medical stores, and a good supply of food. At a tireless run I started off over the backward trail to the camp. I was blaming myself bitterly for not having risked a shot at the grizzly while it was mauling John, and still more for having taken to my heels when he ran. But I appreciated that both of us were equally to blame for having behaved foolishly from start to finish of the incident.

During my absence Little Beaver had done everything possible for John. Then he examined the carcase of the grizzly before starting to skin it; in addition to three bullets in the body, he found ample evidence of the terrific fight John had put up to save his life. Many deep and long gashes made by the hunting-knife were found, though none of them could have proved fatal.

It was nearing sunset when we reached the spot. Little Beaver reported that John still lived, and was now breathing a trifle more strongly, but he had not regained consciousness. The guide believed there was only a slender chance of his recovering from such a terrible mauling. All four of us worked hard to render our patient as comfortable as the circumstances permitted; and next formed a bivouac close to the site of the tragedy. It was only too evident that John could not be carried down the mountain to our camp in the glade. Even if he lived through this ordeal, it would be unwise to attempt such a journey until his strength had much improved. Little Beaver predicted that we would have to wait patiently for some days before John could be moved.

Taking it in turns, we nursed the patient throughout what seemed to us an interminable night. When the new day broke, John was still alive but had not regained consciousness. Little Beaver despatched Billy to the camp with orders to mount the fastest of our horses and gallop to Pueblo, the nearest place with a hospital, and get the services of a doctor. We knew that some days must pass before medical aid could arrive.

John was still living when the doctor reached us and took over charge of our patient. But it was three more days before the sick man recovered consciousness. Our relief of mind was intense, for this improvement indicated that John had passed the crisis and now had a fair chance of recovery. For two more weeks we nursed him back to life and strength. Then, at long last, the doctor pronounced it safe enough to move him by easy stages to the hospital at Pueblo. Fortunately, he withstood the journey remarkably well. Once safely at the hospital, John began to mend rapidly; but a month passed before the surgeon removed the bandages from the many wounds inflicted by the grizzly.

By then my funds were running unpleasantly low. It had become imperative to return to Chicago and find employment, or I should find myself on the rocks. I went to the hospital for the last time to take farewell of John. It was the day when the bandages had been removed, and I found him standing before a mirror, critically examining his reflection. He had become lank and cadaverous in appearance, his handsome face so scarred and horribly disfigured that it was scarcely possible to recognize a single former feature.

He about-turned and faced me with a sardonic grin. The disfigurements made me feel rather sick, and my heart grieved for him. John declared emphatically that nothing could induce him ever again to show himself in the hubs of civilization. He intended to live the rest of his life among the mountainmen in the Rockies. Nothing that I said was capable of shaking this resolve. In my heart I fully sympathized with what he had planned for his future.

That happened many years ago, but it is still vividly remembered. Often there will rise up before my eyes a clear picture of our camp-site at the base of Pike's Peak, surrounded by the stupendous works of Nature which, in all their solitary grandeur, frowned down upon and dwarfed the open glade into comparative insignificance. With a goodly pile of pine-logs on the camp-fire, its cheerful blaze striking high into the blue vault of sky overhead and illuminating the valley far and wide, one could sit cross-legged beside the fire's genial warmth and build fanciful castles in the air.

When camped on broken ground at the base of the grim Rocky Mountains, John could conveniently forget his terrible disfigurements and all other mundane things. To him, under the circumstances, this kind of life would provide immense solace to his heart and soul. He would be living among wild creatures of many species and free to spend his days beside the tumbling, babbling creeks or on the fringe of groves and thickets of timber; and also find immense pleasure in the company of single-minded mountainmen, whose simple talk concerned only exciting hunting exploits. It would be a grand life for John to lead: one, too, after his own inclinations. I frankly envied him.

For a few more years we kept in touch by letters at intervals. Then mine remained unanswered. Finally, Jim wrote to say that John had been killed during a tough fight with a grizzly she-bear. I much doubt if he would have chosen another kind of ending to his life. It is true that man wills, but God disposes.

10

Mountain Sheep in Mexico

IT IS a far cry, of course, from Burma to Mexico. I had returned to London from Rangoon in the middle of 1923; and a month or two later undertook a lecture tour through Canada and the United

States, which ended early in the following year. For a few more months I remained in the United States to complete the writing of a series of articles commissioned by a New York publisher. However, I managed to get in one hunting trip of an entirely novel character in my experience.

When paying a visit to a friend in Arizona, who was aware that I had shot and photographed big-game in various parts of the world, he urged me to try my luck with the mountain sheep in the Mexican deserts. His challenge held out a strong appeal. The more so because I always hankered after something new. I had been unsuccessful, a little over a decade earlier, in securing a trophy of the big-horn of the Rockies, but known better luck with Markhor in India. The temptation to collect a specimen of the mountain sheep in Mexico was far too potent to be resisted.

My host made all the arrangements and engaged the services of a first-class professional hunter, who had taken him out on several occasions. He also generously lent me his battery of rifles, because my own had been left behind in Britain. Fortunately, his weapons suited me admirably. I accepted these kindnesses gladly and stood committed to the adventure.

It was impressed upon me that hunting mountain sheep in the desert regions of Mexico, which are practically waterless, would impose a severe test of human endurance and physical stamina. I gathered that the sport was for the young and physically fit, and my age was then forty-two. But I was hard and tough, having always maintained myself in perfect training. My host assured me that every trophy gained would richly be earned, but they could only be won through toil, sweat and thirst within an arid terrain where the noon temperature hovered around 120 degrees Fahrenheit. Those statements did not put me off.

As a matter of fact, he spoke the truth. If I had fully appreciated all it entailed and the sufferings which must be endured, second thoughts might possibly have caused me to abandon the trip. But when recalling memories of it, I experience no particle of regret and only a gratifying measure of pride in achievement. That reaction, I think, is pardonable.

I set out for Yuma on the Colorado River and situated in the south-western extremity of Arizona. I was to make contact there with the guide and his brother. Bill was a rancher, occasional prospector, much-travelled, and a professional hunter; and he had shot mountain sheep from Alaska to Mexico. No more expert mentor could have been engaged. It was not long before this fact became abundantly patent. His brother, Mike, would accompany the outfit in charge of the transport. Mike also knew a great deal about the ways of mountain sheep and the best methods of hunting them, and was thoroughly familiar with the desert regions where we intended to hunt. Two Mexican *peons*, Lazaro and Francisco, had been engaged by Bill to care for the horses and pack-mules. These two men completed our small outfit.

Early in August, the hottest month of the year, we rode out of Yuma eastwards to Wellton on the Southern Pacific Railway—distant about forty miles. The ride there proved somewhat of a nightmare personally, but furnished a foretaste of what I had let myself in for and therefore was good training. On the Sonora Plains the noon temperature seldom fell below 120 degrees Fahrenheit, and the suspicion was strong that it might even have been higher.

We pulled out of Wellton under the light of a brilliant full moon. Bill and I were riding light, and kept well in advance of the loaded mule-wagon driven by Mike and the pack-animals in charge of the two Mexicans. I reckoned that we averaged four to five miles an hour. Just at first the desert stretched out flatly on all sides in unrelieved monotony towards distant mountain ranges. At midnight we were riding through masses of great cactus, the Saguaro, whose queerly shaped shafts rose to a height of forty to fifty feet above the floor of the desert. Their few branches were set at grotesque angles from the main stem. In the silvern moonlight they looked ghostly apparitions. The entire expanse of desert seemed to be littered profusely with these peculiar growths, but there were few other signs of vegetation.

Bill set a course due southwards to a waterhole situated roughly sixteen miles from Wellton, where he had decided to make our first camp. We arrived there shortly after midnight, promptly bivouacked close beside it, and then awaited the advent of the remainder of the outfit. The water was not of high quality. After the excessive heat of the day the atmosphere now seemed comparatively cool; but the ground still remained very hot to the touch. Mike's wagon and the pack-mules rejoined us about an hour later, bivouacking alongside us.

We broke camp about an hour before dawn. Having loaded two of the pack-mules with necessities and intending to rough it, Bill and I rode off across the desert towards the Tinajas Altas (High Tanks), which were situated on the slopes of a distant range of bare rocky hills. Our objective was four miles over the Mexican border. I explained to my companion that my passport had no visa to enter Mexico, but he told me to forget it as no one would be interested even if we met any human beings, Mexicans or otherwise. Lazaro was mounted on a horse and led the two pack-mules. It had been arranged that Mike and the remainder of the outfit would follow us to the Tinajas Altas, but travel at a more leisurely pace to conserve the stamina of the animals. That ride over the desert proved unpleasantly hot, and it was a relief to reach the water-tanks.

Bill selected a site for our bivouac on a restricted plateau about 200 yards below the lowest series of tanks worn out in the solid rock. Fortunately for us they still contained ample supplies of water, but many a traveller over the desert had arrived there hopefully and found the tanks bone-dry. They died of thirst beside them. Their bones and skulls scattered about the Tinajas Altas provided ample proof. We made ourselves as comfortable as the circumstances permitted, and then waited patiently for the rear party to rejoin us. They arrived about three hours later. For the rest of that day and the night we bivouacked at the Tinajas Altas.

About three hours before dawn I was aroused from sleep by Bill shaking my shoulder vigorously. We enjoyed a good breakfast cooked for us by Mike, saddled our horses, and made sure that all was in readiness for departure. Then Bill and I rode off towards the hunting-ground which he had selected, being accompanied only by Lazaro leading a couple of loaded pack-mules. We rode light. All comforts had been sternly dispensed with. By sun-up we had advanced far into Mexico, and three hours later gained the crest of a high ridge where we halted to gaze around us with field-glasses for signs of our special quarry. Bill soon sighted a bunch of sheep in the distance. Leaving Lazaro in charge of our mounts and pack-mules, we set out on foot to stalk them.

The sheep took fright and bolted, but did not travel far before halting and gazing suspiciously in our direction. We flattened out on our stomachs and remained immobile long enough to restore the animals' confidence, and then we resumed our stalking with extreme caution and stealth. Presently, I came within reasonable range of a fine ram standing at gaze. Although it entailed shooting up a slope and at a trifle too long a range for my liking, yet I tried a shot. Bill's rifle spoke almost simultaneously. To our chagrin, both missed our chosen targets and the bunch of sheep were away at speed. We followed up at a steady run. Two snap shots taken at my ram also failed to register, and I saw both bullets strike the ground over the animal.

Bill's ill-success must have been a case of sheer ill-luck, for he enjoyed a reputation of being a crack marksman. Indeed, later during the day I watched him kill a ram, only part of which was visible, from a range of 400 yards and when every single factor was against him. My own bad shooting I attributed to using a strange rifle, a Springfield, and being wholly unaccustomed to the deceptive light effects. That may be correct or otherwise, but the explanation was accepted by my companion without comment, and no more was said about such a display of indifferent marksmanship. Yet I suspected that he had a poor opinion of the shooting by a man who was known to have done much big-game hunting in Africa and some in India.

The day was now unpleasantly hot, so we decided to abandon our hunting and ride back to the Tinajas Altas camp. The decision came as a relief to my mind. I much wanted a chance to do some target practice with the Springfield and master its performance. At the camp this would not disturb any sheep.

Before dawn the next day Bill and I rode off across the desert. This time we took only one loaded pack-mule in charge of Lazaro, our intention being to bivouac in the area where we hunted sheep on the previous day. Almost certainly the quarry could be located thereabouts, but, as no water was known to be available in this area, Lazaro and the animals would return to the Tinajas Altas after we had selected a site for our bivouac. He was instructed to rejoin us there on the next evening and bring a supply of water for the horses and ourselves. We bivouacked for the night in the dry bed of an *arroyo* (watercourse), but slept none too comfortably because of the hard ground and intense heat which constantly awakened us.

An hour before daybreak we rose, cooked and had breakfast, and then tidied up the bivouac. As the dawn broke we set out on foot to hunt for sheep. The heat was terrific and the going rough, but we kept moving without a pause to rest. After several hours I spotted a fairly good ram at a reasonable range, fired at it and again missed badly to my consternation. I felt very ashamed of such poor marksmanship. It was not true to form. Bill made no comment, and merely grinned; but I had an unhappy feeling that he must think me a real bad shot, and my claimed successes with Markhor in India and big-game in Africa must be accepted with the proverbial grain of salt. If this was what he thought he showed no sign of it.

Not long after this lamentable exhibition, three more sheep were sighted. They were perched precariously on the summit of a large boulder near the base of a hill in the same range where we stood at gaze. All three of them were staring intently at us and obviously feeling an acute suspicion. Acting upon Bill's advice, I waited patiently until the animals had lost interest in the intruders upon their domain. They then sprang down agilely from the boulder, and vanished rapidly out of sight.

I went off alone to stalk them, while Bill took another direction. It was not long before I saw these three sheep again, staring back at me. I succeeded in crawling to within about 100 yards without being detected or alarming the sheep, and then aimed carefully at the best ram of the trio. Whether the run of ill-luck which had dogged me so far had spent itself or I had become more familiar with a strange rifle and the strong light, I cannot say; but my bullet killed the ram outright, and it proved an excellent trophy. My elation seemed justified.

As Bill was hunting for sheep at some distance away, I rough dressed the trophy with much hard work, and then squatted down in the meagre shade of a boulder to rest until he rejoined me. Physical exhaustion and the intense heat made me disinclined to resume hunting. In any case, Bill had told me that the sheep would now be sheltering from the blazing sunshine in rock-caves on the hills where it would be futile to hunt them. There are, of course, always exceptions to every rule. And soon I was given cause to appreciate this fact and able to profit by it.

To my astonishment, I spotted some more sheep on the flank of an adjoining ridge, standing immobile while gazing suspiciously in my direction. Scattered among the rocks were four small bunches of them—three comprising only ewes with lambs, and the fourth all rams. I counted sixteen adult animals in the four groups. Selecting what appeared to be the best ram, I fired at it from a range of 200 yards—too long for my liking; but any movements made in getting closer would probably have sent them all off out of range. I must have hit the ram a trifle too low because it did not drop to the shot. Instantly they were off at speed, as was only to be expected, and the wounded ram went with them. What I had started must now be finished.

I followed up immediately. The spoor was not difficult to trace because the ram was bleeding freely. It travelled for a distance of about half a mile and then I saw it lie down at the mouth of a rock-cave; but the quarry was soon up again and away before I could get within reasonable range for a kill. The ram made an amazingly dexterous descent of the flank of a steep ravine and, when next viewed, was already halfway up the opposite wall but now not more than 100 yards distant. It came to a halt behind a largish rock and with only its fore-quarters visible. My next bullet released the ram from the suffering which I had inflicted.

Because of the heat it was advisable to skin the trophy at once, so I set to work upon this task. Just before completing it I heard a shot from Bill's rifle, and fired also to let him know my whereabouts. Before long he had rejoined me, and heartily congratulated his client on achieving the two successes. Bill had known no luck, not even a sheep coming within sight.

The heads and skins of my two trophies had to be carried down the steep hillside. Bill packed one of them, while I carried the other. I found mine far from simple to manage; not only was the

load heavy and unwieldy, but the going most exhausting. I copied
Bill's method, balancing the head on a shoulder and with a horn
hooked round my neck, and the skin bundled up as best might be;
but the latter was constantly slipping free, which caused delay and
trouble throughout the difficult descent to the level of the desert.

Once there it was mutually agreed that Bill should remain with
the trophies while I trudged across the furnace-like waste to the
bivouac, and then send back the Mexican to him with his horse
and a pack-mule to transport the trophies. We believed that Lazaro
would be there and waiting for us. If not, Bill had decided to wait
where he was until the evening and then come on to join me at the
arroyo. The trophies could be collected by the Mexican *peon* when
he reached us with the animals for our return to the Tinajas Altas.

I arrived utterly spent, soaked with sweat, and suffering from
a raging thirst. It was an immense relief to find Lazaro there with
the animals and a fresh supply of water. Somehow the language
difficulties were surmounted. He seemed to understand what had
to be done and where to locate Bill; and then I sent him off with
the horse and pack-mule. Having quenched my thirst, I rested
until their return. When Bill arrived, he decided to head back at
once for the Tinajas Altas. We rode back through the night. The
heads and skins were cleaned more expertly with Mike's help, and
fortunately the hair had not started to slip. Our task was completed
by starlight.

Up to now we had hunted along the extremity of the Gila Range
and near the El Viejo Hombro (The Old Man) Range. There the
mountain sheep subsisted upon the twigs of a small symmetrical
bush which our Mexican *peons* called El Verva del Baso; but Bill
and Mike spoke of it as the White Brittle Bush. The sheep also
cropped such Galetta grass as chanced to be available, and our own
animals grazed upon it though it was doubtful if they found this
grass to be of a nourishing nature. But, on a desert, animals are
compelled to make do with whatever food happens to be offered. It
is always sparse and indifferent fodder.

Bill and Mike stated that the sheep did not go to a waterhole to
drink, but broke down cactus plants in order to extract the juice by
chewing the pulp. They assured me that this sufficed to quench
their thirsts. Later on, I actually watched some sheep doing exactly
this thing. Mike told me that the rams began to run with the ewes
in October; the ewes lambed down in February; and then the rams,
as also the yearling rams, left the ewes until the following October.
This explains why in August I had seen a bunch of rams and three
bunches of ewes with young but no rams amongst them. For
another couple of months until the breeding season the rams
would remain apart from the ewes.

Bill wished to visit one of his nearby prospecting areas, and I agreed to his temporary defection. Mike offered to take me out after sheep, but I thanked him and declined because I was planning to hunt by myself during Bill's absence, accompanied only by the two Mexicans and three pack-mules loaded with the barest necessities. This idea, perhaps, was somewhat ambitious for a mere tyro. As neither Bill nor Mike offered any objections to it, I did not feel uneasy in my mind. Bill advised hunting for sheep in the Pinacate area, but warned that waterholes were not only few but situated far apart. He said there always was great uncertainty whether or not these would be found dry.

After resting for a couple of days at the Tinajas Altas, I went off into the desert with the two Mexicans and three loaded pack-mules. We rode horses. Lazaro and Francisco assured me emphatically that they knew perfectly well where water could always be located in the Pinacate region. I accepted these statements without question. As it transpired later, this was most unwise and it seemed that still much had to be learned of the character of Mexican *peons*. Lazaro and Francisco had told me only what they thought I wished to hear, having no strict regard for the truth. They came mighty close to landing us all in disaster.

We pulled out from the Tinajas Altas camp late in the afternoon. The next available supply of water was reported to be at the Papago Tank, situated roughly forty-five miles southwards; and both Mexicans insisted that water would positively be found there. I hoped they were not wrong. The first fifteen miles took us over the Camino del Diablo trail crossing the Tule Desert. The route had aptly been named. We rode forward through the night at a walking pace and, though the moon was late in rising, the stars were bright enough to make the trail easily visible. At eight next morning the sun was unpleasantly fierce, but by that hour the foothills of the twin peaks of the Pinacate Range had been gained.

It was then that Lazaro and Francisco appeared to have become hopelessly vague in regard to the exact location of the Papago Tank. Indeed, they failed to find it for me. Quite unexpectedly, I stumbled fortuitously upon an unnamed waterhole in the dry bed of an *arroyo* which was full of water. In reality, it was no more than a smallish rock-basin. As no other supply was known to us, I wisely decided to bivouac beside it. But our animals reduced the water at such an alarming rate that necessity impelled me to cut short our stay at this providentially-found waterhole.

During the second day's hunting around this spot I chanced upon the Papago Tank, which was about fifteen miles to the north-west. It was bone-dry! So much for the reliability of the two Mexicans. They were not even aware of the existence of the water where we bivouacked!

For two days I hunted around for sheep, leaving the *peons* at the bivouac in charge of the animals. I found no sheep, but they provided ample evidence of their presence in the mountain range. For three more days I rode about with Lazaro, leaving the water-hole before dawn, to hunt for sheep over a more distant area. After sunrise it became more devastatingly hot; but at noon a gentle breeze came across the lava-beds, though this was always akin to a hot blast from a furnace door thrown wide open for refuelling.

Reptile life was astoundingly plentiful. Lizards scuttled rapidly away at our approach; a species of toad, with a red speckled back, seemed to be common; and cotton-tails were also fairly numerous. Once I saw a gila lizard, a monster and sluggish creature which is very poisonous. The two birds most in evidence were Gambel's quail and the Sonora (White Wings) pigeon; though many other varieties were also noted, but I could not identify them. The floor of the desert was profusely littered with many peculiar forms of cacti, mesquite and creosote. The Choya cactus seemed to be especially plentiful. The points of its wicked spikes are barbed and extremely difficult to extract without the aid of a sharp knife; and, indeed, I suffered torments from many imbedded in my flesh. It was found next to impossible to get rid of these vicious barbs; and later Mike had to cut out many which still awaited extraction. It was rather a painful operation.

I also encountered thereabouts two kinds of the prickly-pear cactus. Ocatillas were abundant, too. The latter are curious plants, fashioned somewhat like an umbrella with a short central stem; and radiating from it are as many as twenty spokes umbrella-wise. These spokes are generally about six feet long, all profusely covered with diminutive sharp thorns that are concealed by small leaves. When in full bloom the Ocatilla cactus has a flower of flaming scarlet. It is gorgeously beautiful.

On the fifth day I returned to the waterhole about a couple of hours before midday after an unsuccessful quest for sheep, and feeling excessively overheated, weary and greatly disappointed at the negative results of arduous hunting. After a rest and drinking some cold tea, I suddenly decided to go out again after my elusive quarry. I set out alone on foot. Having climbed to the summit of a hill, I squatted down there to search for sheep with my field-glasses. Suddenly I heard a largish boulder rolling down the hill-side and looked quickly in that direction. About a hundred yards away were six sheep at gaze, standing on the rim of a crater-hill; and two of them looked fine ram specimens. Slowly and cautiously,

I raised the Springfield to my shoulder and aimed at the best ram. It dropped to the bullet and must have been killed instantly. The trophy carried a grand spread of horns.

As it was near sunset I decided to leave the prize where it was and trudge back over the desert to the bivouac. Arrived there, I instructed Lazaro to ride off with a pack-mule and bring in the sheep. As my Spanish was limited to a meagre vocabulary and his English negligible, it was difficult to make him understand where the trophy could be found. But his mission was completed in a shorter time than I expected.

Indeed, this was a handsome trophy. The horns measured a trifle less than 17 inches at the base, length 35 inches, and circumference exceeded that of the first two rams falling to my rifle. I set to work by firelight to skin the sheep and clean the head, which took me until well after midnight. I had every reason for feeling elated with this prize, and thought that Bill would be delighted with my success. He and Mike were, too.

As our meagre water supplies were now dangerously low, it was obviously wiser to head back to the Tinajas Altas. Throughout my stay at the waterhole I had felt compelled to dispense with washing and shaving, and a bath would have been welcomed; but those things were an impossibility as every pint of water had to be used for our own and the animals' drinking. After estimating the quantity of water in the rock-basin, I decided that one more day of hunting was possible and then it would be imperative to head back to the Tinajas Altas.

I set out at dawn for the main peak of the Pinacate, and soon after sunrise had got well into the foothills. I kept to the ravines. Before long I sighted a ram upon the flank of a largish crater-hill, but stalking it proved hard and difficult work. An hour passed and still I was not within reasonable range for risking a shot at this ram; and my thirst had now become almost unbearable. With me was only a half-empty waterbottle, so it was wisest to refrain from drinking until after the day's hunting had concluded. The temptation became extremely difficult to resist, but it was imperative to do so.

Then I heard a rock falling and looking towards the spot, I saw the ram walking casually along the opposite side of the gully. It was moving slowly and not more than 400 yards distant from me. I felt tolerably certain that it was still unaware that I was so near, so I headed stealthily for a small ridge towards which the ram was making, and eventually I gained a cluster of rocky outcrops which afforded me adequate cover. I then saw that the animal was only a two-year-old ram, so its life must be spared. The stalk had been a complete waste of time and labour; but that, of course, is all in the luck of hunting. But when it happens, the fact is none the less exasperating for the sportsman.

Not long afterwards, while examining a hilltop through the field-glasses, I spotted two sheep which were half-hidden from sight. It seemed to me that there was an appreciable difference in the dimensions of their respective horns; and one of them, at least, looked worth a shot. I killed the better ram with the first bullet and the other made off at a fast rate. On examining the trophy, I was chagrined and dismayed to find that I had shot a two-year-old ram. Moreover, it was in such poor condition as to be worthless: shockingly emaciated, its hair falling out, and many bald patches on the body. I took its head and as much of the meat as could be carried conveniently, and then headed back across the pitiless sun-baked desert to the bivouac.

That three hours' tramp during the hottest period of the day, heavily laden with the ram's head and meat, proved most exacting and unpleasant. By the time I arrived at the waterhole, I was not only just about dead-beat but also suffering from a terrific thirst. As the rock-basin was now almost drained, it was impossible to assuage my thirst adequately.

How true are the words of Peacock! Although the flesh of a mountain sheep may taste sweeter to some palates, yet that of the valley sheep is much to be preferred. We grilled some of the meat over a wood-fire that night, but it proved so tough that I could scarcely chew my portion. It was also devoid of any real flavour. When little other food is available, no hunter can afford to be too pernickety about the nature of his viands. None of the meat of the mountain sheep of Mexico approached the quality of that of Markhor shot in the Himalayas many years previously. The severe conditions under which the former animals eked out an existence, of course, made them worthless eating; and that is in no way surprising. It was rather like chewing biltong and just about as unappetizing: all the goodness was gone and it had become just desiccated flesh.

As our water supply was now microscopical, there could be no option but to return at once to the Tinajas Altas. I ordered the two Mexicans to pack up, saddle the horses and load the pack-mules, and then we got cracking on the back trail. No time was lost in heading across the Tule Desert. As we were travelling light and had little more than the trophies to carry, good time was made in spite of the difficult conditions. We covered the ninety miles from the Pinacate country in about thirty hours and, viewed from all angles, this could be deemed a creditable performance. But the journey was soul-searching even for the hardy Mexicans, and must have been far worse for our animals.

If my own sufferings were any criterion, then it could only have been sheer agony for the horses and mules.

About three hours after sun-up on the following day we rejoined Bill and Mike at the Tinajas Altas. They congratulated me on the results of my solo hunting, and were generous enough to utter no word of condemnation about the mishap in killing a mangy two year-old ram. Mike made himself responsible for the more efficient cleaning and preservation of the trophies, and performed this task with expert skill. The brothers did their best to cut out many deeply imbedded barbs of the Choya cactus from various portions of my anatomy, but some of them defied extraction. These had to be left until our arrival at Wellton, where surgical instruments could be borrowed for the purpose. After a conference over our evening meal, it was agreed to return to Wellton. I had secured all the specimens of mountain sheep I wanted, and desired to kill no more of the species. At dawn we broke camp and headed towards Wellton.

I parted there from Bill and Mike with sincere regret, for they had proved grand companions. Lazaro and Francisco were rewarded handsomely for their services under trying conditions; but Bill and Mike bluntly refused to accept anything more than the stipulated fee for their professional work. After my return to Chicago, I mailed souvenirs to each as a memento of what had been for me, at any rate, an arduous but interesting hunting-trip. By and large, it had provided some excellent trophies of the mountain sheep of Mexico.

Recollections of that hunt will always remain green. But, whenever I think about the insatiable thirst endured on that brazen desert, I always experience a similar one which seems genuine enough and not just imagination! I think that there can be few men who have not been fascinated by a desert at sunrise or sunset. Even under its blistering sunlight and scorching heat, with the accompaniment of an unquenchable thirst, the magic of a desert's appeal to the human senses will gloss over most of the ills endured in it. At least, that was my reaction to the experience.

(*Right*) Wild fowl in plenty. In the Rockies the abundant bird life gave us good sport

(*Below*) The first elk shot in the Rocky Mountains

Searching for grizzly bear on the slopes of Pike's Peak

Leaving camp in the quest of elk and other game

The camp at an altitude of 10,000 feet on Pike's Peak in the Rocky Mountains

The old-time porter-*safari* of the ex-President of the USA, Theodore Roosevelt, marching over the Kedong Valley to the Sotik region, Kenya, 1909

This young cow died when calving down in Southern Rhodesia, 1928. The carcass of the calf was found about four hundred yards away. The discovery of the carcass of an elephant whose death was natural is a very rare occurrence

A large tusked African bull elephant of Kenya hesitating to charge. The animal was killed with a frontal brain shot soon afterwards

A man-eating lioness in the bush, Kenya. Her suspicions have now been aroused and she is alert for the slightest sound

Three buffalo in the open, Kenya, anxiously watching the intruder and undecided as to whether to attack or bolt

One morning's shoot in 1904: a bull buffalo, cow buffalo, lesser kudu and bull elephant. The elephant tusk was the largest and heaviest ever recorded of those taken in Mount Kenya's forests, the outer perimeter being 11 feet 1 inch and the weight, 169 lb.; the broken stump of the elephant's other tusk (bottom right) weighed 30 lb.

A black rhinoceros
bull advancing to
attack in Kenya

The black rhino photographed on the Sotik Plains, Kenya, when
seemingly charging the photographer. The animal was, however, quite
dead

A section of my porter-*safari* carrying tusks eastwards to cross the River Nile into Uganda

Some of my haul of ivory poached in the Lado Enclave of the Belgian Congo on the west bank of the Nile. This collection was at that time worth £3,000 and had been secured in six months' hunting

Myself at Gondokoro in 1910 at the end of the Theodore Roosevelt *safari* through Uganda

Hamisi bin Baraka (left), my gun-bearer, and Abdulla, the cook, at Nimule, Uganda, 1909

PART THREE

Some African *Safaris*

Adventures are to the adventurous.

Disraeli: CONINGSBY

11

My First Shooting Safari

I LANDED at Mombasa on March 17, 1904, intending to carry out a big-game shooting *safari*, while on leave from my regiment in South Africa. I had three months at my disposal. Travelling by train from the port to Nairobi, I lost no time in putting in hand the arrangements for the *safari*. There were then no outfitting firms operating and no White Hunters had yet taken the field professionally, so everything rested upon my own initiative.

It did not take long to obtain a shooting licence, stores and equipment, African servants, and a body of porters. An expert Swahili gun-bearer, Hamisi bin Baraka, applied for this job on my *safari*. He possessed some excellent testimonials from sportsmen with whom he had been a gun-bearer from the days of the construction of the Uganda Railway. Liking his "chits" and the man himself, I engaged him as my gun-bearer for the next three months. The first estimate of his character and reliability proved absolutely accurate. He remained in my service as gun-bearer for six years, serving loyally, efficiently and courageously, and always proving perfectly reliable in every possible way.

A week after reaching Nairobi all was in readiness to march off to the selected hunting country. I had decided to hunt by myself, though I knew nothing of the country, the language of the natives, the fauna, or *safari* life; everything had to be learned by a process of trial and error. Hamisi knew a little English and so did Sefu bin Mohamed, the Swahili personal servant I engaged. They managed to overcome the language difficulties between myself and the African porters. Sefu had been personal servant to a railway engineer engaged on railway construction work and also with a few sportsmen out for a shoot, and he proved a treasure at all times. Sefu also remained in my service for six years. He procured for me

a passably good cook, Abdulla; while Hamisi collected an efficient
'Ndorobo tracker, whose real name I never learned but I dubbed
him Juma.

These four Africans never once let me down, and I considered
myself lucky in having them in my employ. The porters were all
members of the Wanyamwezi tribe from German East Africa (now
Tanganyika Territory), who were rated as the best carriers in
Eastern Africa. Their headman and the twenty-four porters also
remained with me for six years, often performing prodigiously
long daily marches and proving experts at the work demanded of
them. A Mkamba *syce* (groom) was a good type and looked after
my mule capably, but he left me at the end of the *safari* to return
to his village because of domestic trouble.

Acting on the advice of knowledgeable acquaintances at Nairobi,
I planned to make for Fort Hall, then over the Aberdare Range,
across the Naro Moru plains to the base of Mt. Kenya, then round
the mountain and back to Nairobi through Meru, Embu and Fort
Hall. For a tyro this might be considered an ambitious venture,
but all went smoothly enough. There was no lack of game animals.
The huge congregations of many varieties of species were simply
staggering to behold. Moreover, the *safari* throughout its duration
proved highly enjoyable and fascinating; the more so, perhaps,
because the life was so novel. While working my way about the
base of the Aberdares, by careful stalking and selection I collected
a lot of good trophies—specimens of many antelope and gazelle, a
grand buffalo bull, both bull and cow black rhinoceros, a wart-
hog, four lions and a lioness (the males black-maned animals), and
one male leopard. Then I concentrated upon getting two elephant
bulls endowed with heavy ivory on the Aberdares.

If luck favoured me, I hoped that the ivory could be sold at
Nairobi and go some way towards covering the total costs of my
safari; the current price then for a pound weight was from ten to
twelve shillings, a fair average being ten shillings. We worked our
way over the Aberdares, and en route added a few more good
trophies to the collection. Though we saw a number of herds of
elephant, not a bull amongst them measured up to the standard
I sought. I bided my time, feeling confident that eventually I
should locate two worthy and shootable bulls. There seemed to be
no lack of elephants in the area.

It is not possible to forget the first African elephant I personally
killed, any more than it is to obliterate the memory of the last
one. During the six years between the two incidents a little more
than 400 elephants fell to my rifle. There then existed certain wild
and uninhabited regions of Eastern Africa where a professional
hunter could shoot unlimited numbers without a licence or on a

special *ad lib* one costing an insignificant fee. That is of the distant past. It can never happen again, for the last of those territories—the Ubangi Shari district of French Equatorial Africa—was finally closed to unlimited ivory hunting in June 1932.

All who have hunted elephant in Africa seem agreed that other quarries offer insipid sport in comparison. This I am quite positive about: it is far preferable to face up to an infuriated lion charging, whether or not wounded, than stand in the path of an elephant bent upon mischief. My greatest thrills and tensest moments while hunting in Africa over a longish span of years were derived from encounters with elephants and not lion, buffalo, rhinoceros or leopard.

The majority of hunters maintain that the elephant provides the classic of big-game shooting. I heartily endorse that opinion. When out after lion I never experienced such thrills as I always felt when coming up with a herd of elephant in long grass or really thick stuff, and then began to creep in close for a mortal shot at the best bull. While you peer about for a worth-while beast, every single faculty is strung to the highest possible tension. The huge slate-grey forms are only partially revealed through dense cover, as they stand or move about leisurely within a short distance of where you stand immobile while waiting for a favourable moment to fire. The slightest noise made, an incautious movement or a sudden change in the wind direction may bring down upon you instantly an avalanche of elephants. And it can indeed prove difficult to turn or halt such a panic-stricken stampede.

It is essential first to locate a coveted prize and then manœuvre into a position where the beast can be killed with the first bullet. The wise hunter creeps in to about twenty-five or thirty paces of the animal to be shot. Anything is liable to happen in a second. Believe me when I declare that the odds are heavily against the hunter and the outcome is always unpredictable. Such moments are memories which even the passage of the years cannot efface.

But I have never known moments when lion-hunting which were equally such exciting or dangerous experiences. When standing to confront a lion charging home, you are not so conscious of its size, power or deadly menace as when in the path of an elephant intent upon destroying an enemy. A lion viewed in the open will do its utmost to impress you as being majestic and ferocious, largely by sheer bluff; but an African elephant met in a forest or dense cover, if so minded, can be a demon of destruction. Normally, unless it is wounded or otherwise molested, a buffalo is not vicious and will seldom attack a man if unprovoked. A rhinoceros, being such a stupid creature, almost invariably will go all out to meet any threat of danger rather more than halfway; but it can be turned or sidestepped with comparative ease. A leopard is a cunning and stealthy beast at all times, and its behaviour is often quite unpredictable. But an elephant's reactions when subjected to a threat of danger are an immediate attack in a savagely vindictive manner.

I had been camped for a couple of days at a delightful spot on the lower slopes of Mt. Satima (13,003 feet) while searching for a worthy elephant bull to shoot. On the second morning I started out at dawn and soon spotted a massive bull standing solitary, ears widespread, trunk raised to comb the air-channels for taint of danger, and eyes gazing in my direction. Those wicked little eyes positively scintillated with devilment. Though I could see the entire head clearly enough, the rest of its body was completely concealed by a thick clump of bushes behind which it stood immobile. The distance separating us could not have been much more than fifty yards, and the wind direction favoured me. For some minutes I remained frozen and gazing fixedly at the bull, conscious of a surge of intense excitement not unmixed with fear— a tyro alone with his first elephant.

The trophy was a valuable prize. Covetously I estimated the weight of the pair of gleaming bars of ivory, and guessed each tusk would turn the scale at 100 lb. and over. I faced this bull on my lonesome, for Hamisi (the gun-bearer) had been delayed at the camp when I set out and not yet caught up with me. I badly wanted to become possessed of that heavy ivory, but now hesitated to creep in closer for a killing shot instead of just wounding the animal. While making up my mind what best to do, the fickle breeze suddenly changed direction and placed me down-wind. At once the bull got my scent and bolted. I followed up at a run, but lost its spoor after having covered about a couple of miles; and, as Hamisi had not joined me, I considered it wiser to abandon the pursuit. I returned to camp.

Below the camp-site was a deep valley through which coursed a brawling brook of clear water. It was an ideal situation. I had seen many old and a few recent elephant spoors; and consequently thought my hunting would shortly be rewarded with success. With Hamisi and the 'Ndorobo tracker, Juma, I searched for that solitary bull during three days in succession. I did not get even a glimpse. On the fourth morning, after having almost despaired of any luck, I saw a large dark object moving about in the valley below the camp. Field-glasses disclosed that it was a huge elephant bull (possibly the same animal for which I had been looking), heading straight towards the camp. Grabbing up the .450/.500 Holland and Holland, and a belt of cartridges, I called to Hamisi and Juma to follow me quickly. We set out at once to meet the beast.

Just at first it looked as if the bull intended to walk right through the camp. But it paused abruptly and then turned off to the right along the valley. I suspect that it had got a whiff of man-tainted wind or heard the noises created in the camp. Avoiding trouble for its own sake, I kept steadily in the bull's wake. Presently it came to a halt in a thick patch of bush and tall grass. I could now see its trunk waving slowly from side to side, but the distance dividing us was still far too great for taking a shot. I crept forward as silently as feasible until I was about fifty yards from the bull.

As I stood immobile for a few minutes, the animal displayed evident signs of acute suspicion and was becoming restless. Its trunk was combing the wind for taint. Had the bull seen or heard my stealthy approach? A cold shiver ran down my spine when thinking that this might well have happened; and, if so, I was in for a packet of trouble. To be sure of killing it outright with a bullet into the brain, it was imperative to get closer. But what if it charged me before I was ready to fire? Gradually, my nerves steadied and all sense of fear evaporated like the morning mists before the heat of a rising sun. I crept forward soundlessly and almost imperceptibly, eyes watching intently, every faculty alerted, and rifle held ready for instant use.

Now I was working up-wind. At a distance of about thirty yards from the quarry, I halted again to take careful aim at the brain between eye and earhole. That is one of the most vital spots in the anatomy of an elephant, and generally favoured in preference to all other shots; if the bullet hits the correct spot, the animal goes down as if pole-axed on to the head and fore-knees. Its death is instantaneous. Holding my breath, I gently squeezed the trigger of the right barrel; but, as I fired, the bull plunged forward unexpectedly and the heavy bullet hit it almost at the root of its tail. It must have come as an unpleasant shock and surprise to the elephant. It let out a shrill piercing scream, cutting a ludicrous figure with its spine curved up and tail well tucked in. It reminded me of a pariah-dog trying to avoid a hearty kick on the backside. But this, of course, was no moment for merriment and only for self-preservation; and so I stifled my laughter and concentrated upon the animal.

It made off straight through the bush and down the valley, trampling down everything in its path. The din created was terrific. A fairly stout sapling got between the forelegs, bent over almost double, and snapped off short with a report like the shot of a heavy rifle. I followed up at a steady run, guided by the sounds of breaking branches. Suddenly there came a cessation of all noise, and I realized that the bull must have halted ahead of me. I worked my way to a flank and circled the spot in order to get a clear sight of the bull and a decent chance for the brain or heart shot. But I must have badly misjudged the beast's position, because I suddenly found myself facing the animal at close range instead of being on its flank.

The bull saw me at once and charged all out like a runaway locomotive. It was impossible to dodge that mad rush in such thick stuff, even if I had so wished; and I did most certainly! A frontal brain shot was possible but this is none too easy to make effective; and I dare not accept a risk of failure. The nature of the ground presented no obstacles to that outraged elephant. It smashed down everything in its path like so much chaff, and quickly was almost upon me. I knew the bull had to be killed, or a bad mauling was the least I could expect; possibly the incident would end in my death.

Sheer desperation must have given me the necessary nerve to hold my fire until a favourable moment to shoot presented itself; or it might have been attributable to a temporary paralysis of the brain. I could not say which it was. As the giant towered above me to grab hold of my body with an out-thrust trunk, I felt like a puny atom and the entire horizon was blocked out. I fired between its eyes for a frontal brain shot, but must have hit too high or low as the bullet neither halted, killed nor turned the big beast. The second barrel I emptied into the centre of the chest, but this proved ineffectual in killing or stopping the animal. There was just time to throw myself backwards into a bush. As I fell, I heard the report of another rifle discharged just behind me.

Scrambling hastily erect, I reloaded as fast as possible and then glanced back over my shoulder. The bull had fallen forward on its fore-knees. I saw it stagger erect several times and then go down again; each time, when falling forward, the tusks were driven into the ground. Squeezing myself between the bush and huge body of the elephant, I managed to pass round behind its colossal stern. As I did so the bull stepped backwards and only just missed treading upon me. Working my way rapidly to the opposite flank, I was able to take a brain shot from the side and sent a heavy bullet into the spot between eye and ear as it fell forward once more upon tusks and fore-knees.

At the instant when squeezing the trigger, the bull lifted its head abruptly with the result that my bullet hit too low to prove fatal. On receipt of this additional wound, the bull regained an upright stance. It was then that I realized that its recent conduct was due neither to wounds nor weakness from loss of blood. To my horror, I saw Hamisi rolled up in the beast's trunk. Before there was time to shoot again, the bull flung the gun-bearer through the air with a powerful swing of the trunk as if he was just a truss of straw. Hamisi's flight was halted by the bole of a tree, distant fully twenty-five yards from the spot. Then the wounded bull staggered off into the bush, obviously now "very sick". It vanished out of sight. Running to where Hamisi had been thrown, I fully anticipated to find him crushed to a pulp and either dead or dying.

To my immense relief and amazement, he raised himself on an elbow and greeted me with a sickly grin. His khaki clothing was torn to shreds and liberally soaked with blood. While examining him to find the extent of his injuries, Hamisi explained that he had almost caught up with me when hearing two shots. He had also heard the previous single shot, whereon he sent Juma running in that direction to aid me if necessary in spooring a wounded tusker. It was Hamisi's shot which I had heard as I threw myself backwards out of the path of the advancing mountain of bone and flesh. Before Hamisi could escape, the bull had seized him by the trunk and thrown him heavily on the ground; and next it had tried to crush out his life by battering him with heavy butts from the massive head. The very long tusks had saved Hamisi, for the head was unable to touch him as the points of the ivory buried themselves in the ground.

Hamisi told me that he found himself comparatively safe as long as able to keep his body in the gap between the two tusks. Once he managed to crawl away, but the bull promptly hauled him back with the trunk round an ankle. The animal was making another effort to crush him when I fired into its head from a flank position and thus brought the episode to an abrupt end. The blood smothering Hamisi's clothing came from the elephant and none of it was his own. I made him as comfortable as possible. Shortly afterwards we were rejoined by the 'Ndorobo tracker, who had abandoned spooring the elephant when he heard more shooting. I sent Juma running to the camp to bring back some porters to help in carrying the gun-bearer back.

Before long we had him in bed in his tent, and it was then possible to make a more thorough examination of the patient. His chief injuries were five fractured ribs—three on one side and two on the other; but there was also much bruising and he suffered from severe shock. Having done all possible and made him as comfortable as the circumstances permitted, I set off with Juma to locate the wounded bull and deliver a merciful despatch. It could not be allowed to suffer unduly long from its injuries. About two miles from the scene of the disastrous encounter we found the bull lying dead. Juma went back to camp to bring up some porters to hack out the magnificent pair of tusks and carry them back.

When later put on the scales at Nairobi, one weighed 117 and the other 106 pounds.

I did not fail to profit by the experience gained that day, and the lessons then learned were never forgotten. Errors in technique are pardonable in a novice, but ought never to be repeated. As time went on, I became more and more proficient in hunting elephants and other varieties of big-game; and was learning everything in the hard way, which is the best method of all.

Hamisi's recovery was remarkably rapid. I had wanted to get him into hospital at Nairobi, but he steadfastly refused and insisted on continuing with the *safari*. Finally I agreed but on the condition that Juma replaced him as gun-bearer until such time as he was thoroughly fit to perform this work.

A few days later we broke camp and marched over the Naro Moru plains to the base of Mt. Kenya, camping for a time near the base of that mountain. The site was beside the Nanyuki river, much about where now stands the fast-developing township which takes its name from that stream. I did not think then that I should ever make my home there, but have done so now for the past 13 years. When I was first there in 1904 no single human habitation was visible for many miles around, only vast numbers of wild animals and a few herds of Masai cattle in charge of herdsmen.*

A full and crowded life devoted to big-game hunting with a rifle or camera, or both in combination, is certain to provide one with a great deal of material of interest and value to those who follow after. It is a matter for great regret that many of the famous hunters in earlier times failed to set down on paper their experiences, adventures and natural history observations. Now it is too late and valuable records have been lost to us for all time.

Things have changed a great deal since I first started to hunt big-game in East Africa more than half a century ago; and so have the conditions under which the sport is performed, no less so the habits of many species of fauna. My novitiate in big-game hunting in Africa was immensely helped and guided by reading the books written by famous old-timers—Selous, Cornwallis Harris, Gordon-Cumming, Baker, Burchell, Drummond, H. H. Methuen, and other noted hunters who did publish books.

I wish to state emphatically that not all days of a hunter are rewarding or intensely thrilling, for there will always come the inevitable ones when nothing worthy of recording happens. If in this account there may appear many "narrow escapes" from disaster, it is merely because they occurred at widely spaced

*The account of the remainder of my first *safari* has already appeared in a previously published volume.

intervals of time and were in the nature of highlights in a longish
hunting career. The cat's cream, maybe!

That it was possible to emerge from practically all such nearly
disastrous incidents can be attributed to sheer good luck and
the fact that Dame Fortune consistently smiled upon me. I state
only the truth of each episode, avoiding embroidery or any leaning
towards sensationalism. I am not a Münchhausen of Africa!

12

Pepo: An Elephant Shamba-*raider*

FROM African inhabitants of the district where I was hunting
for an elephant bull endowed with heavy ivory, I had heard much
about an aged and solitary beast which was a persistent raider of
cultivated fields. They had named this "rogue" elephant Pepo (an
Evil Spirit), and believed it was the reincarnation of one of their
notorious former chiefs, whose rule had always been cruel, sadistic
and despotic. Nothing told me about Pepo redounded to his credit.
I was sorely tempted to seek out this bull and put an end to his
gross misdeeds. Already two good bulls had been shot on my
annual game licence, but I still had to get a third, having paid the
additional fee demanded.

For more years than the local people could remember Pepo
had been outlawed by his own kind, making his home in the grim
depths of the forest on a range of hills overlooking the valley in
which I was then camped. It seemed that he was greatly feared by
man and beast, and treated with wholesome respect by all and
sundry. Not only was he a destroyer of *shambas* (fields) with standing crops, but he had earned also an unsavoury reputation as a
malicious man-killer—of at least four European hunters and a
number of Africans, both men and women. It was time that someone put paid to his long-overdue account.

I gathered that Pepo had acquired a far-flung renown for being
invincible. So great was this bull's cunning, so savage and unpredictable his temper, that the Africans spoke of him with awed
reverence and credited the bull with possessing supernatural
powers. Therefore they accorded Pepo the freedom of the district.
Not a man among them dared to raise a hand against him, because
of the belief that if this bull was harmed or killed then the man
responsible for it, and also his relatives, would be made to suffer
severely for such an act of aggression. No efforts were made by these

D*

people to rid themselves of such a grave menace in their midst. Pepo could wander wherever he fancied, devastate standing crops on *shambas*, and kill any human being who had the mischance to be in his path.

They told me that only a few Europeans had ever challenged Pepo's supremacy, and this increasingly rarely. The old bull hated, and also feared, all white men. No other living creature aroused in Pepo's heart such a deadly hate and fear; and the reason for this was that twice white men had wounded him severely with bullets from their heavy rifles. But Pepo managed to elude them and recovered from his injuries. It was believed that this bull's pair of tusks weighed more than 100 lb. each—a worthy prize to gain! I think that this information, more than anything else, induced my decision to become Pepo's executioner.

Before committing myself to the adventure, however, it seemed advisable to learn everything possible about the bull's habits and characteristics. The local Chief proved to be my best bet. He declared that Pepo was so old that his slate-grey hide hung down in folds of crinkles like plus-fours, and was so sagacious that none could teach him a single trick of the *nyika* (wilderness). With passage of the years he had grown more savage and elusive. Pepo had consistently been able to sidestep every effort made by white hunters to collect his ivory. Now he was regarded as being invulnerable. The Chief stated emphatically that wise men left this old bull severely alone. He urged me to do likewise.

I learned that during daylight hours Pepo normally remained in the nearby forest, where no man dared to venture; at night, however, he sallied forth to plunder the crops of the villagers in the valley. Pepo had created a reign of terror. Women were afraid to go to the river to fetch water if Pepo was reported to be abroad. The bull killed human beings wantonly; merely because he hated all mankind and his victims happened to be encountered when he was meandering outside his forest sanctuary. This, and still more, I learned about Pepo. It was not going to be a simple task, but I decided to have a try at shooting this "rogue" elephant and be the richer by his valuable ivory.

It was advisable to have reinforcements. Such a hazardous undertaking was not one for a hunter to tackle alone. Normally, I dislike hunting big-game in the company of others; but this struck me as being an obvious occasion when it would be rash indeed to hunt down Pepo on my own. A supporting rifle in the hands of an experienced hunter was strongly indicated. The hazards could not safely be minimized. A runner was despatched with a letter to two friends, hunting for ivory in partnership, whose camp was some distance away. My letter told them all the facts known to me and declared my intentions. I urged them to join forces with me in an earnest effort to relieve the local people of a grave menace to their lives and cultivated lands. A few days later they arrived at my camp in the valley. Their advent relieved my mind of many causes for anxiety and put quite a different complexion on the proposed hunt for Pepo.

We discussed a plan of operations. It was agreed mutually that, at the start, we should hunt down Pepo separately. If this failed to produce the desired result, then we must launch a combined offensive against the "rogue" bull. Lots were drawn for areas. It was considered that the best hope of contacting Pepo was at night when he was engaged upon raiding the *shambas* of Africans. That first night, with Hamisi in attendance as gun-bearer, I took post on the outskirts of a field of ripe millet and hoped fervently to kill Pepo as he arrived to make a raid upon it. The idea did seem to offer a reasonably good prospect of success, for the bull was known to be partial to ripe millet. It fermented in his stomach and made him drunk. The Chief had told me about having seen Pepo returning soon after dawn to his forest retreat, after completing a night-raid on millet, and he was then obviously intoxicated. If a like situation could be induced, a drunk elephant was more easily killed than one in its sober senses.

My two friends had arranged to maintain watch during the night at more distant *shambas*, widely separated, in the valley; and shortly after night cloaked the land we went off to our respective ambush. For two successive nights not one of us even saw or heard an elephant approaching a *shamba* to devastate the standing crop. On the third night, however, after having been a couple of hours in waiting I distinctly heard an elephant trumpet shrilly once in the far distance. Then all was silent again. If it was the voice of Pepo, assuredly the bull must soon be on his way to raid the crops of the villagers; and I much hoped his destination would be the millet field over which Hamisi and I kept patient guard. If so, there might be offered a good opportunity to drop him dead with a bullet into the brain from close range.

I could picture exactly what must be occurring. Silent as a shadow, Pepo's massive bulk would be brushing through the network of lianas as he headed towards the outer rim of the forest. The bull must know well every yard of that tangled maze of vegetation and giant boles of trees, and be able to pick his way easily and silently to their outskirts. Just inside the edge of the forest he would halt to wait patiently until he considered it was safe to venture down into the valley. He would ponder thoughtfully upon the night's programme. The single trumpet blast indicated that a decision had been made, and also was intended as an arrogant challenge to all and sundry to respect his ancient rights over the district. I fully intended to accept that insolent challenge and see that Pepo met his Waterloo. That is to say, if the bull elected on this night to raid the millet field where I was posted. I knew the others had exactly similar intentions.

Hamisi agreed with me that it was unlikely Pepo would show up for another hour or more. Our ambush had been carefully selected. No wind was perceptible; and if one rose later it would probably blow from the afforested range of hills in our direction, so that no taint of human presence could reach the bull. The night was pitch-dark. So much so that I could scarcely see a hand waggled in front of my face. We had brought with us a Very-light pistol and six white flare cartridges, which would be brought into use as soon as Pepo was approaching close to the ripe millet. The stage was set as rewardingly as we knew how to devise.

A couple of hours must have passed before a slight rustling sound told us of the imminent appearance of an elephant to raid the millet. I much hoped it was Pepo. Both were instantly alerted, eyes peering intently into the veil of darkness, and striving to pick out the giant form now steadily advancing in our direction. It had been arranged that Hamisi was to discharge a Very-light when I gave him a nudge from an elbow, which would afford me a fair chance of taking good aim at a vital spot in the bull's anatomy. A bullet from the .350 Rigby Mauser at very close range should achieve what was desired. Whether a brain or heart shot was taken, of course, must depend upon the actual circumstances when the target became visible to me. In any case, because of the darkness my shot must be fired from an unpleasantly close range and no margin of error was permissible.

The flare from the Very pistol disclosed the massive bulk of an elephant advancing towards us and distant only about twenty paces. I fired for the brain as the bull moved broadside on, but the bullet could not have sped true as the animal did not go down as I fully expected would happen. But the beast halted abruptly. The second bullet must have hit him in much about the same spot. Then the flare went out. Hamisi fired another cartridge but the pistol misfired because the ammunition was faulty; and a third cartridge likewise failed us. There could be no means of knowing to what extent the two bullets had been effective, but it was unlikely that we should be left for long in ignorance.

I had heard the bullets strike hard. They must have given the bull a paralysing jolt to the side of the head and momentarily dazed him with the shock. Then we heard the elephant about turn and retreat at speed towards his sanctuary in the forest. Patently Pepo must have regained full control of his senses with an amazing rapidity, for now the giant was making off at a swift-paced amble. We followed up without delay, anxious to end the bull's sufferings and complete the task to which my hand had been set. We soon realized that on such a dark night it must prove impossible to overtake an elephant in panic-stricken flight from danger. Any further pursuit of the beast that night was just a futile waste of energy. I would have to wait until daylight, when the spoor could be followed more simply. We retraced our steps to camp.

Jim E—— had returned to camp before us, after another fruitless vigil at his ambush further down the valley. He had heard my shots and was eager to learn what kind of luck had befallen me. A few minutes later his partner, Harry B——, joined us. The story of my encounter with Pepo had to be retold for his benefit. It was agreed that all three of us should go after Pepo and search him out in his forest retreat, leaving camp before dawn so as to arrive at the outer edge of the timber as soon as light enough to see the spoor. We had not the slightest doubt about where Pepo would have made for, and inside the forest was the most certain place to locate him for a killing.

I argued that Pepo, knowing that he must be pursued relentlessly by the hunter, would be positive to make for the most inaccessible portion of his domain. The bull would travel down-wind but, when assured that the pursuit was outdistanced, probably make a wide half circle and travel back on a parallel course to take the hunters unawares. That is a trick often played by elephant and buffalo. We all realized that we were up against a tough proposition, the outcome of which must remain unpredictable. But the iniquitous career of Pepo had to be terminated by whatever means happened to be available for the purpose.

At the false dawn we left camp, accompanied by our gunbearers, trackers and a dozen porters to carry essential supplies. All strode off towards the hills and forest surmounting them. We intended to live rough, bivouacking at night, until our task had been completed satisfactorily. I do not think one of us deluded himself into believing that the next few days would be either comfortable or pleasant, or even that they would lack grievous personal danger. Dirty, very dirty work was in store for us. And well we knew it.

As the sun rose over the eastern horizon we discovered the spot where Pepo had entered the forest. We followed the path made by him. My competent 'Ndorobo tracker was never once at fault and led us unerringly forward through a tangled maze of giant trees and matted undergrowth. We pursued Pepo for many miles until we emerged suddenly on a fairly wide clearing covered with high grass and scattered clumps of bushes. The time was then nearing

the hour of sunset. Up to this point our progress had been none
too pleasant and all were feeling excessively weary. We decided
to bivouac on the spoor for the night and resume the hunt early
next morning. Food and sleep had become a necessity.

When light enough to see a few yards ahead, my 'Ndorobo
tracker led us over the spoor of Pepo. Before long, however, it
became abundantly apparent that the bull had started to double
back on a course parallel to the one taken earlier. He was working
his way back into the heart of the forest. Our advance now had
to be contrived with the utmost precautions against any sudden
surprise encounter with our quarry. The slightest relaxation in
caution might involve one or all of us in dire disaster.

After a brief conference, it was decided that our best policy was
to split up and go forward on more or less parallel lines in order
to cover as much ground as feasible. This would lessen the chances
of being caught in any ambush devised by Pepo. Having drawn
first blood, I claimed the right to be allotted the central course
on the bull's spoor. Harry went off to my right and Jim to the
left, each accompanied by his own gun-bearer and tracker. The
porters were ordered to follow about a hundred yards in my rear.
I warned them sternly to move onwards as noiselessly as they knew
how and that no talking was permitted. If they heard any shooting,
they must halt immediately and wait until summoned to advance
again.

Jim and Harry whistled softly to advise me that they were in
position. I whistled back to acknowledge their signals and for all
to proceed as previously arranged between us. With rifle held
ready for instant use I kept close upon the heels of my tracker. I
felt the utmost confidence in his skill. This 'Ndorobo, Juma, had
been my tracker for several years and proved himself to be the most
expert of any known to me. Up to now his spooring of Pepo had
been perfection. I knew that he would not fail to locate our quarry
for a killing shot, provided that Pepo was still anywhere in the
vicinity.

Many thoughts passed through my mind during the course of
the next two hours. I was trying to think exactly as would Pepo.
It is highly advisable to know something of the working of an
elephant's brain and thus be able to anticipate its actions and
reactions when being relentlessly pursued by a hunter. This sixth
sense can prove invaluable. But the gift is not possessed by all big-
game hunters; otherwise there would have been recorded a far
fewer number of tragic endings to ivory hunting.

I believed that Pepo would be consumed with a desire to be
revenged upon the man who had injured him so severely and
knowing a lust to kill. Possibly he had realized that several hunters

were camped in the valley, and all of them determined to take his life. Pepo would have winded them, know exactly what to expect, and fully appreciate the meaning of this sudden invasion of his domain. The bull definitely would know that the red flag of danger was hoisted.

Supreme confidence in his skill, cunning and ability to outwit any serious threat must have been rocked badly by the encounter at night beside the millet fields. It would have scared him quite a lot. Pepo had known a very narrow escape from sudden death; and the ache and throbbing in his head resulting from two bullet wounds must have rendered a none too amiable temper now positively sadistic. He would go all out to act really tough. At thought of his loss of face and the gnawing pain he was enduring his temper would boil. And he would be determined to make the hunters pay dearly for that attack upon his life.

Wisdom dictated that he ought temporarily to seek out pastures new; at any rate until such time as the hunters abandoned their quest and withdrew from his domain. Yet, before doing so, he might be obstinate enough to carry out one more night-raid upon the millet *shambas* in the valley. He would think this was due to his self-respect. That raid could be carried out swiftly and noise-lessly during the night, but he must be back in the shelter of the forest before the mists of early morning began to evaporate under the warmth of an African sun. Pepo would bide his time until all was quiet and still in the valley. Now he was probably hidden effectually in dense cover to await the opportune moment for launching that lone-hand raid. In the meantime, he rubbed a sore head against the smooth bole of a giant juniper tree to ease its ache, itch and painful throbbing. The two head wounds must be worrying him a great deal. But the gentle massage against the tree would somewhat soothe the maddening irritation set up by these injuries. All this, and still more, was passing through my thoughts as I followed close behind the efficient tracker. How correct or otherwise were those surmises only time could show.

Until nearing sunset we combed the forest industriously for Pepo, but failed to contact him. Finally, on a whistled signal from me, the others converged upon the spot where my party had halted. We discussed what was best to be done. They were told exactly what my reading of Pepo's movements and intentions amounted to, and this was accepted without either of them questioning its probable accuracy. It was decided to return to camp for the night. Jim offered to post himself in ambush beside the field of millet situated nearest to our camp, while Harry and I rested.

It was already dark when we reached our tents, bathed and

changed, enjoyed sundowners and then had an excellent dinner. Later Jim went off with his gun-bearer to take up post; and for a while longer Harry and I sat by the log-fire yarning about ivory hunting. By now all was hushed in the valley. The Africans had ceased singing, dancing and drum-thumping, and retired into their huts to sleep. The distant chuckling of a scavenging hyena shattered the stillness of the night with its maniacal laughter. The abominable sounds ebbed and died away. They were shortly succeeded by the deep-throated coughing grunts of a night-hunting lion. As the majestic challenge to the wilds reached its zenith of power, the roaring shook the valley with a snarling bellow.

Harry went off to his tent to have a sleep, leaving me seated beside the fire and listening to the queer noises of the African night. Large painted moths fluttered out of the darkness to beat their bejewelled wings while palpitating restlessly about where I sat. From all sides now arose a shrill and grating trilling noise, as the nightly chorus of tree-hyraces got under way. Presently, I was startled by a hoarse bark close at hand, repeated several times in rapid succession, as a bushbuck doe sounded the alarm. A few moments later it was repeated more shrilly, but cut short as a predatory leopard pulled the doe down in death. On hearing that throttled death-cry, I knew well enough what had just transpired.

If my suspicions were correct that Pepo intended a raid on the millet this night before making his get-away into another district, just about now he would be emerging from cover in the forest to descend into the valley. The golden sickle of a young moon hung in the sky overhead, as if entangled in the black trees of the forest. Now the African night was tranquil and serenely somnolent. I felt tolerably sure that Pepo was now on his way down into the valley, and sat listening intently for sounds of any movement in the direction of the cultivated lands. And suddenly I heard the dulled movements of a heavy animal advancing towards where Jim and his gun-bearer were in ambush. But no shot was fired.

Jim told me later that Pepo had almost approached close enough for a shot, when the wind direction suddenly changed and he must have got a puff of man-tainted breeze. Pepo knew well all that this implied. Instantly the bull whirled about and sped away from the danger zone, before Jim could take a shot likely to prove effective. He heard the bull crashing down everything obstructing its passage. Jim decided it was futile to follow up that night, so he and the gun-bearer returned to camp.

We knew that Pepo would go back into the shelter of the forest, feeling supremely confident of his ability to escape from any pursuers. The bull would travel down-wind until he gained the forest, where danger would be behind him and safety ahead.

As the dawn broke we were once again on Pepo's spoor. I suspect that the bull could not have been deep in the forest when we began to follow him, and that a slight but unmistakable whiff of man-tainted wind reached him or he had heard our movements through the tangled undergrowth. It was impossible to move soundlessly. Pepo must have managed to get noiselessly in our rear and without any of us being aware of it. We heard absolutely nothing to shatter the restful silence of a newborn day, save only our own movements, the gentle rustle of a breeze through the dense canopy of foliage overhead, and the twittering of many birds in the treetops. My 'Ndorobo tracker led the way. I was close upon his heels and Hamisi just in rear of me with the second rifle. Jim walked a few paces behind Hamisi, followed by his gun-bearer and tracker; but Harry was dawdling behind at a distance of about fifty yards, while his gun-bearer and tracker kept about midway between him and those of Jim. In view of what followed, those positions must be borne in mind.

Suddenly, with a shrill and infuriated scream, Pepo charged full tilt at Harry from about thirty yards behind him. Harry swung about at once, rifle to shoulder, and fired a bullet from his .450/.500 rifle into the forehead of the huge bull. It failed to kill. But the shock stunned Pepo and made him swerve slightly off course. Neither Jim nor I could shoot because Harry stood in our direct line of fire and with his back towards us. The density of the undergrowth on either side of the track prevented a change of position to shoot with any degree of safety. Both saw and heard Harry make another frontal brain shot at the bull, but this second bullet was equally ineffective. Pepo just shook his massive head. Trumpeting loudly, the bull charged all-out at Harry, who was reloading the rifle since his gun-bearer was not near enough for an exchange of weapons.

A moment or two later Pepo was upon Harry. We saw him hurled violently to the ground, with the long tusks stabbing and ripping at his body; and then he was seized around the waist by the trunk, lifted on high and flung against the bole of a giant tree. A nerve-shattering scream of agony froze the blood in our veins; but a second later that dreadful sound was cut off short. As Jim and I ran back to his aid, I saw Pepo prodding savagely at Harry's prostrate body with the tusks and heavy fore-feet stamping upon him.

When not more than twenty paces distant I fired a bullet into Pepo's head, taking the frontal brain shot. My aim must have been a trifle too high or low for a kill, but the frontal brain shot was never my *forte*. Pepo did not go down, but whipped around and made off at a rapid rate; and the dense wall of trees and vegetation quickly concealed him from our sight. We let the bull go. Harry demanded all our attention.

But there was nothing that we could do. He was dead. His body had been mangled into a twisted and broken parody of a man; and the sight almost made me violently sick. The only service that we could render Harry now was to give his remains a decent burial; and sorrowfully this was done before we made our way back to camp. We ought to have followed up Pepo and put him out of his sufferings, but neither Jim nor I had any heart for it. We were too badly shaken by the ghastly death of our companion, and in no shape to undertake such a formidable task. Both agreed that it would be foolhardy to attempt it until our nerves steadied.

Once, as we trudged in silence through the forest to descend into the valley, we heard a loud trumpet blast of savage triumph and exultation. The sound rang sonorously through the stillness of the aisles of giant trees, echoed over the valley, and eddied back and forth between the hills. Without any doubt, it was Pepo mocking and challenging the universe.

We felt tolerably sure that Pepo could not survive for any length of time from the serious head wounds inflicted. But neither Jim nor I felt disposed to make certain of the "rogue" bull's death. Early next morning we despatched the trackers, gun-bearers and a party of porters to search for the carcase, hack out the grand pair of tusks, and bring the ivory back to camp. They found Pepo's body about a mile from the spot where Harry had been killed. On weighing the tusks, it was found that they gave 105 and 98 pounds of ivory respectively.

By right of drawing first blood, this pair of magnificent tusks were mine. But I derived no satisfaction from their acquisition. I would have surrendered them gladly, as well as a great deal more, if this could have restored Harry to life. Jim had told me that his partner was unmarried but had been maintaining a widowed sister in South Africa. So I insisted that Jim should take the ivory and sell it for her benefit. As I had been responsible for involving Harry in this hunt for Pepo, which had ended so tragically for him, this seemed the least that could be done.

But Harry's death was a high price to have paid for freeing the local African population from the deadly menace of Pepo, the "rogue" bull which had constituted himself the "Lord of the Forest".

13

Facing Elephant Stampedes

WHEN hunting elephants for their valuable ivory, almost anything is liable to happen. Having shot some hundreds of these animals in Africa, I have been given every reason for knowing this.

Often one reads about a herd of elephants charging *en masse* in panic-stricken flight. I believe that the movement is then not a deliberate charge with lethal intent, but far more of an unreasoning desire to escape from danger threatening them. I much doubt if a herd ever does actually charge a hunter as a compact body. It is, nevertheless, a nerve-shattering experience when a stampede does happen. The forest resounds to the crash of their terrified flight from the danger zone, the noise resembling that made by an avalanche down a mountainside.

There was an occasion while motoring through Sumatra from north to south when I came near to being overwhelmed by a landslide which suddenly came tumbling down the side of a mountain upon the roadway not more than a hundred yards ahead of the car. It just missed us and completely blocked the roadway. The noise created by the immense fall of masses of earth, rocks, boulders, and large trees cascading down over the roadway was paralysing. After the tumult had subsided, a thick fog of dust blotted out the landscape. It filled my eyes, mouth and nostrils. When this lifted finally, I stared at a path of desolation which was every bit of a quarter of a mile in width.

The stampede of a large herd of elephants can be even more terrifying than that. As soon as the herd's initial panic has ebbed, it can vanish from sight without making more than a faint whisper of sound. Trees have been knocked over or uprooted, bushes and high grass flattened, and there remains over everything a thick haze of dust which is slow in lifting. I was compelled to face up to a fair number of elephant stampedes in my early hunting years, and liked the experience less and less. One occasion stands out as the worst, for the herd suddenly swung around and returned in panic-stricken flight in my direction. One such incident is bad enough in all conscience, but to endure it twice within the course of only about five minutes was absolutely nerve-shattering.

One day when hunting for ivory on the west bank of the Nile, almost opposite Nimule, I encountered a large herd of elephants numbering approximately 800 animals—bulls, cows and calves of varying ages. The grass stood from six to fifteen feet in height. The whole countryside was studded with bush and acacia thorn-trees, yet the only sound made by the herd was like that of a light breeze stirring the grass. It was little more than the echo of a sigh, such as one may frequently hear in a field of wheat. It was astonishing that such a large number of huge bodies could move collectively across this type of terrain so noiselessly. Had they been feeding while on the move, the constant snapping off of branches from trees and the contented rumbling noises peculiar to this species must have been heard distinctly.

Often I have been spooring a herd on the move and keeping fairly close up on the tail of them, but then unaccountably lost contact. The spoor would have been simple to follow if there had not happened to be so many other quite recently made ones. I was unable to hear the movements of this herd. Only when I located their mounds of steaming droppings was it possible to determine positively which path these animals had taken. If sound alone had been my guide, it is unlikely they would been contacted again that day.

On another morning, shortly after dawn, I picked up the fresh spoor of a smallish herd not far distant from Nimule *boma* on the east bank of the Nile; and one pad-mark in the dusty track clearly indicated that a giant bull was with them. The measurement of the circumference of a pad-mark affords a reasonably accurate estimate of the size of the animal which left the impression, and also gives an idea as to the weight of ivory carried. This is by no means an infallible guide and I have been deceived on several occasions, only discovering on coming up with the herd that the bull's tusks were unrewarding in the matter of size and weight.

As it was the beginning of the breeding season, I knew it likely that this bull would be well in advance of the cows in the herd; and hunting it, therefore, would prove dangerous work. Hamisi and I discussed the problem for some minutes before a decision was reached to proceed. Hamisi was rather against following up the bull to make a kill, but another careful measurement of that large pad-mark changed his mind. He now thought that the bull would prove a good prize and it was worth accepting the risks involved.

Closely followed by Hamisi, and my excellent 'Ndorobo tracker leading over the spoor, I set off in the wake of the herd. It was easy enough to follow them through the high elephant-grass, for they had left a path as wide as Fifth Avenue in New York; but, unsuspected by us, we got amongst the cows. I could hear nothing and see no animal either ahead or around me because of the tall grass. Suddenly Hamisi tapped my shoulder and signalled to drop flat on the ground; and, though I knew no reason for doing so, I was wise enough to obey his signal at once. He crawled silently alongside and whispered: *"Tembo, bwana!"*. Still I was unable to see anything of any elephants nearby though the gun-bearer was pointing to a spot just in front of where we lay on the ground.

I strained my eyes and ears. Every faculty had become keenly alerted, and the rifle was thrust forward in readiness for raising it swiftly to the shoulder for a shot. All at once I heard a curious sibilant kind of sound, closely resembling the gentle kiss of a light wind through foliage. *Swish—swish—Swish!* not another sound could be distinguished and no particle of an elephant was visible. But suddenly my eyes registered a slight movement near a tree to my immediate front, and I almost shouted in sheer surprise. Close to me, so that I could easily have rested a hand on a hind-leg, stood immobile a large elephant cow. I crawled back hastily, and likewise did the gun-bearer, only almost to bump into another cow. Females of the species are taboo to a hunter on a game licence. It was at this moment that I realized we had inadvertently got into the middle of the herd and were now surrounded by the cows. A most unpleasant situation, indeed!

We dared not move, though much desirous of getting clear from a decidedly unhealthy predicament with the least possible delay. But in the circumstances our departure from the scene was not easy to accomplish, and I decided to wait patiently until such time as the herd moved onwards. The cows were not showing the slightest inclination to go, but appeared to have settled themselves in this spot to enjoy their customary noontime siesta—normally between ten in the morning and three in the afternoon. My watch told me that the time was eleven. This was most provoking. It seemed likely, too, to develop into a dangerous situation for us before very long. So far there had been no wind of much account, but it might soon strengthen and disclose our proximity to the herd. Then we were destined to know a whole heap of trouble.

The time dragged on interminably. We remained motionless, legs and arms becoming cramped, and scarcely even daring to breathe. At frequent intervals, I tested the wind and found there was none to give us away. At last, I could stand the strain no longer and decided to break the tension for good or ill, being so desperate I was prepared to accept big risks to free ourselves one way or another from this dangerous situation.

Cautiously I took the spear from the tracker's hand, gradually raised myself erect, and swung the weapon to wallop the rump of the cow with a hearty blow. This was the only target that offered, and so well proportioned that a blind man could not have missed. I struck with all my power, the steel head of the spear hit the cow's posterior with a resounding thud, and the shaft broke into three pieces. I dropped the portion left in my hand like a red-hot coal and took the rifle from Hamisi's outstretched hand. As I grabbed the weapon from him I heard his chuckle—a rare event for Hamisi!

The cow sprang into life, emitted a shrill and ear-piercing scream, tucked her tail well in, and was off into the bush. When last viewed she was travelling fast. All around us now could be heard sounds of great activity, for the grossly insulted elephant cow had started a positive riot. The remainder of the herd were crashing off noisily through the grass, bushes and timber in the wake of their outraged companion, trumpeting loudly and creating devastation in their paths. Several of them passed far too close to us for our liking. But all headed well away from our position and caused no injuries. I never saw that cow again. Moreover, I did not particularly desire to do so.

Realizing that the herd had cleared off from our immediate vicinity, we trotted forward after the coveted bull, chuckling in amusement at the gross indignity inflicted upon the surprised cow. Making a wide detour, we tried innumerable times to get in between the cows and bull. But these efforts failed. All that happened was that we bumped into the cows and young bulls, who were now feeding as they travelled onwards. The wind had now risen and was unfavourable for us, because it was constantly changing direction. It was approaching sunset when I called off the day's hunt, admitting defeat in favour of returning to camp. It had been lucky for us, of course, that the herd had moved away instead of in our direction; otherwise the day might well have ended in a tragedy. For three more days we searched for the big bull, but without success. I did not again contact the herd.

When an elephant wishes to create a din it can make more noise than any other animal in the wilderness. A herd of several hundred of this species, such as one commonly encountered on the west bank of the Nile during much earlier years, will trample down the entire cultivated acreage of an African village and destroy all the standing crops. In doing so they make as much row as a tornado or earthquake. Elephants revel in raiding the cultivated lands of long-suffering Africans, causing in a single night terrific devastation and reducing the wretched cultivators to the brink of starvation. If a cyclone had been in progress it could not have done more damage than a herd of elephants on the rampage through growing crops. That is why the Game Departments of Kenya, Uganda and Tanganyika established elephant control operations, which served to teach these marauders to leave severely alone the works of mankind. Some of the raiders, if caught red-handed, are killed and the others driven away from human habitations. These animals are quick to appreciate that crop-raiding does not pay.

The majority of instances of herds stampeding *en masse* are due to the animals having been frightened. The power of scent being the strongest sense in the elephant, it is only natural that they should strive to gain a position up-wind with least possible delay. It is their best chance of smelling danger from the front. In doing so, they often appear to come deliberately for the disturber of their privacy and may then rush over the hunter or photographer in their frenzy to get up-wind. At such a crucial moment their sole object is to gain a favourable strategic position for either attack or defence. It is not actuated by any desire to kill or injure the human cause of their fright. Every living creature prefers to face any threat of danger rather than to be kicked hard from behind.

Should a herd of elephants (or buffalo) do this on being startled by the unexpected appearance of a human being almost invariably it splits up into two sections in order to pass on either flank of the intruder. I have experienced this a number of times with both species, and am never likely to forget the paralysing fear suffered during those brief but tense moments. Such incidents can be most unpleasant. But I am not convinced that at such times the animals are especially dangerous for the hunter—provided always he keeps cool and stands perfectly immobile throughout the ordeal.

When a herd of elephant suddenly comes all out in your direction, trumpeting shrilly in anger or intimidation, it is sometimes feasible to turn them without having to slay a single beast. A bullet fired at top of the skull will nearly always achieve this desirable object, but it can never be reckoned upon as a certainty. When facing a mass stampede it is far more advisable to stand absolutely immobile where you are; but, admittedly, this does take a good deal of self-control. The most natural reaction is to bolt for cover behind the nearest large tree, which can be suicidal in the majority of instances. The slightest movement made by the hunter or his gun-bearer immediately discloses their exact whereabouts, and the result is almost certain to be some kind of disaster. Whenever we acted wisely in freezing, the stampeding herd passed on either side of us and we suffered no harm. Such experiences are not those after which any hunter hankers.

Generally speaking, when an elephant charges with lethal intent, the trunk hangs down in front of its chest with the tip curled inwards to the forelegs; but I have had them come at me, screaming with fury and trunk extended straight out to grab hold of my body. If the trunk is curled up and held straight down before the chest, the only target offered is a frontal brain shot into the forehead. A number of professional elephant-hunters, either friends or acquaintances, have been killed because their nerves played them false at the critical moment. Most of them had been hunting this species successfully for a long period of years without once experiencing any serious kind of mishap; but they had been after ivory too long and should have quit earlier.

Once when hunting elephants in the Belgian Congo a large herd stampeded suddenly in my direction. By a strong effort of will I stood frozen in their path, though aching for wings to make myself scarce. Had I been a block of stone, I could not have contrived a greater degree of immobility. I just gripped the rifle and stared at the oncoming avalanche of huge bodies, widely extended ears, thundering feet and flashing bars of ivory. My ears were deafened by the terrific noise of their passage and shrill trumpeting. As the herd crashed through the bush and trees, leaving behind a wide wake of desolation and destruction, I was conscious chiefly of a paralysing and ghastly fear. Until the stampede had passed and left me uninjured, I was incapable of uttering a sound, of thinking, or of acting. The noise rang in my ears and brain for a longish time afterwards, and it was only possible to hear Hamisi with difficulty when he spoke to me.

The picture conveyed to my brain was filled with gigantic slate-grey bodies ever coming nearer and larger, of waving trunks, of huge outstretched ears, and of gleaming tusks of ivory. The earth shook and quivered to the heavy pounding of large feet on the ground as the herd passed me in rapid flight from the cause of their panic. Fear has been defined as "a painful emotion caused by impending danger or evil; a state of alarm; anxiety for the safety of oneself or of others." It is every scrap of that! Fear can be a great deal more, too, if judged by the emotions created when facing up to a herd of elephants, perhaps several hundreds strong, when in a panic-stricken stampede. And well I know it.

Even after the ordeal was over and no damage done, I still stood rooted to the spot and unable fully to grasp the actuality of a providential escape from being killed or injured. How long this endured, I do not know. I was recalled to my senses and the immediate necessity for getting away to a place of safety by a gentle touch on an arm by Hamisi. He had stood stoically at my elbow throughout those tense moments. Hamisi could always be trusted implicitly never to abandon his employer in times of serious danger; it was not the nature of this courageous Swahili gun-bearer to think only of his personal safety. Not once in six years when in my service did he fail me in the slightest degree.

I turned my head to stare incredulously at his face. He was grinning broadly. With a shrug of his shoulders he silently pointed a finger in the direction we ought to go, turned and led the way.

At that instant we heard the huge herd of elephants returning towards us. Once again we froze in our tracks to meet this unexpected dire threat to our lives. Once more we were called upon to suffer the ordeal, but the herd divided to pass on either flank and soon left us far in their rear. Then I followed Hamisi, saying no word.

Had he noted the hallmarks of the ghastly fear I had known? If so, he gave no sign or even hinted at it. Hamisi was far too loyal and efficient a gun-bearer ever to attempt to make capital out of his employer's momentary lapse into weakness. We had hunted in each other's company far too long a time for any possibility of there to exist other than friendship and complete understanding between us. When master and servant have faced death shoulder to shoulder, year in and out, there is forged a bond between them which transcends all others. Any idea of the so-called "colour bar" has no place in that deep sense established of mutual loyalty, consideration, understanding and perfect companionship while out big-game hunting. Speech is unnecessary. Actions and co-operation in all things alone count for anything. And it had always been thus between Hamisi bin Baraka and myself.

Because of all this, neither he nor I ever referred to that terrifying test of our manhood. Such things are best locked up in one's own private skeleton cupboard. Yet I was never really able to conquer an instinctive dread during the first few seconds of facing up to an elephant, though once the issue had been joined beyond recall my entire outlook always changed immediately. I became cool and collected, nerves quite steady, and was able to cope efficiently with the situation.

There was another occasion while hunting for ivory on the west bank of the Nile when I had a nasty experience when trying to cut out a magnificent old bull from the centre of a herd which must have numbered fully 900 bulls, cows and calves. I was accompanied by Bill Bennett, who was not long embarked upon a career as a professional elephant-hunter and had persuaded me to let him join up for three weeks' hunting. Hamisi was my gun-bearer and Bill had his own. The local Africans told me that there were a few big tuskers in this particular herd, but both of us felt inclined to be sceptical. It is unusual to find heavy tusked bulls in a herd, for these are much more likely to be leading a solitary existence or accompanied by one or two chosen companions. Bulls with herds are mostly immature or in the prime of life, and normally do not carry worthy ivory.

We contacted the herd. Our information had been correct, but it became necessary to abandon the hunt that day because the two bulls wanted were always surrounded by younger males and many irate cows. They would not let us get near enough to the grand patriarchs to take a safe brain, heart or shoulder shot. Neither of us felt inclined to accept any undue risks. Time and again, we had striven to get in close to the best bull but never were able to approach nearer to it than the outer ring of vicious cows guarding him. Immediately they winded or heard us, the entire herd scattered in every direction; while the cows shepherded the two big bulls clear of the danger zone.

In a large herd, such as this one, there will always be found cows cursed with extremely vile dispositions and ugly tempers. These are mostly old animals. The instant they become aware of any danger threatening, all crowd around the bulls to protect them. This renders it practically impossible to get in close enough to take a safe shot at the coveted bull. In this instance, some cows frequently charged deliberately towards us, though many others remained on guard over the two big bulls and hustled them away. That day had certainly been crammed with thrills—enough of them, indeed, to satisfy even the most adventurous spirit.

Two days later we again contacted this herd and once more endeavoured to get in near enough for a shot at our selected bulls. This time we managed to creep within close range without alarming the vicious cows, largely because the wind direction was favouring us. It then became apparent that there were four old bulls worthy of our bullets. One by one, at no minor risks and with the exercise of infinite patience, we dropped all four of them with brain shots. Long before this had been completed, however, the cows were charging haphazardly all over the place and our situation was extremely dangerous as well as being unnerving. Anything was liable to happen at any moment. It had been agreed mutually that on this day we would accept risks, but we had rather spoken out of our turn. If we had known all this might entail, I think that we should have reconsidered the decision.

Immediately the last of the four bulls had died from my bullet into the brain, we deemed it advisable to remove ourselves temporarily from the scene. We wanted to allow sufficient time for the enraged herd to calm down somewhat and move away from the carcases of the four bulls. The cows were charging about hither and thither in search of the enemy, and a sudden change in the wind direction would spell disaster. It was a critical situation for us, because we were still surrounded by the infuriated herd of elephants. Time and again, I tested the wind direction by dropping sand from my hand; and, luckily for us, it remained constant and blowing towards where we stood in a state of indecision.

We got down on knees and hands, and then started to crawl

cautiously up-wind from out of the midst of the herd. My heart was in my mouth. Those tense and anxious minutes dragged by slowly and seemed like an eternity. In crawling we were often so close to cows, which had now become stationary and were quest-ing for our wind, that it would have been simple to pat them on a leg in passing. Hamisi and I had taken our own lines of with-drawal, for now it was a case of every man for himself. I had no idea where Bill and his gun-bearer were, and did not even try to find out or even glance around for Hamisi. I was far too concen-trated upon getting clear of the herd for any other thoughts.

Suddenly I found my way blocked by a dense ring of cows, a forest of legs and waving trunks, and a sea of burnished ivory. For a brief time I hesitated, being at a loss about what best to do. Then, taking my courage in my hands, I crawled onwards to pass under the belly of the nearest unsuspecting cow; and, when clear of her, tested the wind. It was still blowing favourably for me. Next I started to crawl behind another immobile cow, but she raised a hind-leg and only just missed planting it down on the small of my back. I almost screamed aloud in fright. Now my heart was pumping like a dynamo and sweat pouring down into the eyes, obscuring my vision. The stench was nauseating. Few animals, lest it be the camel, have a stronger odour than elephants. In their habitual haunts the air is permeated with this aroma and stagnant with it for a long time after they have moved far away. The smell is not exactly like that of a bed of violets. A farmyard is attar of roses in comparison with the vile stench which saturates the ground, trees, vegetation and atmosphere where elephants have stopped for a time.

Ahead could be seen still more legs and swinging trunks, with tusks showing here and there; and to the right, left and rear of me it was the same. I crawled onwards slowly, careful to make the least possible noise, testing the wind direction constantly, and missed being trampled upon a dozen or more times. No words could adequately describe what I endured during that nightmare crawl to a point outside the herd of elephants. I was conscious chiefly of an urge to rise and run; no less so of a sickening state of fear. It was a ghastly experience.

I crawled clear of the outer fringe of the herd, rose and walked steadily away down-wind. Now it was possible to breathe more freely. My nerves steadied, heart ceased to race uncomfortably, and every faculty now was keenly alerted. When I was about half a mile away my legs gave way under me and I collapsed on the ground in the shade of a large tree. I had even forgotten my companions for the time being. But, no matter how great might have been their need, I was physically incapable of going to their aid. It had all been rather more than enough for one day. After a time I took a long drink from the water-bottle—cold tea, milkless and sugarless, which is the best thirst quencher for an elephant-hunter.

Some time passed before Bill Bennett, Hamisi and the other gun-bearer rejoined me. All had known similar dreadful experiences, were badly shaken and unnerved; and Hamisi was more so than I had ever known him to be. He and the other African looked yellow about the gills, and both were shaking as if from a severe attack of ague. Bill seemed to be much in about the same state of mental and physical exhaustion as myself, which says a great deal. His face was as white as a sheet. I suspected that my own showed no more colour than well-laundered linen.

We rested in the shade for a couple of hours, and then headed back to camp. Next morning we returned to the spot with a gang of porters to recover the valuable ivory won; and there was no sign of the herd except that rank and musty odour heavily tainting the atmosphere, mounds of their droppings, and a sea of devastation created during their stampeding. The four pairs of tusks were hacked out, and with them we returned to camp. All were exceptionally good ivory. The biggest bull's pair weighed 121 and 113 lb. respectively; while the other tusks were all over 90 lb. each. It had been a profitable day's hunting, indeed!

But as I accompanied our haul of ivory back to camp, I kept on asking myself if the prizes were really worth all we endured in the winning of them. Were they? Many may consider that they were not. But I believe the majority of elephant-hunters would think otherwise. The pursuit of ivory can prove a most fascinating and hazardous adventure, but also is distinctly rewarding if reasonably successful. At least, it can honestly be stated that I knew of none better during my youthful years.

14

Adventure with Man-eating Lions

Tell me, if you were turned into a lion,
what sort of a one would you be?

MARTIAL

WHEN a lion degenerates into a confirmed man-eater the loss of human lives in the district can be considerable. It is far worse when a "troop" of lions happens to be involved in this ghastly reign of terror; and the latter circumstances are less unusual than when a single beast is engaged upon man-eating. It is rare for such cunning and vicious beasts to be content with other prey. A very true saying is "once a man-eater, always a man-eater". But I am not convinced that man-eating among lions is an hereditary trait, as some have argued, but far more of an acquired vice.

Until such horrible pests are exterminated, they can prove a deadly scourge to the African population. To terminate such a gruesome situation is never a simple proposition. The task is always fraught with peril for those embarked upon it. It is seldom that the final curtain is rung down in a day or night. The killing of such brutes may entail days, weeks or even months of arduous hunting with an ever-present danger overshadowing the hunter. Well I know it, too. I became deeply involved in such a duty on a number of different occasions in Africa.

As a general rule during earlier times in East Africa either the Game Department or European Police Officers were saddled with this onerous and thankless task. In Kenya, from 1904 to 1909, it often fell to my lot; but this was welcomed rather than otherwise. On this particular occasion I was touring the outlying areas of an extensive district over which I had been placed in police charge, travelling by porter-*safari* and doing any hunting that chanced to come my way. I was accompanied by my stout-hearted gun-bearer, Hamisi, and my 'Ndorobo tracker, Juma.

Upon arrival at the *boma* of an isolated district one evening I was informed by the District Commissioner that a "troop" of man-eating lions were on the rampage in his area and their menace had been unduly prolonged. Reports of grim tragedies amongst the African population had been reaching him with a depressing regularity. He urged me to undertake the job of wiping them out. As this was likely to take some time, before accepting the challenge I demanded a covering order from him so that no trouble would overtake me if I were too long away from my official headquarters. This was readily forthcoming. With this cover I was content, because in those early years the extermination of animal pests was accepted as a part of a Police Officer's maltifarious duties.

The D.C. did not know the exact total of victims, but thought it might well be as high as fifty men, women and children over the past two to three months. Indeed, he assured me, it was an unending tale of tragedies. From the reports reaching him, he concluded that the man-eaters were chiefly operating to southwards of the *boma*. In view of all he told me, it was obvious that drastic measures were demanded to put an end to this reign of terror created by a "troop" of lions. In accepting the D.C.'s challenge, not for a moment did I delude myself into thinking that the execution of these pests would be a simple matter.

I went out next morning at dawn with Hamisi and Juma to comb the countryside for the "troop" of man-eaters. The head-man of a village at which we called for news, informed me that these lions had been close to the village during the night. Shortly after proceeding onwards, I encountered a small group of Africans standing on a pathway. All of them were obviously terrified. They reported that a man had been taken by the man-eaters about a couple of hours earlier when heading for the *boma* to seek employ-ment. They indicated the signs on the path. Blood and pug-marks of a large lion were to be seen clearly on the sandy soil, while the spoor led off from the path into a thick patch of thorn-bush.

Although appreciating that it was likely to prove unrewarding because too long a time had lapsed since the taking of this man, I decided to follow up the spoor. Candidly, I disliked the nature of the terrain into which we must go. As we advanced my dislike increased. A tunnel through the bush, in which we soon found ourselves, was so narrow and thorny as to make it impossible to swing a rifle except to cover a few yards ahead. Visibility was far from good and, if the man-eater happened to be there, an escape from a mauling or worse seemed negligible.

We had forced a way into this forbidding thick stuff for a dis-tance of about 100 yards, and then I suddenly spotted a fragment of dirty blanket caught on the thorns. I examined this and saw it was blood-soaked, attached being a few coins strung together through a hole in their centre. Discarding this pathetic object, we continued to force a way onwards but now very alert to deal suitably with any situation arising. The smell of blood and lion grew momentarily stronger as we crept forward. After covering about another thirty yards we emerged upon a small clearing, where the grass had been flattened out. In the centre was the head of the luckless victim of the man-eater, and nearby also the hands and feet. A few licks from a rough tongue had scalped the head. Some of the larger bones had been stripped clean of flesh and then discarded.

There was nothing more that could be done. The man-eater had vanished and by now would be far distant, so it was futile to follow up its spoor. Most of that day we searched the countryside for the man-eaters but did not even glimpse a single lion.

For another five days we hunted around for the "troop" but met with no success. The brutes were proving cunning and elusive. I began to despair of luck favouring our sustained efforts to put paid to their long-overdue accounts. Hamisi and I agreed that our only hope of success rested upon the taking of a victim being reported to us without any delay, which alone might provide a reasonable chance of finding the brutes gorging upon the body.

Although the local Africans were living in the shadow of sudden and violent death, yet not a single man amongst them would volunteer to participate in an organized sweep of the area where the man-eaters were operating. Like the District Commissioner, they had passed the buck to me. These Africans expected miracles to be performed on their behalf, but it just does not work out that way with man-eating lions.

On the morning of the sixth day I struck camp and marched back to the *boma*, hoping that the D.C. might be able to persuade some of the tribesmen to assist us as beaters in making a wide sweep of the countryside. It looked like being a vain hope, but was our best chance of gaining success. But the D.C. failed to induce, any Africans to volunteer their help. They continued to be supinely unco-operative. More and more it was being impressed upon my mind that the task must prove a heartbreaking one, while the fall of the curtain on these human tragedies would be unduly delayed. Moreover, we were hunting for the man-eaters in a particularly unfavourable type of terrain.

The D.C. informed me that takings were still being reported to him; and during the next four days at least six more Africans became victims of the brutes, though these cases were not reported to me quickly enough to be of any real use in finding the man-eaters. By then I was nearly at my wits' end as how best to cope with this grisly situation. Scouring the country for the man-eaters appeared to be unproductive toil, but I made camp near the *boma* so as to get information of a taking without undue delay.

Five days later, after an early breakfast, I was making preparations to go out on a whole day's sweep of the countryside. Suddenly I heard terrified voices shouting loudly and distinguished in the babel the word *simba* (lion). A few moments later an African police-sergeant ran up to report that a young woman, the wife of a constable, had just been taken by a man-eater. He told me that she was walking along a path leading to the police-lines, and in full view of them all, when a large lion sprang out of the high grass, struck the woman down with a blow from a fore-paw, and carried off her body into cover of the high grass. He had seen the grass going down and dividing as the man-eater made off with its victim in the direction of a belt of forest situated about a mile from the *boma*.

It may seem rather callous of me, but I felt really glad to get this report within a few minutes of the tragedy. It afforded a reasonable chance of finding the brute gorging its victim. We wasted no time getting on the man-eater's spoor. The sergeant and bereaved husband, both armed with Martini-Henry rifles, volunteered to join our party. I was at two minds about accepting this offer. Hamisi, Juma and I were capable of looking after ourselves, but the two volunteers not so. Indeed the likelihood was that we should have to look after them, and this additional burden was a little too much. They were so urgent, however, in pleading to go with us that I reluctantly agreed to take them.

The grass through which the man-eater had carried off the woman's body was high, thick and tinder-dry; and if we followed directly over the brute's tracks, inevitably our advance must be too noisy. That would seriously reduce our chances of overtaking the brute before it got well concealed in the forest to enjoy a feed on human flesh. The hefty blow from a paw to the woman's head must have killed her instantly. It is a customary habit of man-eaters when claiming a human being, and a merciful trait in the character of the species. This, therefore, was not a case of rescuing the woman alive but of killing the brute responsible for the outrage.

Instead of following the spoor of the man-eater, I decided to proceed by the shortest route to the fringe of the forest-belt. A narrow native path led there from the *boma,* and then skirted the timber to the leftwards. It was my hope that the man-eater would not hear us and be unsuspicious of being followed. We might be able to intercept it before the brute and its burden could get too deep into the thick stuff for a gorge. And this proved sound strategy. We had not penetrated far inside the edge of the forest when was heard a savage and intimidating growl from our quarry. This note of warning was almost at once succeeded by sounds of a heavy body forcing its way through the undergrowth. Our man-eater had bolted. The two policemen, in spite of my stern orders to advance noiselessly, had moved carelessly in our rear and made a bit too much noise. This sufficed to scare the man-eater from its victim.

Now we were faced with a tough proposition. It would not be simple to locate the beast for a killing shot; but, at least, we had established a contact with one of the horrible pests preying upon the local population. That was something gained. If fortune favoured us, the fact might be turned to good account. Slowly and cautiously, I headed directly towards a largish patch of thick grass in a small open glade and from where the ominous growl had seemed to come. Every faculty was alerted. Indeed, this was imperative if I wished to retain a whole skin. Hamisi was close on my heels, Juma slightly in rear of him and carrying a .303 Lee-Enfield carbine, and the two policemen walked about ten yards behind us with their rifles.

At the base of a giant wild-fig tree we found the body of the unfortunate woman. It was not a pretty sight. Momentarily, I experienced a sense of acute nausea and my stomach revolted at that ghastly object on the ground. It was as much as I could manage to prevent myself from being violently sick. Even during the short time that had lapsed since she was taken, one leg and both arms had been devoured. This made me suspect that more than one man-eater had been on the body and, if this surmise happened to be correct, the ultimate outcome was quite unpredictable. The speed with which this lion had carried the woman's body over a distance slightly in excess of a mile might have astonished me but for the fact that I knew an authenticated instance of a notorious man-eater in Northern Rhodesia which had carried a woman victim for seven miles and only once put down the body for a brief rest.

From the spoor around the corpse, which was extremely confused, I deduced that there must have been three beasts—a lion and two lionesses—at the "kill". Hamisi and Juma insisted that a lion and three lionesses had been present. Which of us would be proved correct, only time could show. The fact remained that we were confronted with an unenviable situation, and one which called for careful planning to deal suitably with it.

There seemed every likelihood that the brutes would not readily relinquish their meal, but presently might return to the spot. If they did, it would provide a chance to kill one or more of them; always provided that our tactics were soundly devised. The first essential was to create an impression that the human invaders of the man-eaters' preserves had withdrawn, and thus it was safe for them to come back for a resumption of the gorge on the woman's body. With this in view, I ordered the two policemen to go back to the path skirting the fringe of the forest-belt and make as much noise as they could while progressing. They were then to take post on the path, turn back anyone coming along it from either direction; and if they heard shots to get back to the *boma* at best speed. On being warned that the man-eaters were on the rampage near at hand, no time would be lost by any African in making himself scarce.

Hamisi, Juma and I waited beside the woman's body until the loud voices of the policemen ceased, which assured us that they had gained the path and taken up post there. Then as noiselessly as possible, we climbed up into the wild-fig tree. It was a huge one with dense foliage, overlooked the remains of the woman, and had two stout limbs at a height of about six feet above the ground which would easily bear our weights. The foliage provided adequate concealment for us. All that was necessary now was to

E

wait patiently until the man-eaters returned for a resumption of their interrupted meal. We settled ourselves as comfortably as the circumstances permitted, and hopefully waited for the next move.

I have always disliked being perched in a tree over a dead or "live" bait for a tiger, lion or leopard which had to be killed. But there was something especially abhorrent in sitting upon a cast-iron bough over human remains—horribly mutilated—which were being employed as bait to lure the man-eaters to their ultimate destruction. Indeed, it needed some time to bring myself to the stage of regarding the wretched woman's remains as no more than just dead meat. But the suspicion was strong that neither Hamisi nor Juma was feeling in the least bit squeamish about this.

No words were exchanged. Any essential movements were contrived as soundlessly as feasible. The period of waiting seemed to me interminable. It was Hamisi's keen hearing which first detected the stealthy approach of the brutes. He drew my attention to their advent by making a slight sibilant hissing sound through the teeth. We had been comrades in big-game hunting far too long a time for me to misinterpret the meaning of that soft note of warning to be keenly on the alert. Then I heard, too, the cautious rustling in the long grass directly in front of our position.

For some time longer, possibly ten minutes, it was impossible to distinguish the forms of the brutes. Then I saw some tawny-coloured shapes pacing to and fro behind the screen of parched yellow grass, though it was impossible to distinguish them clearly. Until positively assured that the intruders had left the coast clear for them, they would not venture to advance boldly up to the "kill". After a time these movements ceased abruptly. I cautiously raised the .256 Mannlicher-Schoenauer to my shoulder in readiness to shoot when an opportunity offered. Out of a corner of an eye I saw Hamisi push forward the barrel of the .350 Rigby Mauser over the fork of a branch and prepare to back up my first shot. Juma was holding ready the .303 carbine, with which he had learned to shoot with a reasonable degree of accuracy. All we now wanted was for the lions to emerge from cover and provide us with simple targets. Then rapid and accurate shooting would be imperative.

We waited impatiently for another fifteen to twenty minutes. Nothing stirred. I was tempted to think that the brutes must have suspected instinctively all was not exactly as it looked, and had once more withdrawn to a point of safety. Then a black-maned lion's head suddenly poked cautiously through the screen of grass and bushes to survey the ground ahead. I could not have been more distant than twenty-five yards from our tree. I saw its eyes blinking rapidly, as if the strong glare of the sunlight hurt them after being in the subdued light of thick cover. Never until this moment had I realized that lions blinked their eyes so much. It is characteristic of the species rarely to glance upwards into trees, whereas tiger and leopard may often do so at intervals during an advance. Thus, though its eyes quested this way and that, the brute failed to look upwards or see us in the wild-fig tree. Our luck was in.

As I took deliberate aim for a shot into the lion's head, a second face, that of a lioness, was thrust through the grass to have a look-see; and two fawn-coloured shoulders, seen only imperfectly, indicated the presence of two more lionesses. So Hamisi and Juma had been correct. The "troop" consisted of a male and three females. How they could have been so cocksure of this fact passed my comprehension, for my own eyes had only been able to identify the spoors of a lion and two lionesses.

Hamisi and I shot simultaneously. He killed the lioness where she stood with a bullet into the chest, which raked her body to take the heart and lungs; but my own shot at the lion failed to drop it. No excuse could pass muster for this lamentable failure on my part, for the beast had been a positive "sitter" at such close range. More-over, I was not a novice at hunting lions. I knew perfectly well that their foreheads slope backwards from the nostrils but this fact is concealed by a tuft of hair adorning the forehead. It just happened that momentarily I forgot this, and with nearly disastrous results. Shooting downwards from a tree, instead of from ground-level, at a lion's head does make a clean kill less likely; but due allowance for this difference ought to have been made. My bad marksmanship on this occasion was unpardonable.

As our shots shattered the depressing silence of the glade in the forest, the wounded lion and two surviving females agilely whipped about and started to bolt from the danger-zone. I fired a raking shot into the lion's stern, heard the thud of the bullet striking its rump, and saw the beast limping back into thick cover. Hamisi shot at one of the two lionesses and dropped her dead with a bullet into the heart; while my third shot registered a hit in the right shoulder of the lion. It uttered a ferocious growl of mingled pain and rage, bounded into the air, and vanished out of sight. The third lioness got away unscathed before it was possible for any of us to shoot at her.

Some may think possibly that we had accomplished none too bad a morning's work. In about three hours after the woman had been taken, we had caught up with the man-eaters, killed two lionesses and thrice wounded the lion—how severely had yet to be learned. That sounds just fine on paper. But we did not delude ourselves into thinking it was any too good. Ahead of us was some real nasty and dangerous work to be done, which might well end tragically for one or more of the party. An unwounded lion normally presents no serious difficulties in its killing; but a wounded one, more particularly a confirmed man-eater, is an entirely different proposition. We were holding the wrong end of the stick. Within the next hour or more almost anything was liable to happen. But the wounded lion must be given a merciful despatch with the least possible delay, and the unwounded lioness also killed. As we had sown, so must we now reap.

It was necessary to follow up both beasts through the worst imaginable type of terrain for our personal safety. To be frank, I was feeling none too happy about the prospect; and do not think my two African companions liked it any better. It was agreed between us that we should keep close together and wait hopefully for any spot of luck which might come our way.

Juma was quickly on the blood-spoor of the lion. He followed it up with myself close behind him and Hamisi a few paces in rear of us. Blood smears upon the grass were simple enough to track, and its frothy nature indicated that the lungs of the beast had been hit. Before we had progressed any great distance it became abundantly evident that the lion and lioness had not travelled far in company. Two distinct tracks now became perceptible through the high grass, both heading in the same direction and parallel to each other at roughly twenty yards apart. The width dividing them increased with the distance covered.

Hamisi begged for permission to go off after the lioness by himself, but I sternly rejected this suggestion. It would have been supreme folly for us to separate. Under the prevailing conditions, I believed unity was strength. The lioness was almost certain to rejoin her mate before too long, and then our chances of bagging both beasts would be enhanced. We continued to follow the spoor of the wounded lion.

Anyone who has pursued dangerous big game through high grass and thorn-scrub will readily conjure up a picture of what the next few hours were like for us. It can be a fascinating and enthralling business, but always hazardous, for those taking part in such an adventure. There are the terrific heat, a deadly monotony and sense of frustration, but withal intense excitement; and either acute suspense or bitter disappointment. Those things are inevitable for anyone embarking upon such a task. An extremely wary approach to every patch of bush or high grass is imperative, and then only to discover that your quarry is not concealed there as fully expected. It has all been a waste of energy. There occur often, too, a quick tightening of the grasp upon one's rifle and accelerated heart-beats as the grass parts suddenly to let out an inoffensive duiker or impala. Always one is working completely in the dark, just feeling the way, and knowing well that all the dice are heavily loaded in favour of the beast being sought.

It might have been wiser if we had gone after the lioness first of all, which would have allowed sufficient time for the lion's wounds to stiffen. But the obligation existed to make a quick end of a thrice wounded creature, and this could not conscientiously be avoided or even unduly delayed. Moreover, I am Irish and therefore have an impetuous nature. We kept steadily upon the spoor of the wounded lion and at any moment expected to make a contact with it.

Eventually the spoor led us out of the high grass on to a large expanse of open countryside, where the grass was short and visibility more favourable in all respects. The area was approximately two miles in length by three-quarters of a mile in width. It was littered, here and there, with clumps of bushes; and trees of varying girth and height were scattered about, these for the most part being the umbrella-topped acacia thorn-trees. As we emerged from the suffocating depths of grass and on to this more open ground, Hamisi nudged my elbow and excitedly pointed a finger straight ahead.

Then I saw a lion resting in the shade cast by an acacia thorn-tree and not much more than 300 yards from where we had halted. All were agreed that it was the wounded man-eater. I examined the beast with field-glasses and, while doing so, it rose to its feet in slow time and with evident difficulty. Now there was no room for doubt about it being our quarry. The wound caused by my raking bullet was clearly visible on the brute's stern. But it was impossible to see either the head wound or the shoulder one as the beast was facing away from us.

Probably the lioness was not far off and, true to form, would charge boldly and instantly if her mate was killed. It is indeed rare for them not to do so. On the other hand, the male will disappear if the lioness is killed or injured. The male beast is not noteworthy for its gallantry. It is a wise policy, therefore, to take a lion first and deal suitably with the lioness when she promptly charges home. This makes sure of getting the male, and probably also the lioness. I much hoped that both ambitions would be gratified, and the last two members of this "troop" of man-eaters forced to pay the penalties of their crimes.

As I was about to squeeze the trigger, Hamisi touched my arm and whispered urgently: "Don't shoot, *bwana*." His finger pointed at a nearby patch of bushes. "I've just seen the lioness—*there*! The lion's wounds are now stiff, so it can't move away fast. You **can** kill it later. The lioness will charge soon now, for she's seen us. Thus both will be killed."

I knew this reasoning to be sound, but did not accept his advice. I aimed at the lion's heart as it stood broadside on to us, and dropped it dead on the spot. I caught a fleeting glimpse of the lioness as she slithered around some bushes a short distance away; and then she gave tongue, as a lioness nearly always will when her mate has been killed. She spoke with a nerve-shattering roar of fury, which told me exactly where she was and what to expect from her. But in this particular instance I had guessed wrong about the intentions of the lioness for she did not charge instantly. Why not, I am at a loss to explain. In about ninety-nine cases out of a hundred a lioness will do so.

Instead of charging promptly, she wilfully invited us to attack her. The devil of it was that she had taken refuge in some unpleasantly thick cover and where we could see no further than a yard to two around us. Moreover, the lioness kept on shifting her position, making it extremely difficult to keep tab on her whereabouts. But I knew positively that she was waiting patiently for one of us to make a mistake and thus could be taken off guard; and then someone would be made to pay dearly for killing her mate and the other two females. The winning tricks of the game were definitely held by her. A man-eater is supremely cunning at all times; this one sure had us guessing, because of her unexpected behaviour.

We played tag with the lioness all around and inside of that nasty patch of scrub-bush. The game must have lasted for an hour or more, though the time seemed much longer to me. We saw nothing of her, though we knew for certain that she was close to us within that dense cover. Sometimes it was her powerful stench that warned us where she was; at others, she disclosed her position by angry snarls or stealthy movements. All this was nerve-racking in a space giving scarcely room to swing a rifle. Once she emitted a deep coughing grunt from behind a bush, but I could not see even a speck of the tawny body; and yet, all the time, I was conscious of her amber eyes glaring balefully at me through the vegetation. We were striving our utmost to ring down the final curtain upon this drama of the wilds, but still far from achieving this desirable result. Eventually, too, she made complete fools of all three of us; and, mark this well, not one was a novice at lion hunting.

After a particularly savage and menacing snarl, I was leaning forward to peer through the bushes when she suddenly let out a devastating roar from my rear. It shook me badly. I spun around on one heel with rifle to shoulder, knowing a lust to kill this elusive and tantalizing brute. But there was nothing visible at which to shoot. At that moment Juma collected a thorn in a bare foot—a wicked three-inch-long spike from an acacia thorn-tree. Placing the .303 carbine on the ground, he went down on a knee to extract the offending thorn. I much doubt if he was further away from me than five or six yards. My recollection is that Juma must have been about midway between me and the lioness, while Hamisi stood close behind my right shoulder with the .350 Rigby Mauser held ready for a quick exchange with me. At the same moment was heard the crashing of undergrowth and out came the lioness from cover like a cork out of a champagne bottle. She attacked from the far side of the tracker. Here was the opportunity for which she had been waiting patiently, and now was swift to make the most of it.

Rifle was at shoulder to sight for a killing shot, but momentarily I held my fire. I saw the lioness rise in a spring. Juma, acting upon some heavensent instinct, dropped flat on his face to the ground. It all occurred so rapidly that my memory of the sequence of events is confused, being left with only a blurred picture of what actually happened. But my recollections are that the spring of the lioness had been directed too high and, once launched, she was unable to check it. She had sprung out upon a man bending down on one knee, but he had dropped flat as she rose off the ground. The result was that her body sailed over the prostrate tracker.

The lioness landed about midway between Juma and myself: a ferociously snarling mass of vindictiveness and murderous hate. Before she had a chance to recover her balance for a spring at me, a bullet from my rifle raked her body through the chest and laid her low. She did not move again. By then Juma was on his feet and almost touching her, and putting a shot into her head to make certain. While it lasted, the situation had been extremely tense.

What we had set out to accomplish had been achieved. All three felt justifiably elated, for on a single day had been wiped out four vicious and persistent man-eating lions. We much hoped that this had accounted for all members of the "troop", though the District Commissioner thought it numbered six brutes. Much time and labour had been expended upon the destruction of these horrible pests, which unduly long had been responsible for a reign of terror in this area. The going had often been tough. It was heartening to know that now four of the brutes had been executed summarily for their past misdeeds. We could only trust that no more of them were left to roam at large. Yet one never really knows. In Africa so very often the totally unexpected is liable to happen.

The shadows of the night were lengthening fast over the parched countryside as we briskly walked back to our camp at the *boma*.

It had been dark for a couple of hours when we reached our tents, excessively tired but content with that day's work.

For a week longer I remained in camp there, just in case other man-eaters might have escaped retribution. As no more reports of takings reached us, it was decided that the entire "troop" must have been exterminated. I packed up, struck camp, and set off on the backward trail to my headquarters station. Some weeks later I received a letter from the District Commissioner, informing me that no more human victims had been claimed by man-eaters in his area.

So that difficult job had been completed satisfactorily.

15

African Buffalo

THOSE who have an intimate acquaintance with the African buffalo (*Bos caffer*) will not think me guilty of exaggeration when I state that it is the grandest of the bovine genus. The superb head, great sweep of horns, impressive boss and frontlet, and massive bulk all combine to emphasize this creature's colossal strength. In action these qualities are confirmed. A buffalo trophy is seldom secured with ease by a sportsman and generally only after having experienced some "tense moments". The prize, therefore, is deemed the more worthy.

In spite of being subjected to periodical epidemics of rinderpest, to determined thinning out under game control operations, and to shameless butchery by African poachers or ruthless *biltong* hunters, the buffalo appears to be holding its own in a miraculous manner. Game Departments in Africa have reported a steady increase in the numbers of this species within recent years. So much so, indeed, that lately herds around Nyeri in Kenya made themselves such a destructive nuisance to farmers that drastic steps had to be taken to reduce their numbers. Buffalo are believed to be recovering from recurrent outbreaks of virulent animal diseases and man's destructive hands in many other parts of the continent. They breed approximately at the same rate as domestic cattle, a cow producing a calf about every year; and this fertility seems to have offset losses through mortality attributable to diverse causes.

The species mostly favours swampy or thickly vegetated types of country for its habitat. Normally, they will be located near water and facilities for wallowing; both of which are essential to their wellbeing. Nowadays, sportsmen anxious to obtain good buffalo trophies must go further afield than during earlier years, and work much harder to satisfy their ambitions, because these animals have learned the wisdom of keeping well away from settled areas. Many of their former habitats are now rendered impossible for them, and by necessity the species has become far more nocturnal in habit.

Acknowledged experts at big-game hunting have expressed diverse views on the subject of the "dangerous" qualities possessed and exercised by the African buffalo; but all of them placed this species high on their lists, some even according it the premier position. Personally, I award the African buffalo third place on my list of dangerous wild animals. Above it, I would place only the elephant and tiger.

But however one rates these animals, the African buffalo can never be rated as a weakling, cowardly or an unworthy quarry to hunt. Indeed, very often it can prove a highly dangerous beast to encounter and will always take the utmost advantage of any lack of precaution on the part of the hunter. No kind of liberties may ever be taken with *Bos caffer*. No other species of big-game in Africa—except perhaps the elephant and rhinoceros—is more resolute in carrying the fight to anyone attacking it with lethal intent. A wounded buffalo will always savagely attack a hunter if it is still capable of charging. When coming to terms with an assailant, it will prove relentless and of the utmost ferocity in its onslaught.

If a buffalo does charge, then it means business. The nose is thrust out straight ahead, shoulders covered by the massive sweep of horns, and the beast offers small chance of a bullet hitting it in any vital spot. Unlike the domesticated bull, the buffalo keeps the eyes wide open to watch its enemy. The head is only lowered at the last moment; and, at all such times, it is never simple to halt, turn or kill the beast.

Some individuals of this species, hunted in various parts of Africa, have occasioned me moments of the intensest anxiety until they were finally killed. Buffalo are endowed with excellent powers of scent and vision, and also have keen hearing; assets which render them really formidable animals to hunt.

If unmolested buffalo will generally display little of an aggressive spirit. Under such conditions it is rather a shy, quiet, retiring and comparatively inoffensive beast, whose chief desires are eating, getting into thick reeds or dense bush, mud-wallowing, resting in a secluded spot, and the reproduction of its kind. Evidence of a natural truculence, so often charged against the buffalo, has not

E*

often been my personal experience. For what it may be worth, I think that the bestowal of a reputation for inherent savagery in its general disposition is unwarranted; and the sole exception is when it has been wounded or subjected to constant persecution by mankind. Selous, whose knowledge of the fauna in Africa was perhaps unrivalled, gave the buffalo an evil repute; and so have other hunters since his time. But not every experienced hunter will endorse their verdicts.

Many years ago now I was hunting buffalo in the Tana river region of Kenya where, in those times, big-game had been little molested by man. A herd of about sixty buffalo, of both sexes and with a few calves, was located; and an especially grand bull was seen to be standing in rear of them, aloof and dignified as became the herd bull. I coveted that trophy. After a number of vain attempts to work round behind the herd for a reasonable shot at this magnificent specimen, in which I was hampered greatly by frequent variations in the wind direction, the others became somewhat disturbed and inquisitive but still appeared to be non-aggressive. Finally, as then it was late in the afternoon, Hamisi suggested that we should make our way through the herd, as the wind now favoured us and was constant for the time being, in order to get a shot at the herd bull. Frankly, I did not much favour this idea.

Some imp of mischief induced me to risk this foolhardy action, though I knew well enough it was a mad undertaking. We set off at a trot, side by side, towards the herd. The animals raised their heads to watch us, but did not move off or even display any signs of an aggressive spirit as we ran through their midst to the rear. Indeed, Hamisi and I actually pushed aside by hand some of the animals obstructing our passage! Once in rear of the herd, I dropped the bull dead where it stood. Then the entire herd went off in a panic-stricken flight. Although this action succeeded when past experience suggested that it could not, I do not recommend others to imitate such foolishness. Never again did I do it. Through greater experience gained of this species, I acquired a far more wholesome respect for *Bos caffer* in its natural environment.

If surprised, the general attitude of the species is that of suspicious curiosity, and this shortly will be followed by a sudden stampede away from the threatening danger. The entire herd will crash its way through the bush for some distance, then halt to look behind them with much snorting, and next resume their flight. Once an animal has been wounded or its anger aroused, however, it can be the most resolute and ferociously vindictive beast of all the major species of fauna in Africa. A really enraged buffalo, with a foe at its mercy, is incredibly sadistic and intensely destructive.

There do occur occasional instances of a solitary bull or cow charging a man when unprovoked and then displaying immense ferocity. But I think that this can be explained by the fact that it has been wounded on some previous occasion, and past experience taught the animal to hate as well as fear all mankind. Unwounded and little molested, however, they are often known to stand immobile and pose admirably before the lens of a camera at a distance of fifty or less feet before suddenly withdrawing from the spot. That has happened to me on several occasions. Not unlikely, an insatiable bovine curiosity accounts for such a placid attitude. In the Queen Elizabeth National Park, Uganda, groups of buffalo can be viewed grazing contentedly beside the roadway or lying down there while reflectively chewing the cud. The animals do not even deign to pay the slightest attention to passing motor-vehicles or their human freight.

Once in Kenya a buffalo bull deliberately charged me from out of a largish herd, immediately after I had killed a grand male amongst them. I had no wish to kill unnecessarily a second one, certainly not an animal of lesser worth; so I shouted loudly while waving my rifle vigorously above the head, hoping that this might stampede the entire herd and they would take this aggressive bull with them. It failed to achieve my purpose. The second bull came on resolutely, leaving me no option but to kill it in self-defence. An examination of the carcase revealed the presence of many bad sores on the gums of the mouth, primary symptoms of rinderpest, which probably explained this unprovoked attack. I can suggest no other logical reason for its unusual behaviour.

A startled herd will frequently stampede blindly in the direction of a hunter and, having passed beyond him, sometimes about turn unexpectedly to reverse the direction of their panic-stricken flight. When a herd, unaccustomed to molestation, happens to be located in open-country, I believe that the likelihood of a charge *en masse* is remote. The animals are generally content to stand immobile while staring steadfastly in the direction of any human intruders, heads raised and horns laid back in a challenging manner. Finally, their insatiable curiosity will often induce them to advance at a slow walk, moist nostrils held high and questing the air-channels for taint of danger. It is rare to find a really aggressive-minded individual in a herd. Their curiosity satisfied, normally the herd about-turns when some distance away and ambles off leisurely into the nearest available patch of cover. More than once that was my experience. Many others have told me that it resembled their own observations.

Viewed as may be, a savage and deliberate charge made by a wounded and vindictive buffalo is *not* something to be courted.

Once a beast has made up its mind to kill, only the death of the man or itself can be the logical outcome. When a buffalo does charge a hunter with malevolent intent, the odds generally favour the man armed with a powerful and accurate modern rifle rather than the beast. However, even the most expert marksman is liable to fail in killing, stopping or turning such a deliberate attack; and then he must pay the inevitable forfeit. This is usually exacted in full measure. Like Shylock, wild beasts in the animal kingdom are not bashful in demanding their pound of flesh.

Once having got a man at its mercy, a buffalo will not desist from savagely mauling him, sometimes even after death has ended the victim's sufferings. On all such occasions a buffalo can be a fiend incarnate. I write this with a knowledge of the evidence recorded by others who had the misfortune to suffer such an experience but were lucky enough to survive. Fortunately I was spared such a ghastly mauling.

Even though mortally wounded several times, a buffalo will frequently continue with its charge. There was an occasion when I hit a charging buffalo severely with five successive bullets from a .450/.500 Holland and Holland rifle. All of them should have killed it. But they did not. The bull came on in that vicious charge. It went down dead just behind where I was standing ready to send a sixth bullet into its shoulder, and with Hamisi beside me waiting to make a rapid exchange of weapons. How it managed to survive and still come on at us, after five heavy bullets had hit in vital spots, is quite beyond my comprehension. All I do know is that it did. The vitality of that buffalo bull must have been amazingly great.

What exactly is in the muddled bovine minds when a herd of buffalo appears to be making a massed charge at a sportsman and his gun-bearer? Terrifying as this may often be, in actual fact it is far less dangerous than the individual charge made by a wounded buffalo bull or cow. I believe that few hunters have been mauled or killed as the result of a massed stampede, but quite a number by a single beast when it was bent upon venting its spleen. After having experienced both types of incidents on several different occasions, I must admit that I would far prefer to face up to a massed stampede than a solo charge; and many hunters have confirmed that their opinions were the same.

The procedure of a massed charge, or panic-stricken stampede, of a herd of buffalo rarely appears to vary materially. The entire herd forms a kind of scrum facing the danger-point; and then, after an appreciable pause which impresses the hunter as being pregnant with dire threat and peril, the bunched animals advance slowly towards him. Next they accelerate the pace. Yet I have never once known such an advance to be pressed right home to its logical conclusion; and on two occasions was able to check it by firing a couple of bullets into the ground—a yard or two ahead of the leading animals in the centre. To my way of thinking, at any rate, it was doubtful if those shots were the determining factor in the next development. When distant from me about twenty yards, the herd wheeled slightly and split up into two separate sections from the centre of the formation. These sections passed only a few yards away on either flank of Hamisi and myself. No sort of attack was made upon us.

For some years I believed the explanation was that the movement was not at the start in the nature of a deliberate charge but far more of a blind and panic-stricken flight towards the point of danger. Later, however, I became less satisfied that this theory was correct. I am now tempted to think that, when disturbed from up-wind, buffalo have no exact knowledge of the nature or position of the danger threatening them. Instinct impels them to attain a more favourable strategic position and, in order to accomplish this, they take a chance by stampeding down-wind. In so doing, not infrequently they pass uncomfortably close to the hunter.

Once well beyond the suspected source of threat, and now cognizant of its nature and locality, their initial state of panic changes to a mastery of the situation. From that stage it becomes an easy movement away, provided the hunter does not persist in trying to get on terms with them.

Buffalo also have a disconcerting habit of about-turning to charge back over the same ground but from up-wind. At all such times a hunter will be extremely fortunate to escape with a whole skin. It always struck me that massed stampedes of buffalo were half-bluff and half-charge, which was much influenced by a leave-it-to-your-partner attitude and therefore more or less ineffectual.

Hunting buffalo, whether the Asiatic or African varieties, demands a considerable degree of physical endurance, a sound knowledge of its general habits, an immense measure of patience, and steadfast nerves when in a tight corner. Indeed, it is rare for an easy target to be offered. Shooting at a buffalo in the wrong place, that is to say a non-vital part of its anatomy, is merely an act of senseless cruelty and certain to land you in serious trouble. It is infinitely wiser and more humane not to fire at all until there is a reasonable chance of killing the animal outright.

A wounded beast often may get away before there is any possibility of finishing it off, and then will suffer intense pain until relieved of its lingering torments by death. If not too severely injured it is certain to retaliate at the first chance upon an entirely

innocent human. For this reason it has now been made compul-
sory, under threat of punishment in a Court of Law, for all hunters
wounding any major species of the fauna to report as soon as
feasible the circumstances to the nearest Game Ranger or District
Commissioner. Steps are then taken to locate and kill the beast.

It is seldom a simple matter to track down a wounded buffalo
and, unless it is contacted and killed quickly, the quarry may not
be seen again by the hunter. There is always a considerable ele-
ment of danger for the pursuer. Knowing this, it is incumbent
upon all sportsmen to do their utmost to kill outright or, at least,
hasten the completion of a task which they have started. Although
it is not always practical, the precept of one bullet one animal is
undeniably sound in theory. However, there need be no sense of
shame if, after the first shot has proved ineffective, two or more
others are necessary to deliver a merciful despatch. After all, it is
the first wound which counts most.

When after buffalo it is advisable to make an early start from
camp so as to reach their usual haunts as soon after daylight as
practicable. It is then, and also late in the afternoon, that the
species emerges into more open country to graze. A swampy area,
forest, salt-lick or mud-wallow are the most probable places in
which to look for buffalo; and African villagers will generally co-
operate in telling you whereabouts to find them. The Africans are
inordinately partial to the beef, and make their shields from the
hide. They know well that a hunter will take only the head and
surrender the remainder of the carcase to them. As a general rule, I
found it advisable to follow up any buffalo spoor which displayed
obvious signs of having been made during the previous night or
evening. That is, always provided that it was picked up early in the
morning.

Once I was after buffalo on the Mau Plateau of Kenya, accompanied by a friend from Johannesburg who was desperately keen
to secure a good trophy of the species. We left at the false dawn.
It was freezingly cold, for the altitude was above 8,000 feet. A
drizzling rain added nothing to our comfort. Within a mile of
the camp, Juma picked up quite fresh buffalo spoor and, after
following this for some time, we sighted the herd. For the most
part, the animals were lying down in rather high grass and chewing
the cud. Unfortunately, we disturbed them before we were able to
fire a shot; and the herd galloped off into cover of the nearby
forest. For the best part of that day we kept after them, but were
never able to get a reasonable chance of shooting one of the big
bulls. As it was then growing late and we were both exceedingly
tired, we wisely decided to abandon their pursuit and retrace our
way to camp.

When at no great distance from it, we came upon tracks which Juma insisted had been made quite recently by buffalo. Neither of us knew enough about spoors to argue with him. Hamisi was inclined to agree with Juma's verdict. Late as it was, we hopefully followed up this spoor under the impression that it had been made by another herd which had passed only a short time earlier.

The trail led into the forest and eventually brought us back to the spot where we found the buffalo resting early in the morning. It then became obvious that we had got on the spoor made by part of this herd before daybreak. So cold and damp was the weather that the grass cut by the sharp hooves of the buffalo had remained perfectly fresh and unwithered throughout the day; but if there had been a hot sun, of course, it would have shrivelled rapidly. The spoor of this species will vary greatly in its appearance, according to whether it is exposed to the sunshine or remains in the shade; but that knowledge was only acquired later in my hunting career. We arrived back at camp long after dark, weary and footsore, and without a single trophy to show for a hard and long day's hunting.

My first and second intimate encounter with buffalo was staged in the bamboo forests on the higher slopes of Mt. Kenya, soon after my arrival in East Africa. On the first occasion I was hunting alone, having travelled with a porter-*safari* over the Aberdares to the base of Mt. Kenya and there camped for a week while shooting. On the first morning I set out with Hamisi, Juma and a dozen porters to hunt on the slopes of the mountain; and in a matter of a few hours had killed a good bull and moderately worthwhile cow buffalo; also in the bag was a grand kudu, a species rarely known thereabouts. Next I saw an even better buffalo bull just inside the fringe of the bamboos. The animal offered anything but an easy target, and my bullet only wounded it badly. I followed up at once. Then a "rogue" elephant bull butted unexpectedly into the picture and was killed with the third bullet fired at it.

In the excitement of dealing with the elephant the matter of the wounded buffalo was completely forgotten. To the best of my recollections, this was the only occasion when I did not make an earnest effort to complete the killing of a wounded beast. For this lapse from grace, perhaps I may be pardoned in view of all the attendant circumstances. The first two buffalo had been shot easily enough; and so would also the third if it had been more clearly visible to me. But the shot was fired through bamboos which obscured my aim. It should never have been attempted.

On the second outing after buffalo in this same area I was accompanied by John E———. He had recently arrived from South

Africa, on leave from his regiment there, and persuaded me to take him out on a shooting *safari*. We had with us four excellent Wanderobo trackers, but five days passed before their efforts produced any tangible results. By then both had almost begun to despair of success. On the sixth morning, however, two of the trackers arrived in camp to report having marked down a small herd of buffalo, comprising three bulls and five cows. They stated that this herd was feeding in the forest not more than five miles from camp, so we went off with them at once to the spot. After a tiring tramp over rough ground we came upon the small herd.

Two of the bulls carried exceptionally massive horns, but none of the other animals appeared worthy specimens. As John had yet to get his first buffalo, I agreed to stand by and let him have the first shot at the best bull; while the other good bull must take its chance with either of us. I did not particularly want one and hoped John might drop both animals, intending to kill only if forced to shoot in self-defence. That might well prove necessary.

The small herd was extremely restless and suspicious. For a longish time it was impossible to approach near enough for a shot as the animals were constantly on the move away from us. We followed them relentlessly. At last they stood immobile to stare morosely in our direction. We crept forward stealthily, making full use of every scrap of cover and keeping tab on the changes in the wind direction. From a reasonably short range John fired at the best bull, while I covered the second one with my rifle. He was a good shot, but whether due to inexperience or excitement I do not know, the bullet missed a vital spot and struck the ribs with a resounding thud. Wasting no time, I let drive at the second bull and dropped it dead.

The other animals, now thoroughly alarmed and enraged, took complete command of the situation. I stood my ground, ready to shoot at John's wounded bull; but this beast denied me an opportunity. The next moment it was almost on top of us. I was far too fully occupied to observe what John was doing, because I was watching for a chance to drop the charging bull. It thundered past me so close that I could easily have touched its body with an outstretched hand. Why the bull did not gore or trample me underfoot, I just do not know. I plainly saw the blood frothing at its mouth and nostrils, and the massive head lowered for deadly execution; but, fortunately, it ignored me and went on to vanish into the bamboos.

A few seconds later the remainder of the herd galloped madly past us in the wounded bull's wake. As they came, I saw them divide and pass to each side of where we had taken cover behind a small tree. As soon as they had disappeared, I glanced around for

John. Until that moment my mind had only been half aware of what was transpiring around me, and every second I had expected to be tossed skywards or bowled over to be trampled under galloping hooves. For a little time I could see nothing of John, so I feared that the worst might have happened. Then I saw him step out from behind a large bush and calmly light a cigarette. That made me laugh. It served to break the tension, and soon we were both laughing. Afterwards neither could account for this sudden burst of merriment, for it had been no laughing matter.

We left one of the trackers to mark the dead bull and followed the stampeding herd. The wounded beast had to be finished off as quickly as feasible. Time pressed and we were a longish way from camp; but, after covering a distance of about a mile, the herd was again sighted, halted in an open glade. Our quarry was standing in the centre of the others, and easily singled out because of its grand spread of horns. The bull's massive head showed above the back of the other animals but offered no good target for a "settler". It was snorting angrily at intervals and uttering deep bellows of pain. Hamisi suggested that I should try and kill the bull, while John and himself covered me with their rifles; and this was mutually agreed between us. Keeping careful tab on the wind variations and as soundlessly as possible, I crawled in closer by gradual stages until enabled to see clearly the vulnerable shoulder of the bull. Taking careful aim, I fired and the bullet sped true to the mark. The bull went down to it. As the beast struggled to rise, a second bullet ended its sufferings.

At sound of the first shot the others charged straight at us. It was an awe-inspiring spectacle, but I was granted no time to admire it because the animals were almost on top of us. I did the only thing possible and jumped agilely behind a tree's bole, which seemed so much smaller than it was in actual fact. As I did so, two shots rang out in rapid succession from my left rear; and a third bull was seen to stagger, come down on its knees, and then roll over on to a flank. One of the cows did likewise. The other four cows thundered past on either side of my tree-refuge. We let them go. Both had had rather more than enough for one day, though neither admitted it. Hamisi was more honest. He bluntly counselled a return to camp because all were suffering from strained nerves.

The memory of those cruel and widespread horns, so unpleasantly close, did not encourage any desire for a repetition of the experience. Even if we were tempted to get still another buffalo, the game laws prohibited it; the hour was growing late; and we had a long way to walk back to camp. Having collected the heads of our trophies, our party headed down the mountainside for the camp. It was long after dark before we arrived there, feet feeling like lumps of lead at the extremity of our legs.

John was delighted and triumphant. His last two shots had been placed as accurately and courageously as anyone could have desired. They made full amends for his indifferent marksmanship earlier in the day.

16

Some Buffalo Encounters

As a general rule a head shot at any beast—other than elephant, hippopotamus, or crocodile—is to be deprecated; but it does happen occasionally that a sportsman must accept any chance offered or lose his quarry. It may well be confined to the head. The hunter concerned must be the judge.

From my experience I think that a bullet just behind the shoulder is the most advisable shot to take at a buffalo. When aimed from broadside on to an animal this generally, though not always, proves fatal. If the hit is slightly in advance of the vital spot, fracturing the shoulder, the buffalo will be at your mercy for another bullet to kill it. There exists a possibility, however, that the beast may travel for a short distance if the bone has been perforated but not fractured; yet, even so, the perforation normally will cause the shoulder to break under the heavy weight of the beast.

A shot taken from right angles to the body, far back through the ribs, is quite useless and never proves quickly fatal. The bullet merely inflicts a cruel wound, which will cause the animal intense suffering and probably a lingering death. Such a shot should be taboo. It will rarely furnish a trophy. The wounded animal may be followed up for several days before you are able to come to terms again with it, while the chances of doing so and killing the quarry can be regarded as remote.

A bullet hitting high up in the loins, thus perforating the liver, is nearly always likely to prove fatal; but the death of the beast is not so rapid as when a shot has been placed well behind a shoulder. In the former case the buffalo may travel a longish distance, fight hard to preserve its life, and take much lead before finally succumbing.

The loin shot should be taken at a spot about nine inches below the termination of the dorsal ridge. If no better target presents itself, such as when a buffalo is standing broadside on and with its entire body, except for one hindquarter, concealed by cover, I found that the best policy was not to delay in taking a shot in the fond hope of a better one becoming available later on. Fire to fracture the hip-joint. It is then improbable that the beast will escape from you.

Should the animal be standing in full view and facing you, a bullet into the centre of the chest will mostly prove fatal, though the death of the beast is not so rapid as from a bullet behind the shoulder. If, on the other hand, a buffalo is standing still or moving away with only its hindquarters visible, then I would always advocate a shot under the root of the tail. The bullet will rake the body and penetrate the vital organs. Only once, I am glad to say, was this particular shot forced upon me and then it had been taken solely to prevent the escape of a severely wounded animal. If there had been an alternative shot possible, I would not have aimed under the root of the tail. In such cases, even if the aim is not perfectly accurate, one or other of the hip-joints or hind-legs may be fractured; but should a foreleg be broken, the animal can still advance on three legs to attack. A buffalo suffering from a fractured hip-joint is incapable of travelling far or fast and, if followed up immediately, it is feasible to finish off the animal with another bullet without experiencing much difficulty.

A shot fired diagonally behind the ribs in a line with the opposite shoulder can prove deadly in its effect. Indeed, I have known this to happen several times. The bullet rakes the vital parts of the beast before fracturing the far shoulder. If only the head is visible, as may so often occur, with the nostrils elevated and head showing over cover to glare balefully at the intruder, a shot fired into the cartilage of the nose, plumb central and slightly above a line drawn between the nostrils, will penetrate the brain and drop the animal dead where it stands. Frankly, I disliked being forced into taking this shot at a buffalo because the margin of possible error seemed far too great.

When following up a wounded buffalo, I always considered it advisable to fire a bullet into it at an angle through the forehead —between the eyes, behind an ear or in rear of the horn bosses. Normally, this will shatter the brain and kill the beast instantly. Humane and sportsmanlike behaviour demands that a wounded beast must be put out of its sufferings as soon as practicable, and that is now also a legal obligation in many African territories.

One thing to avoid is coming upon a buffalo suddenly and unexpectedly, and then being charged before the rifle can be used. The animal comes at a high speed, and unless it can be seen from some distance away, holds the winning cards. In all such eventualities the hunter's ability to defend himself adequately is negligible.

Because a wounded buffalo traverses the densest type of cover available and the pursuer cannot possibly discover whether it is travelling rapidly away or has concealed itself in some thick patch of cover, the utmost caution is advisable. It is quite likely, and often so, that the wounded beast is hiding up with lowered horns and waiting patiently to charge the pursuer when he is only a few yards away. As a wounded buffalo will sometimes travel for many miles, frequently making good its escape, it ought to be obvious that every minute wasted is to be deprecated. Notwithstanding, great circumspection in tracking the beast is essential.

Once when hunting elephants in Uganda I shot a buffalo bull which had an exceptionally good horn measurement. On this occasion I was compelled to risk a head shot. It might well have escaped if I had not chanced that shot. I was returning to camp after failing to get a good elephant, which had been spoored most of that day but got clear away from me, and accidentally stumbled upon the spoor of buffalo. This was fresh enough to invite following up.

After a time I saw a single buffalo bull out in the open near the edge of a forest-belt. It was feeding and seemed unsuspicious of any danger. Halting at once, I despatched some of my porters to make a wide detour and drive this bull towards me. Presently I advanced slowly and stealthily, but after covering about thirty yards again stood immobile behind a largish bush. I had not been in position for many minutes when Hamisi nudged an elbow and pointed ahead, when seeing that the buffalo had now started to walk in our direction. It offered a difficult target. Then the bull stopped abruptly to stand and gaze, so I sighted and fired instantly because knowing that the beaters were fast approaching from the rear and this would scare the beast into a panic-stricken flight.

The bullet must have hit a trifle off the fatal spot in the head, for it did not kill outright. The bull promptly bolted. We followed up immediately, but did not expect to see the beast again except after a prolonged pursuit. I felt mad with myself for risking that head shot and missing the bull's-eye by so small a margin. A short distance further on, however, I saw the wounded bull roll over and fall down the slopes of a hillside into a deep valley. We scrambled down in its wake. On gaining level ground, we saw the buffalo struggling to rise but it was experiencing difficulty in standing; and from close range I sent two bullets into the shoulder, which settled the business. The bull went down dead on to its side.

After being wounded and running for some distance, the beast must have become giddy from the effects of the bullet in its head and, as it fell at the edge of the steep hillside, rolled downwards into the valley. I was indeed lucky to get that grand trophy with such comparative ease. It might so well have proved a nasty business to complete satisfactorily, and I would have had only myself to blame for anything which happened amiss.

Two days later I had the unenviable experience of being charged unexpectedly on the same morning first by an elephant and then by a buffalo: fortunately for me, *not* at the same moment. I say "charged", though that term is not strictly applicable. The two animals almost over-ran me. I do not believe that either beast showed any lethal intent. The two incidents furnished a clear-cut example of how wild animals, on occasions, are apt to run headlong and blindly into the danger which they desire to avoid. When suddenly startled, they are prone to lose control and make an ill-considered rush in the direction of the danger threatening them. I think that most wild creatures are liable to bolt at you instead of in the opposite direction (as wisdom should dictate) but do this more from panic than anything else.

On this particular morning I was in the open when an elephant bull, solitary and a single-tusker, rushed straight at me. Obviously it had not the slightest intention of delivering a malicious charge. I fired two shots at the beast without effect and no time was available to reload. Hamisi had not accompanied me that morning and so was not present to take a hand in the business. I leaped swiftly aside to avoid being bowled over. It was a near thing, and far too much so to be in any way pleasant. Rapidly reloading, I went after that elephant. It fell down dead before another bullet had to be expended, both shots having registered in a vital spot. One had shattered the heart and the other the lungs. The single tusk was of light weight, which fact was most annoying because it counted on my year's game licence; a plea of self-defence would not have been acceptable, as it had much been overworked in the past.

The incident with the buffalo occurred later that morning. The encounter with the elephant had rather upset my nerves, and this buffalo completed my discomfiture. I had returned to camp to send out some porters to collect the tusk of the elephant. Then, this time with Hamisi, I went out again to try for a pair of heavy tusks. Soon we picked up the spoor of a solitary buffalo bull and followed this for a longish distance, when we came upon the form where it had been lying down. The open hoof-marks leading away from the form showed that the buffalo had taken alarm and galloped off. Possibly it had winded us before we approached near enough to hear its flight; at any rate, neither Hamisi nor I had heard it rushing off at a gallop.

A stern-chase of this creature is always likely to become a long

drawn out affair. A solitary buffalo, which might often have been
hunted, is usually a cunning beast and leaves little enough to
chance; but, if it is alarmed early in the day before having had
time to lie down and chew the cud, it is within the bounds of
possibility to contact the beast before too long. If seriously alarmed
after performing this essential function, it may be followed vainly
until late in the afternoon. The likelihood is, however, that you
will not see the beast again. It looked like ending that way with
this buffalo.

It kept in the thickest cover available. The hunt was both pro-
tracted and wearisome but, finally, we emerged upon a large open
space in a forest glade. Beyond that point I decided not to proceed.
Frankly, I was fed-up and ready enough to call off the pursuit.
Then, to my astonishment, I spotted the quarry, a really grand old
bull, slowly retracing its way at an angle to where Hamisi and I
had halted. Why it was coming back is anyone's guess. I knew of no
other men hunting in the neighbourhood; but it was possible that
the beast had been disturbed by some Africans.

I estimated the range to be about 300 yards, which is (or should
be) prohibitive for taking a shot at any species of big game. So I
waited, tense and patiently, for the animal to come within 100
yards so as to make sure of killing outright instead of merely
wounding. Suddenly, and with no sort of warning, the bull
lowered its great head and charged full tilt at us. I fired at the
nostrils, and distinctly heard the dull thud as the bullet struck;
but it failed to halt or turn it. The two local African trackers with
me immediately bolted. Hamisi shouldered up with the second
rifle, for he would never have even considered deserting me when
in a tight corner. Whenever most needed, he would be at my elbow
and automatically make the exchange of weapons. I did not have
to glance around because so smoothly, quickly and expertly did
he perform his duty on all occasions; and in moments of the gravest
peril his presence beside me always inspired confidence.

The wounded bull galloped madly past us, not more than a few
yards distant. I sent another bullet into the shoulder as it went
by, but had made insufficient allowance for the speed at which the
beast was travelling. It was hit too far back to prove instantly
effective. Hamisi exchanged rifles in a second. The next bullet
struck the bull's hindquarters, bowled it over, and ended the hunt.
I fired a "settler" into the brain to make sure of its death. It had
been warm work. I was greatly relieved to see the bull lying dead
on the ground, and believed that Hamisi was no less so. The
trophy was a most rewarding one, for the spread of horns,
measured over the curves, registered forty-three inches.

I consider the greatest difficulty experienced in tracking down big-game is that the hunter so often finds himself at the mercy of varying changes in the wind direction. Where the spoor leads there must he follow, whether up or down wind. Sometimes, for several days in succession, he may know the bitter disappointment of hearing the quarry, having winded him, racing away out of range. He may not even get one opportunity to fire a shot. Such an eventuality, however, is one which no skill or expert knowledge of jungle-craft can surmount.

When hunting buffalo in a forest, it is imperative to move noiselessly and never speak above a whisper. But that is equally applicable to the pursuit of all species of big-game. When knowing the quarry is near at hand, a hunter must be extra cautious and exercise patience in waiting for a favourable moment to shoot. Many a grand trophy has been lost irretrievably because of rushing the final stages and then shooting too soon.

It was my preference to tackle a solitary bull rather than try to get one out of a herd. The animals in the latter graze habitually in long lines, heads facing up-wind, and their flanks guarded by the old bulls. They may have to be stalked down-wind, which mitigates against success. Be as careful and experienced as you may, the fact that cows are in the herd makes it incumbent never to shoot until positive that you are aiming at a bull. Usually, in a small herd there will be found only one male beast worth a bullet; and the chances are great that the first beast offering a good target is not the one you have selected for killing. Even the most expert of hunters are liable to commit errors and, in some instances, these are quite unavoidable.

Notwithstanding every possible precaution taken, some cows deceive you into believing that they are big bulls, both by their darker coloration and spread of horns. Even the expert may know self-reproach because he has killed a cow in the honest belief that he was firing at a bull. To make certain of the sex, you must either see the animal's head from the front or view the entire herd on open ground. A mature cow appears to be a large beast, her horns quite frequently being of almost equal proportions to those of a bull.

Exceptionally good heads have been shot in a herd. But the herd-bulls, generally speaking, are animals in their prime of life and whose spread of horns really bear no comparison in size to those on an aged solitary bull. I knew of one herd which was an exception to the general rule, for it contained a number of bulls with truly magnificent heads.

One day while hunting over the Aberdares I had a narrow escape from being gored or killed by a solitary buffalo bull which had been wounded severely by someone else previously. No chance was offered for taking careful aim and, much against my principles and better judgement, I risked a difficult shot. The bullet hit the bull in the neck instead of the shoulder as intended, and it charged home immediately. No vestige of cover was available, and only one more cartridge remained in the magazine. Hamisi, with the other rifle, had gone off on the spoor of elephants in an attempt to locate for me the herd's whereabouts. As the buffalo's head was held low to cover the chest, I was not offered much of a target for that one bullet; and there was no time to reload the magazine. I jumped to one side and shot rather forward into the shoulder. The bull went down for keeps not more than five yards from where I stood. That had been far too close a call for my liking.

About a year previously I was hunting over rather a swampy region and, soon after leaving camp at daybreak, picked up the spoor of a solitary buffalo bull. Hamisi and I tracked it for some distance through the fringe of the swamp. The bull was feeding a good deal, but also travelling at a fast rate; and probably we followed it over the major portion of its night's wanderings. We also trailed the ground covered by it during the early hours of that day.

The sun was high in the blue sky and the heat insufferably intense when we reached a patch of dense cover through which the spoor led. Our hopes of success evaporated. Under such conditions I knew the bull would probably be lying down and chewing the cud. Any chance of locating it when feeding in the open was slight, though we carried on over the spoor. But now our advance, of necessity, was infinitely more wary. After proceeding for some distance through the thick stuff I heard the rush of the bull as it bolted, probably after having been alarmed by some slight noise we had made unwittingly. It was quite impossible to determine how much further that bad patch of cover extended but, just on the chance, I ran forward and almost immediately came to the edge of an open glade. The bull was cantering across the latter. As it was about to enter the far patch of thick cover. I risked a shot but one which was not really justified.

Then I advanced cautiously towards the spot where the bull had vanished from sight, feeling almost sure that my bullet must have missed. To my astonishment, Hamisi showed me a fallen leaf liberally bespattered with fresh blood. We continued to follow up, found more blood, and then came upon the quarry standing broadside on. I shot at the shoulder, and the bullet dropped the bull dead.

On examining the carcase, I found that the first bullet, fired from directly behind the bull, had merely scored the ribs and not cut deeply. It had missed the portions overlying the intercostal spaces, then entered a foreleg and lamed the beast. It was a lucky snap shot. That I had hit the beast at all was just a fluke. All things considered that fine trophy had not been deserved, for it was unpardonable to have taken a snap shot from such a longish range. The only excuse which can be offered is that I lost my temper when seeing the bull about to make good its escape after such an arduous and prolonged chase. But *that* is no excuse at all. A hunter should *never* under any circumstances allow ill-temper to gain the upper hand of him.

There was another occasion while hunting in Uganda along the east bank of the Nile when I shot a buffalo bull through the lungs, which ordinarily proves fatal. Unfortunately, this time it did not. The bull got clear away from me, though I followed up at once to give a merciful despatch. The frothy and light-coloured blood smears provided evidence that the beast had been hit through the lungs; and so, as long as sufficiently light, I continued after it. Several times, at long intervals, I closed with the bull but was given no chance to take another shot at it. Darkness forced me to abandon the hunt and return over the long trail to camp. I had left myself nasty work to be done next day.

Before dawn Hamisi and I started out again after that bull, picked up the spoor where we left it on the previous evening, and fully expected to find the beast lying dead further ahead. But it was not to be. We followed its spoor over a long distance without even glimpsing the bull. Hamisi discovered where it had rested during the night or early morning; but its hoof-marks clearly showed us that it had bolted in alarm from its form. It is possible that the bull either had winded us or heard our approach. Its departure from the spot appeared to have been vigorous, which astonished me in view of the bullet wound in its lungs. Although four more days were devoted to trying to locate the wounded beast, yet we never set eyes upon it again.

As all signs of bleeding had ceased and the bull seemed to be travelling strongly, it was my earnest hope that the poor brute had recovered and was not condemned to die a lingering death in torment. I had done all in my power to finish it; also offered a handsome cash reward to any African bringing me truthful information about the wounded bull's actual whereabouts. These efforts failed and, as time pressed, the quest was abandoned with intense reluctance.

The loss of a grand trophy was not what really mattered, but I did hate knowing myself to have been instrumental in causing this buffalo unnecessary sufferings. Sometimes, strive as hard as you may, such an occurrence is not avoidable. In this particular instance my bullet should have killed the bull, but did not; while

everything possible had been done to complete the task to which
my hand had been set. No more than that can be expected of any
big-game hunter.

17

Vigil at a Salt-lick

WHILE ivory-hunting on the west bank of the Nile, in the
erstwhile Belgian Lado Enclave, during 1910, I suffered a harrow-
ing and nightmare experience. The incident chiefly concerns two
species of wild animals—elephant and buffalo; but other creatures
also came into the picture, and a horde of viciously biting red ants
contributed to a most horrible night. The details are still vividly
recollected, though it is now more than half a century since all
this occurred.

That morning I had contacted a large herd of elephants, shot
four heavily-tusked bulls out of it, when the remainder lost no
time in making themselves scarce. Leaving Hamisi with a gang
of porters to hack out the four pairs of tusks and rejoin me at an
arranged rendezvous, I proceeded on my way to the Nile with the
main body of the *safari* and a large number of tusks previously
collected. The intention was to cross over the Nile into Uganda
and there sell the ivory to a Greek or Asian trader. My hunting
had been exceptionally profitable.

It was nearing sunset when I realized that I had lost my way.
At such a late hour it was futile to try and regain the correct path,
and much wiser to wait until early next morning. I decided to
bivouac on the edge of an extensive clearing in the heart of the
forest where we had just arrived, and selected a site close to a
small stream. Most of the porters must have been lagging behind,
for they failed to join us at the bivouac when darkness clamped
down over the countryside. With me were only Abdulla, the cook;
a second gun-bearer, a Mganda recently employed and as yet
untested for his worth; and four Wanyamwezi porters, who had
for some years served me well. Worst of all to contemplate was the
fact that the laggards had my tent and bedding, all food and drink
supplies, and the rations of my African followers. I did not mind
sleeping rough, because I was quite accustomed to it; but strongly
resented being bereft of food, drink and bedding. Unless the headman of the *safari* located us, it would be necessary to get such sleep
as possible while lying on the hard ground and to share the *posho*

(mealie-meal porridge) of the new gun-bearer. Both prospects left me cold. Indeed, I heartily disliked the night's outlook.

Although painfully aware of hunger and physical exhaustion, yet I welcomed the providential finding of this site for a bivouac. Nevertheless, I would not have felt so pleased if knowing that the spot was a much favoured salt-lick of wild beasts and habitually frequented by them in considerable numbers. That knowledge was only acquired during the night. As a matter of fact, I had never been there before and the area was unknown land to me.

I watched the Africans building a fire at the base of a giant tree, idly noting that the dry sticks soon blazed up bravely. The flames appeared pale and almost invisible in the fading sunlight, while thin vapours of smoke danced frenziedly above them. A *sufuria* (metal cooking-pot) was propped on three stones over the crackling fire, and the cook squatted on his haunches beside it while stirring the boiling *posho* with a stick. The other Africans were huddled around the fire, all busily occupied in plucking leeches from bleeding legs and then thoughtfully cutting them into small pieces with sharp knives. I sat with my back against a tree at a short distance from them, smoking a pipe, and longing miserably for some food and drink. My waterbottle of cold tea was empty. Acute resentment mounted. It had been a hard day's hunting since dawn, we had marched far and fast after killing the four elephant bulls, and it had been terribly hot. Now to be deprived of the solace of any comforts was too much.

Soon the gentle murmur of bird and insect life, which always precedes the clamour of the sunset hour, was beginning to purr all around me. The stream sang drowsily while flowing over the stones and boulders littering its bed. The Africans, except Abdulla, stretched themselves in ungainly poses before the fire, rolled over on faces and were sound asleep immediately. The last leech now dismembered, they could slumber until awakened to stuff themselves with the *posho* being cooked.

Suddenly a loud tumult shattered the stillness of the clearing. Abdulla screamed shrilly in fear and to warn his sleeping companions, but this was drowned by the trumpeting of an elephant nearby. In my ears it sounded not dissimilar to the whistle of a factory steam-siren. There followed the explosive crashing of branches torn down from trees, a rending of the dense undergrowth, and the heavy movements of a giant through the forest. On the instant the cook had swung himself agilely into the nearest tree and swarmed up it like a monkey. Not until the topmost fork was gained did he pause even to glance down below. The others had awakened at the first moment of alarm and with an agile leap that took them some yards towards trees, for an African

can fall asleep in the manner of an animal and just as abruptly be in complete wakefulness. In a few more seconds all had perched themselves aloft in the highest forks of adjacent trees; and from their respective refuges were now scolding and chattering like panic-stricken monkeys.

All of these things had transpired before I appreciated the extent of the danger which now threatened me. Then I hurriedly scrambled erect. As I did so, two long and gleaming tusks, a trunk held menacingly aloft, two fierce small eyes, and the enormous bulk of a dingy slate-grey and crinkled hide appeared in full view. It was only a short distance from me. I dodged quickly behind the bole of the tree, thus sheltering from the onslaught of this enraged and shrilly squealing elephant bull. A moment more, and I had swung myself upwards into the tree and climbed to a position of comparative security high up on a fork.

The elephant charged at the fire, scattered the burning logs far and wide, trampled the *sufuria* as flat as a pancake, kneaded my dropped pipe and tobacco pouch deep into the ground, and kept up a spate of ferocious trumpeting. This endured for no longer than a few minutes, though it seemed to me more like hours. Then the large bull whirled about clumsily and, still screaming with fury, vanished amongst the trees as suddenly as emerging therefrom. I saw no more of it. Indeed, I had no wish to do so, and had already had rather more than enough of its company. The Africans and I remained on our perches in the treetops, intently listening to the beast's progress sounding fainter and fainter in the distance. Finally, even this noise ebbed and died out.

"How is it possible to understand such anger?" demanded the Mganda gun-bearer, with the aggrieved and half-surprised patience typical of an African. In their long-enduring souls any calamity seldom arouses more than a mild display of disgust. He received no reply from his quaking fellows in adjacent treetops. All were far too paralysed by fear to be capable of commenting upon the startling incident now happily concluded, even if feeling so inclined and which they certainly did not.

I regarded sorrowfully the flattened *sufuria,* and no less so the fragments of a treasured briar pipe and battered tobacco pouch. I had no replacements for them, so those comforts were now denied to me, Even worse was the fact that our only food had now been ruined and scattered broadcast; so all must go hungry that night. The Africans, still jabbering like scared apes in the trees, shook the boughs upon which they perched precariously, with the violence of terror consuming them.

Now satisfied that the disturber of our peace had withdrawn

and was unlikely to return, I scrambled down from the tree and ruefully surveyed the scene of devastation. I shouted angrily to the Africans, commanding them to join me on the ground and assist in salvage work; but they continued perched aloft, shuddering and chattering like magpies in excited voices. Not one of them would budge. I bawled curses at them, but neither commands nor this angry tirade had any effect. Terror held them chained in the treetops. This obstinacy angered me still more, and I threatened them with all manner of severe punishments; tried to bribe the trembling wretches with promises of rewards if obeyed; flung stones up at them, which they dodged with ease; and, finally, even condescended to entreat them to descend and help in collecting the remnants of our property. I might just as well have conserved my breath.

A great fear having driven them aloft, some considerable time was needed before sufficient confidence could be restored for them to confront once more the manifold dangers of life upon ground-level. I could cheerfully have wrung all their necks like a fowl's, but knew myself incapable of getting within grasping reach of any of them. Perforce, the idea of persuading any of the panic-stricken wretches to rejoin me that night had to be abandoned.

When the sun went down in a blaze of glory and night began to clamp down upon the clearing, I was feeling exceedingly ill-tempered. Much time had been wasted senselessly. I was acutely conscious of hunger, but knew it could not be appeased that night. The shock to my nerves caused by the elephant was making itself felt, and I disliked intensely the prospect of sleeping on the ground while the Africans remained perched in their refuges. The idea of searching for essential materials to erect a crude shelter, unless assisted by at least one African, made no sort of appeal. Finally, I elected to seek such repose as possible at the base of the tree under which I was irresolutely standing. There seemed no other choice.

High above the topmost branches of the trees the moon, not yet at its full, was now showing pale and watery. I strove to comfort myself with the thought that it would remain fairly light until about three hours before the dawn. A large log-fire could be contrived to keep me warm and protect by its blaze; and, with this thought uppermost, a wholly unexpected difficulty presented itself. My only box of matches was gone. I recollected having left it beside pipe and pouch when startled out of a doze by the elephant's sudden invasion. For about half an hour I searched for it with feverish diligence and a mounting anxiety, but without avail. I gave it best.

For a time I toyed with the idea of making a fire by friction, but scrapped that too because it would be a prolonged process and great exertion. I surrendered unhappily to the inevitable. Again I cursed, fluently and angrily, the Africans in the trees, the mothers who bore them, the fathers who sired them, their male and female relatives to the third generation, and fervently consigned all and each of them to everlasting perdition. Also were said many bitter things regarding Fate and Destiny. This outburst served to relieve my pent-up anger, but achieved nothing more than that.

Finally, I stretched myself upon the warm earth between the huge and stout buttress-roots of the large tree. There I was protected by a low rampart of very tough wood on either flank, my body occupying the space enclosed by the roots. Only from the hips to feet was I exposed to attack. Although hoping that the roots would serve to protect me adequately against all wild beasts during the hours of darkness, yet I felt none too happy about my predicament.

Presently the silvern and ethereal light of the moon began to flood the clearing and surrounding forest with a soft radiance, lending a ghostly and mysterious aspect to the immediate environment. The moonlight peopled the clearing with fantastic shapes and shadows. I must have dozed off for a time. Suddenly I was awakened by a faint but crisp sound, and sat up to listen with every faculty alerted and heart beating tumultuously. Far off on the opposite bank of the stream, a dry branch snapped with a sharp report. Again and again this was repeated. But now several branches of trees seemed to be torn down simultaneously. There came to my ears a swishing noise, as of green leaves being stripped from boughs by some giant's ruthless destructiveness. Then, for a brief time, silence once more reigned.

Gradually, however, the sounds were heard again, louder and more distinct, and approaching closer to the clearing. For the best part of an hour these noises persisted. Then I heard a soft squelching sound succeeded by a popping note, also repeated many times, and later I clearly distinguished the sound of water being splashed over heated bodies. The meaning of them all was interpreted correctly. I knew that a herd of elephants must be feeding on their way to the stream, but now had arrived there to quench thirsts and bathe hot bodies in its waters.

The night-wind was blowing over the stream to where I now stood erect with rifle in hands, thus the herd enjoyed their ablutions at leisure and entirely undisturbed by the close proximity of man. For some time they splashed and wallowed noisily in shallows or deep pools of the stream. Then I heard them floundering out of the water on to the near bank; and next travelling slowly through the thick stuff to get up-wind before venturing out on to the clearing. It was just possible to distinguish the surge of the bush as the big animals ploughed their way through it, but the tread of the giants made no perceptible sound. Except when the branch of a tree was snapped off and stripped of its foliage, the passage of the herd was amazingly quiet. Tainted wind from the Africans in the treetops passed over the elephants though, from time to time, I knew, the moistened tips of trunks would be combing the air-channels for hint of any danger threatening them. Then they must have winded me. Suddenly there arose a deafening tumult of trumpeting and shrill squeals that shattered the stillness of the night. This was quickly succeeded by the herd's panic-stricken flight.

I listened to the crashing and tearing sounds as they sped through the trees and bush. There were moments when I imagined that they were charging straight for me and my life was in grievous peril. Yet, with the knowledge born of ripe experience, I realized the sheer impossibility of ever feeling certain about the direction in which elephants will move when bolting from sudden danger. A few minutes later, however, I was assured that the herd was headed away from the clearing in uncontrolled panic. As the noise ebbed in the distance, I was conscious of an immense flood of relief.

Once more I settled myself as comfortably as feasible between the buttress-roots, steeling my upset nerves to endure the balance of that night which was so filled with alarms and ghastly nightmares. Again and again, while the light of the moon still held, wild beasts of different species made their way cautiously to a point upwind. Each time human taint was wafted to them and warned that a threat existed on this clearing. They fled rapidly from its vicinity.

I distinguished the loud blowing and snorting of a rhinoceros, gruntings of forest hogs, an abrupt and startled bark from an alarmed reedbuck, the shrill whistle of a diminutive dik-dik, and many other familiar sounds of the wilderness. Each was succeeded by the snapping of dry twigs or crashing of rent undergrowth. All those diverse noises conclusively informed me that the clearing was a favoured salt-lick of the animal kingdom, but the creatures had winded me and hastily withdrawn from it. Every different sound heard was at once identified. I realized that my present position was none too secure.

I again sought refuge in the higher branches of the big tree. Before long, however, the acute discomfort created by an uneasy perch became still more insupportable because of ferocious attacks from a vast horde of disturbed red ants. The insects swarmed all over me, biting like a pack of mad dogs. Soon they had forced me to brave the perils on ground-level, though I hated deserting the comparative security of my perch high up in the tree. I preferred to risk disaster on the ground to the certainty of being driven demented by these savage insects. Once more on the ground, I cursed the Africans fluently with a venomous tongue because they could endure a physical torture which I was incapable of supporting in spite of stoical efforts to do so.

When the moon set, a black pall of darkness shut down over the clearing and its surroundings. Although I sat or reclined at the edge of the salt-lick, which was unusually large in extent, it was not feasible to distinguish the branches of trees against the skyline or even see a hand before my eyes. The impenetrable gloom now enveloping me wrought already overstrained nerves to a pitch of agonized intensity which became almost unbearable.

Next, a fresh horror was added to my unpleasant predicament. The larger species of game were no longer approaching the salt-lick from up-wind, yet I knew well that they were now swarming over the clearing. From time to time I could hear some unidentified beast floundering through the nearby stream or treading softly upon the kneaded earth within a few yards of my refuge. Moreover, hordes of bloodthirsty mosquitoes and sand-flies were attacking me savagely; and I knew these pests came from the congregation of wild creatures assembled around the salt-lick.

These insects fastened greedily upon every exposed portion of my flesh. As I was wearing only khaki shorts and a bush-jumper, a generous field was offered for their blood-feast; and they lost no time in making the most of these opportunities. Mosquitoes nestled in the hair, buzzed maddeningly without cessation, and stabbed me individually and collectively. They were shortly reinforced by masses of sand-flies, the combined forces attacking savagely and rendering me almost insane from the fierce irritation set up. But there was absolutely nothing that could be done in self-defence against this massed assault. It just had to be endured as best knowing how.

Every once in a while some unidentified beast passed so close to me that I could hear distinctly the crisp sound of its cropping and gentle rhythm of breathing. Occasionally some of them winded me. The sudden strike of sharp hooves on the ground or an angry snorting and blowing told their own tale. I knew exactly what had happened. All this time I could see nothing, only hear what was transpiring all around the buttress-roots.

Several times I shinned up into the tree, but weary limbs could discover no particle of rest there, and the viciousness of the red ants soon compelled a descent to ground-level. I was acutely conscious of feeling strong resentment at the knowledge that my

African followers were capable of enduring such a fiendish purgatory without complaints, whereas this was entirely beyond my capacity; and with the realization of that truth, my smouldering rage knew no bounds. But cursing them supplied no panacea.

About an hour before dawn I was suddenly startled out of an uneasy and fitful doze by the sound of some large animal passing near at hand. I could distinctly hear its movements; even more clearly than those of other creatures peopling my waking nightmare. As I lay inert and listening fearfully, there were suddenly heard a mighty blowing, then a ferocious snorting, and next the thunder of hooves pounding over the hard surface of the clearing. Some beast, as yet unidentified, was charging murderously towards me.

I was stretched out on my back with the sloping buttress-roots flanking each side of the body. The beast passed above me, doing no more harm than a hoof pinching the fleshy portion of an exposed thigh. It cut as cleanly as the blade of a sharp knife. I could feel the warm blood trickling down the leg but was unconscious of any pain. Continuing to lie flat, too terrified even to move and almost choked by the wild beating of my heart, I clutched the .350 Rigby-Mauser in the right hand. Yet I fully appreciated that it would be futile to shoot at an unseen beast, for a wounding must only serve to accentuate the existing degree of peril.

The invisible animal was apparently not yet finished with me. The reek of a hot and pungent breath upon an upturned face, which nearly deprived me of reason, assured that some huge beast was now astride my prone body. I was in deadly danger and my life probably would be forfeited. From the odour of its breath, I realized that the attacker was a buffalo and my situation must be regarded as desperate. The temptation to shoot was almost overpowering. But I dare not risk only wounding and not killing outright such a vindictive beast. I laid down the rifle and instinctively felt at my belt for the hunting-knife, a long and keen-edged blade from which I was never parted when out hunting. Drawing it from the sheath, I grasped its hilt in the right fist. I was resolved to sell life dearly and, if needs be, go down fighting to the last gasp of my breath.

Presently, to the accompaniment of much blowing and snorting, some hard object was gradually being insinuated beneath my prostrate body. I moved slightly to sidestep this new horror, clinging desperately to the roots flanking me. Again and again, first on one side and then on the other, this hard prodding substance strove resolutely to insert itself beneath my body; but I pressed flat on the ground, offering as little opening as possible for anything to be

F

forced beneath me. At each prod I was bruised and dull pangs of pain shot through me. The determined attack was making me feel faint. I was gasping for breath. My body seemed to be slowly but surely pounded to death by the brute astride me.

How long this ghastly ordeal endured, I have not the slightest conception. But it seemed that an eternity passed, during which every single energy of mind and body was concentrated upon preventing the beast from securing an advantage. The buttress-roots partially protected me, so I strove to cling tenaciously between them. It was a desperate effort to accomplish. I began to believe that the end of my life must be inevitable. When a new day began to break my horrible plight remained unchanged, except that the powers of resistance were weakening. I thought it would be impossible to last much longer.

Up to a certain point the dawn in Africa comes up rapidly enough, though the sun takes its time to rise above the eastern horizon. One moment all is as dark as a fathomless pit around you; another, a new sense is vouchsafed of actual form; and a minute or more later there is an ability to distinguish colours, which comes with something akin to surprise. All in a moment one can see, after having been unable to do so. And now I was experiencing all of those peculiar phenomena in their correct rotation. A dim green manifested itself in the grass on the salt-lick; the whitish coloration of a nearby stone was perceived; and the greyness of a tree's bole became perceptible. Each was revealed to me as a new and unanticipated quality in a familiar enough object. In a few more minutes I was enabled to see my surround-ings with a measure of clarity, and what the eyes disclosed was definitely not reassuring.

I stared up at a vast bulk standing over me: a creature with heaving and formidable shoulders, and endowed with a ferociously massive head depressed towards my body. As yet, however, those features were only viewed in dim outline. But I knew for certain that the grim and murderous assailant was a gigantic buffalo bull. Its dark hide synchronized with the receding darkness of night. The few scattered bristles, instead of the customary short and smooth hair, told me that this was an aged bull and therefore the more pugnacious. Soon I could perceive the ears below the great spread of horns. I reckoned that the latter measured fully thirty-five to forty inches over the curves, while the bosses must be all of fifteen inches in depth. Here, indeed, was a mighty beast, endowed with the strength of a giant and imbued with unbridled ferocity. I did not give much for the chances of conserving my life. I thought them about zero.

Then, as the light steadily increased in strength, I could distinguish clearly the dark hide, great belly, heaving flanks, massive head and throat, smoking nostrils of a flaming scarlet, and wicked eyes glaring down at me with murderous hate. My hand felt for the rifle but failed to contact it. Almost before realizing what was being done, I grasped the hunting-knife in both fists and, with a strength born of sheer terror and desperation, drew its long and keen blade swiftly across the bull's shaggy throat. The blade cut deep into the flesh. A torrent of hot blood gushed forth like a fountain into my face. It almost blinded me.

The buffalo, snorting loudly with mingled pain and anger, strove again and again to gore me with its cruel horns; but the buttress-roots baffled all these efforts. Meanwhile, the knife's blade was sawing savagely at the bull's throat. Soon the buffalo was experiencing that deadly nausea which presages death, and fell forward heavily upon its knees. Once more it floundered erect. Then the bull reeled away from me, sank again to the knees, and a stream of blood was pumping from a wide gap in its throat. A few seconds later it collapsed on the ground. After repeated attempts to rise and tearing up the earth in its death agony, the huge bull lay still in death.

Then, I think, consciousness must have deserted me. The next thing remembered was when my injuries were being treated by the faithful Hamisi. I learned later that he had arrived with the remainder of the *safari* about an hour after sunrise and then was told the details of the night's ghastly events. Abdulla, the cook, and the Mganda gun-bearer would have been certain to make the utmost of that grim story and depicted themselves as heroes. As Hamisi skilfully disinfected and bandaged my injuries, he grinned and pointed at the carcase of the buffalo, commenting laconically: "Yonder is much good meat, *bwana*." And that was all he had to say on the subject.

Hamisi claimed to be a Mohammedan, though an unorthodox follower of Islam. To reassure his religious scruples, I told him: "The bull's throat was cut with my knife before it died. While performing *halal*, I murmured *Bishmillah*—in the name of Allah, the All-Merciful and All-Compassionate. It is lawful therefore for you to eat its meat. The throat was sawn like a log of wood, and the killing done in accordance with the rites of Islam."

"It was well done, *bwana*." He then shouted to the *niapara* (headman) of the *safari*: "Get busy on skinning and cutting up the buffalo. Then see that plenty of its meat is cooked for all to eat. The *bwana* and I have a great hunger."

Naturally enough, I could not contemplate spending another night at this salt-lick, so I insisted upon a resumption of the journey to the Nile in the cooler hours of the late afternoon. Hamisi tried to dissuade me, but to no purpose. Painful as was the gash in my thigh and the bruising suffered, we marched onwards at the appointed hour. Walking over the rough ground proved agonizing but, fortunately, I was tough. In a few more days the injuries had become just memories of the past and had healed remarkably well. I knew myself exceedingly lucky to escape from being killed or suffering a more severe mauling; but the devil looks after his own.

Never again could I be persuaded willingly to spend a night near a salt-lick.

18

Black Rhinoceros

OF ALL the major species of African fauna perhaps the rhinoceros (*Diceros bicornis*) furnishes the most fruitful topic for arguments amongst sportsmen. Opinions in regard to this creature's dangerous qualities and characteristics are diverse. Some famous hunters placed the beast fourth on their "danger list". Others of great experience rated it as the most dangerous, but I do not agree with them. The subject is really influenced by individual encounters in the field with this stupid and ungainly beast; but is generally conceded that occasionally the black rhinoceros can cause much bad language and prove an unmitigated nuisance.

I have known both those reactions, but never likewise with its relative the square-lipped (or "white") variety. Although not personally ranking the black rhinoceros as a serious danger to man under ordinary circumstances or as a menace to property, yet I will admit that it can be a formidable foe sometimes. If so inclined, it can give a hunter unpleasant minutes. The beast is as full of whims as a badly spoiled child, and its contrariness of spirit will frequently be exercised at the wrong time for a hunter's liking.

The besetting sin of the rhinoceros is an insatiable curiosity— a fault which it seems incapable of curing or checking. Largely on account of its poor vision and a highly developed curiosity, this creature is prone to follow the dictates of its keen sense of smell whenever any form of danger comes to its notice; and given the scent, no matter how faint, of something strange and suspicious, it will advance at once in that direction in order to investigate at close quarters. It does not wait to see what this may be, but depends upon its nose rather than eyesight for enlightenment. A whiff of man-tainted wind, and it immediately feels impelled to satisfy its curiosity. Moreover, it does. A rhinoceros never waits for trouble to come to it, but goes all-out to meet the threat rather more than halfway. This beast prefers to start a fight rather than have one forced upon it; and, while admiring its pugnacity, I have often been given every reason to resent it.

Personally, I have always considered the black rhinoceros to be a blundering, capricious and brainless fathead. Nothing seems to teach this beast even a modicum of commonsense in its relations with mankind or other major species of fauna. Nevertheless, it can be a good sport and always give you a lively run for your money when encountered on the veld of Africa. It is devoid of fear. Challenge, no matter how unwittingly, its nearby presence and the fight is instantly carried to you. It gives battle in a determined manner and with no half measures. I know of no beast more consistently resolute in meeting danger at once and face to face; and that spirit, combined with its other characteristics, makes it a doughty foe for a hunter to attack

This marked trait may explain why so many sportsmen insist that it is an ugly, useless and dangerous beast. Some have advocated the ruthless extermination of the species, but such a policy would be unwarranted on any ground. Granted, the rhinoceros and cultivated areas do not make a happy mixture. But the animal is perfectly well aware of this truth, and thus normally keeps away from settled districts. It has been quick in conforming with the rapidly changing conditions of its existence, which is well for both man and beast.

The number of casualties resulting from ill-starred encounters, or because of poor tactics employed by a hunter, with enraged rhinoceros do not warrant an assumption that this beast is a genuine menace to human life. Not once during my hunting career in Africa did I have this kind of personal experience. But perhaps I was unduly favoured with good luck when in close contact with individuals of this species. Yet it is impossible to deny that the rhinoceros not only appears ever ready for a first-class row, but can prove inquisitive to an uncomfortable extent. The rhinoceros strongly believes that attack is the best form of defence, and normally adheres to this sound strategy.

I have expressed the opinion that this creature is a crass idiot and will never learn through experience. That is true. Time and again it has provided definite proofs of being the supreme dunce in the animal kingdom. The elephant is unique amongst beasts of large size in that, with its growth, there has also been a marked development in brain power. In order to demonstrate what I mean, a comparison will be drawn between the two species as I have known them in the wild state. That makes a fair enough comparison, for the rhinoceros is the nearest in size and weight to the elephant.

Both species are found in the same regions of Africa. Each formerly wandered about freely over open plains, but during the past half-century a very marked change has occured in the habits of the elephant, though not so in that of the rhinoceros. The former has learned through bitter experience far more readily and permanently than the latter. As a general rule the elephant no longer favours open country, whereas the rhinoceros continues to roam over the plains and thereby is subject to the grave risk of complete extermination. And in these modern times, when the horns of the rhinoceros have assumed a profitable export trade, that danger is never really absent. Poachers are not concerned with the ethics of fauna conservation or the trusteeship of the game for future generations, only with the acquisition of profits through their unlawful and despicable enterprise. In the case of elephants, however, the risk of ultimate extermination is not so serious because the difficulties in hunting illegally for ivory are greater than for the horns of rhinoceros. Those considerations place a brake upon ivory poaching, though this is still being done by gangs of Africans on a largish scale in National Parks and Game Reserves.

Elephants now will only traverse open spaces under cover of darkness, because they are aware that danger lurks there for them during the hours of daylight. No elephant in those regions where they are hunted regularly would be so foolish as habitually to spend its days on the open plains. That habit ceased many years ago. Moreover, it is the fixed custom of elephants to seek rest in shade during the hottest periods of the day—ten in the morning to three in the afternoon. On the other hand, the foolish rhinoceros has never abandoned its habit of frequenting open spaces by day or night. Although the elephant is wisdom personified, yet the rhinoceros continues to be a brainless, chump-headed and obstinate dunce incapable of altering its age-old habits to conform with the changed conditions of present-day existence.

The vision of both species is indifferent. In consequence the elephant rapidly learned to seek refuge in those areas where sound and smell counted far more as protective measures than good eyesight. The powers of scent and hearing possessed by both species compensate to a large extent for the handicap of defective eyesight.

Black rhinoceros are browsers and subsist upon the foliage of trees and bushes, whereas the "white" variety are grazers and subsist mainly upon grass. The former generally feeds in the evening, night and early morning. It may occasionally be viewed on the move when a day is cloudy and rain falling; and, like most wild animals, is seldom found at any great distance from water. They resort there to drink in the evening and at dawn. After the early morning drink this creature has a confirmed habit of wallowing in the mud, the latter subsequently caking on the body to help in smothering the tick infestation on the softer and thinner parts of the hide.

Normally, this beast sleeps during the hottest period of the day. If a hunter suddenly disturbs it, resentment is shown in no undecided fashion; while a really peeved rhinoceros can prove liverish indeed. Neither man nor beast likes to be awakened suddenly while enjoying a peaceful siesta. How exceedingly wrathful and obnoxious a suddenly disturbed rhinoceros can be, I think only those who have experienced what ensues could possibly appreciate. The moments that follow are extremely lively and especially dangerous for the disturber of the slumbering beast. One should expect nothing else.

Both varieties of this species are comparatively simple to stalk, always provided that their bird-sentinels do not chance to be on duty. Previous to any attempt to get within easy range for a shot, the experienced hunter will first inspect his quarry carefully through field-glasses. Should he detect any tick-birds perched on the beast, it will be realized immediately that the utmost caution must be exercised throughout the approach. After a long and tedious stalk, the hunter is frequently detected by these birds and an alarm instantly sounded; and, more often than not, a coveted trophy will be lost. Should the birds be perched on a rhinoceros, a hunter is well-advised to make his stalk rapidly. Just so long as keeping up-wind and not exposing himself, he will most probably get within easy range for a shot at the beast and without being baulked by the tick-birds' sudden disturbance.

Whenever alarmed the rhinoceros moves off with its head elevated; and if a cow is accompanied by a calf, the latter follows in the wake of the mother instead of preceding her. If warned of danger by the tick-birds, the beast may charge more or less blindly. As likely as not it comes directly towards a hunter, who may imagine that he has been seen and the charge is made deliberately. By no manner of means, however, is this invariably the case. The poor eyesight of the beast operates against a hunter being seen, and it just gallops blindly towards the spot where it suspects the danger to be or follows a false direction in a state of panic. It is never simple to explain satisfactorily the reactions of one of these ugly creatures, for they are far too brainless for man to fathom the workings of their mind—if they are blessed with one, which I am

inclined to doubt! It is expecting too much of this beast to look
for any show of intelligence. You would be disappointed.

They have been seen when viciously prodding with a horn at
the ground tainted by man's feet; and they have a habit of returning, time and again, to the same midden. Their droppings are
scattered far and wide over the spot after having made themselves
comfortable, this being done either with the horns or feet. I have
often come across one of the open-air latrines of this species, the
droppings being either old and dry, comparatively so, or quite
recently deposited. From such places a hunter can pick up a
freshly made spoor and follow up until the beast is sighted.

The black rhinoceros is morose, irritable and always unpredictable. When wounded, it often charges straight at the hunter. If
he manages to sidestep it in time, usually but not invariably the
beast will continue straight ahead and not about-turn to seek out
its enemy. They have been known to charge, without the slightest
provocation, a span of oxen or donkeys drawing a wagon and even
through a camp. While doing so, the beast lunges with the cruel
horn to right and left. In a brief time it has inflicted serious
casualties amongst men and beasts.

During the construction of the Uganda Railway there occurred
not a few incidents when an infuriated rhinoceros charged a train
between Tsavo and Nairobi. Mostly, these beasts came off second
best. It was not even an uncommon event for one of them to be run
into (or over) on the track and killed. In much earlier years upon
the Athi and Kapiti Plains there used to be a considerable number
of this species, and I frequently saw them from a train when they
were close to the track. The species was very plentiful around
Sultan Hamoud, where they became a persistent nuisance and
terrified the construction gangs of Punjabi coolies. At odd
moments each day they made a habit of turning up to see how
the work was progressing and would stand to gaze at the labour
force from an unpleasantly close distance. Being intently watched
by a rhinoceros while at work is not conducive to concentration
upon the task in hand.

I noticed that rhinoceros would frequently stand motionless
when first threatened by a man's approach, probably waiting to
locate definitely the spot from which danger was likely to come.
It is also not improbable that they were striving to avoid detection
by remaining immobile; but I am not at all convinced that the
latter is correct. Primarily, I think, they are merely waiting for
some hint to disclose the exact location of the danger they had
heard or winded.

If a hunter keeps his wits about him when attacked by a rhinoceros the odds are generally in his favour. As the rhinoceros weighs

roughly three tons, it can hardly attain high speed. Its defective vision, too, must be a severe handicap at all times. If the beast is charging down-wind, the odds are that you can safely stand your ground to kill it with an effective shot; but, all the same, it is seldom easy to put down, for the hide resembles the quality of armour plates on a cruiser. The neck is the most vulnerable spot at which to shoot, for the bullet is almost certain to fracture the vertebra. A bullet in a shoulder may cripple it but is unlikely to penetrate to the vital organs of the beast, though such a wound provides time to finish it off with a well-placed shot in the neck.

I always thought that the most peculiar feature about this species is you generally bump into one when least expecting it. You may hunt them assiduously over an area where they are well known and never glimpse even one. For instance, I devoted a week to the search for a grand bull along the banks of the Stony Athi river, and did not find it. That, of course, is all in the run of a hunter's luck. But three days later in a different area when concentrating on lions, I secured three good specimens of rhinoceros within an hour after leaving camp.

The species rarely exceeds a height of five feet at shoulder; length from tip of nose to base of tail, eleven feet; circumference of barrel, about ten feet; and weight, approximately three tons. It may be added that the length of its anterior horn measures up to forty-three inches, while that of the posterior one up to twenty-one inches. It cannot be rated as a beautiful beast; and, indeed, it is far from being so. It is entirely useless for man's needs. But the horns supply a profitable export trade and find a ready market in the East, being ground down for sale as an aphrodisiac. Whether this is effective or just so much moonshine, I am unable to say.

But it cannot be argued reasonably that this ugly animal has no rightful place in the clever pattern of Nature's devising. Indubitably, it has. If such was not the case, then the beast would not have been created. But what this useful purpose is, I much doubt if anyone can determine with certainty.

19

Some Rhinoceros Episodes

To be candid, I have never much liked the rhinoceros, largely because of those occasions when these animals wrecked my porter-*safari* and created irreparable damage to my personal property.

F*

Indeed, some of them afforded me ample cause for dislike. When selecting a camping-site it is never wise to pitch your tent on an old rhinoceros path; but I learned that in my novice days, and never again made the same mistake.

I was on a duty *safari* with a friend in typical rhinoceros country, and we camped for the night in thickish bush. It was cut up in all directions by old and wide paths made by the species. Not suspecting the likelihood of any trouble from these beasts, we pitched our tents on an open space in the bush and close to the bank of a river. The site looked ideal. The *safari* had travelled a long distance that day, the sun had been overpoweringly hot, and all were exceedingly tired. I had not the heart to order our porters to clear another site, as they had carried sixty-pound loads all day and it was necessary to rest them all as much as possible so as to be fit enough for another long march next day. Consideration for the physical wellbeing of African porters is as essential as that for animal transport.

In the middle of the night a rhinoceros ambled along the path upon which our tents were standing, collided with and then wrecked them. Then it passed on its way. I do not know its sex, which does not much matter. Neither of us suffered an injury, but we did feel angry. I grabbed my rifle and struggled clear of the wrecked tent. The moon was almost at the full, so I saw plainly the black stern of the beast lumbering off through the bush. I fired a shot in that direction to hasten its departure, aiming wide because I had no wish to kill or wound the beast unnecessarily. We might so easily have fared far worse.

On another day, when hunting lions upon the Athi Plains, Hamisi suddenly drew my attention to a grey mass ahead of us and softly warned: *"Kifaru, bwana."* I had noticed nothing until he pointed to the spot. We crept towards it cautiously and then saw a large rhinoceros bull lying down on its side. Patently, it was asleep. Legs were doubled up and there could be noted no signs of movement except its heavy breathing motions; and not until we were within fifty yards of it did the beast suddenly awaken. Without rising, it raised its head off the ground and looked around suspiciously. As far as I could judge, it had not seen, heard or winded us.

Suddenly it scrambled erect and stood facing us where we had halted, obviously weighing up the advisability of a charge in that direction or a swift withdrawal from the scene. I feel sure it could not have seen us, but a change in the wind direction might have carried a whiff of human taint and warned the beast of danger threatening.

I was hunting lions, not rhinoceros. I experienced no temptation to injure this beast, but merely wished to observe its reaction to our close proximity. So I waited, fully prepared to shoot if the need arose. Several minutes passed. The bull appeared still undecided what to do, but finally made up its mind. It started towards us at a walk, broke into a lumbering trot and lowered its head; and now we knew that it intended to take offensive action. It was, of course, unwise to continue being inquisitive. I aimed with deliberation and killed the bull with the first bullet, before it broke into a gallop for the final stage of the charge or "demonstration". The specimen was not a particularly good trophy, so I regretted being the instrument of ending its life; but dictates of self-preservation ordained this curtain to the chance encounter.

Very often a rhinoceros, after being hit with a bullet in a vital part of its anatomy, will perform a queer kind of death-waltz. This is generally a sure indication of imminent death, but not always the case. It is far wiser and safer therefore to take no chances and give the beast a "settler", otherwise it may still be capable of causing casualties. As the animal falls dead, frequently may be heard, as I have experienced, a screaming whistle not dissimilar to the escape of steam from a locomotive. As a human being dies with a deep sigh, I presume that this whistling sound is the death-sigh of a rhinoceros but magnified because of the greater size of the beast.

Once I was ordered to Makindu as prosecutor in a most unsavoury criminal case. The four accused were Asians employed on the railway, and the details of the charges filed against them were especially revolting. The Town Magistrate of Nairobi, Ranald Donald, travelled with me by train to adjudicate. Many witnesses were called for the Crown; still more for the defence; and all were prepared to commit perjury shamelessly. In consequence, the trial detained us at the Dak Bungalow in Makindu for a matter of four days.

Makindu is on the Tsavo Plains, about 211 miles from Mombasa and 119 miles from Nairobi. This was a noted area for big-game and bird shooting. Lion, rhinoceros, buffalo and elephant were then abundant thereabouts. The area now constitutes the eastern boundary of the Tsavo National Park—a fairly recent creation and the scene of great devastation during the past few years committed by gangs of African poachers, against whom drastic measures have had to be taken—with some success. Views from Makindu of the rounded summits of the volcanic Kyulu Hills and of the snow-capped heights of Mt. Kilimanjaro (sixty miles distant) are entrancing. During clear weather from some points on the Kyulu Hills I have seen Kilimanjaro to the southwards and Mt. Kenya to the northwards.

In my opinion the bird shooting around Makindu was then

quite unexcelled by any offering elsewhere in East Africa. I always found this to be true. Early each morning, before the Court sat, and once again after tea, Donald and I went out to enjoy a couple of hours with our shotguns. The "bags" were always large and of great variety—greater and lesser bustard, francolin of diverse sub-species, guineafowl, spurfowl, sandgrouse, quail and snipe figured regularly in our shoots. It was rare to return with less than a hundred birds, and several times the total was double of that. Every day we despatched birds to friends at Nairobi, and their recipients must have been truly sorry when our duties at Makindu terminated.

On the last morning's shoot a fool rhinoceros butted into the picture and completely ruined our sport. We would not have minded this so much if the beast had refrained from committing graver sins. Armed only with 12-bore shotguns we were placed at a decided disadvantage in coping with the situation, and, further-more; neither of us had anticipated bumping unexpectedly into any kind of serious trouble. Our gun-bearers had been left behind at Makindu. We had only taken with us four local Africans to carry back any birds shot; and my two smooth-coated fox terriers, both grand sporting and courageous dogs, completed the party. The dogs had taught themselves to point and retrieve as to the manner born, and became really first-class gundogs.

I had just shot a brace of sandgrouse when a much disturbed rhinoceros bull emerged from the bush and galloped over a path all-out for me. Neither Donald nor I had the slightest inkling that any of this species was anywhere near at hand, so it caught us wholly unprepared. There was only one thing to be done, and that without any loss of time. Each shinned up the nearest tree as speedily as able, unmindful of cruel thorns lacerating our flesh during an undignified ascent—even these were preferable to having the horn of a rhinoceros thrust through the body. Unfor-tunately, I dropped the shotgun in my haste to attain a safe refuge in the tree.

Once out of reach of this infuriated rhinoceros, time was avail-able for taking stock of the situation and learning how Donald had fared. He also was aloft in a tree, but had retained possession of his shotgun. He shouted across to me that there was only one unexpended cartridge in the gun and his ammunition bag had been dropped when climbing the tree. I suggested that he should conserve this one shot to tickle up the beast, in case it marooned us for an unconscionable time. He laughed and called back: "Fat lot of use a No. 4 would be!"

The birds shot that morning had been abandoned by the four Africans, who now were also safely perched in other trees. The rhinoceros advanced warily to the heap and sniffed at it. A moment later it set to work in making mincemeat of the birds in a most thorough manner; and, having done so, next turned its attention to my shotgun, sniffed it, and tossed the weapon skywards. As it landed, the beast proceeded to stamp upon the gun. I groaned unhappily, for that shotgun was by Daniel Fraser of Edinburgh and had cost me sixty guineas. Time and again, the brute repeated this unpleasantry; when finished with its new toy and bored with it, that shotgun was not worth sixpence. I could have wept.

Nothing could be seen or heard of my two terriers, and I wondered what could have happened to them. Later, it was found that they considered discretion to be the better part of valour and had made a beeline for Makindu. Wise little dogs, too!

The rhinoceros now advanced to my tree and had a good sniff at its bole. I climbed higher into the long-thorned acacia tree. My refuge proved not only most uncomfortable but terribly painful, and for some days afterwards I was kept busy upon extracting tooth-pick thorns from my body. Many of them had broken off short and the points were deeply imbedded in the flesh, so these had to be cut out with the blade of a sharp knife. It was a painful process. We were forced to remain as unwilling prisoners in our respective trees. My temper was severely frayed. The gross absurdity of our predicament did not make any sort of appeal to my Irish sense of humour. Indeed, I was *not* amused! All I wanted was to become revenged upon our cantankerous jailer and be free to make our way back to Makindu. Neither was a possibility. And we were now long overdue in Court to conclude the trial of the four prisoners.

I shouted across to Donald and suggested that he should tickle up the posterior of the rhinoceros with his sole remaining shell. I was hungry and wanted my breakfast. But he bluntly refused to expend the cartridge on such a futile purpose. The beast now appeared to have come to an anchor at the base of my tree and inclined to enjoy a siesta for a time. Another hour passed slowly, and the animal had not moved but seemed to be asleep; and by that time we both had had our fill of being tied to perches in trees, felt thirsty and hungry, limbs cramped, bodies converted into thorn-cushions, bored and angry about our predicament, and were desperately eager to be rid of this pestilential rhinoceros. Once more I suggested a shot at the broad rump of the rhinoceros in the hope that this might wake up the beast and send it off from our vicinity. Donald agreed. He was now desperate and ready to do anything likely to secure release from his painful perch aloft.

Probably the animal was more startled by the sudden discharge of the shotgun than hurt by any of the small lead pellets, for its hide was so tough that the shot could not have achieved more than tickle. It did prove, however, instantly effective. The ugly brute woke up with a loud and angry snort; then, to our intense relief, trotted off into the thick bush and vanished from sight. We waited a full fifteen minutes before descending to ground-level. Having retrieved any reasonably sound remnants of our property, we hurried back to Makindu for a belated breakfast before resuming the Court's sitting. On the way we kept a watchful eye for our tormentor or any others of its kind, but saw none.

Immediately after the Court had delivered judgment and imposed a heavy sentence upon all the prisoners, we agreed to go back and try to extract retribution from that annoying rhinoceros. The indignities and sufferings inflicted upon us called for some kind of drastic punishment. Both felt convinced that the particular beast could be recognized again with ease, for ample time had been given us to note every single characteristic of its personal appearance.

After two hours' spooring, our quarry was located in the dry bed of a small stream. It died to Donald's first shot. Neither of us had the slightest compunction over that killing. It had been guilty of flagrant "Contempt of Court".

The majority of my encounters with this species were practically unsought and unpremeditated. It was seldom that I had any special wish to kill them and, in most instances, merely acted in self-defence or in protection of private property. On a number of occasions a rhinoceros was met on open plains or in bush-country when I was not engaged upon hunting. The animals insisted upon joining battle and made themselves such unmitigated nuisances, that it became imperative to put an end to their nonsense. I could quote a number of incidents where a spirit of aggressiveness was displayed to their own ultimate disadvantage.

There was an occasion when I was returning to Nairobi from a duty *safari* to Fort Hall, and we were marching across the plains because this was a shorter and more interesting route than following the rough track alleged to be the roadway. The porter-*safari* was passing the base of El Donyo Sabuk mountain (7,000 feet) when a rhinoceros suddenly launched an attack upon us. When least expected, a bull appeared from behind a large clump of bushes and acacia thorn-trees. It advanced menacingly in our direction. The loaded porters, marching in single file, did not like the look of things one little bit. The beast was too distant to have seen us. It probably heard the porters chanting or got a whiff of man-tainted wind. This old and cantankerous rhinoceros seemed to resent strongly our advent in its preserves, so at once launched a violent onslaught upon the cause of its irritation.

If I had been allowed any choice, the ensuing argument would have been sidestepped—even though the beast carried an exceptionally long and slender anterior horn, a far better trophy than others falling to my rifle. Moreover, I was in the Ukamba Province and at that time this species was rigidly protected by the Government. No specimen was permitted to be shot in the Province. But a ca'canny policy was denied to me for the rhinoceros was spoiling for a fight. It got what it wanted.

The animal's ponderous and resolute advance at a walk quickly changed into a brisk trot. The head was lowered, tail held erect, and the charge delivered at a gallop straight for the line of porters. Rather than have one of them injured, I fired a bullet into the ground just in front of its forefeet in the hope of turning the beast off its course, which generally proves quite effective. But I might just as well have saved that cartridge. Instead of turning the animal, the whine of the bullet ricocheting past its head only infuriated it still more and the speed of the charge was stepped up. The porters had halted to stare at the beast, seemingly undecided whether to stand fast or bolt for the nearest refuge.

Head well down now, it was obviously bent upon mischief. This was no time to indulge in any pandering to sentimentality, so I shot again and the bullet hit the base of the anterior horn. But this neither halted nor turned the animal. It held on its way straight for the centre of the string of halted porters, as if nothing more than a fly had stung it. This proved too much for the nerves of the porters. They dropped their loads to the ground, fled incontinently to the nearest trees, and climbed aloft. Hamisi shouldered up to me, second rifle loaded and thrust forward to make a swift exchange of weapons. I was using a .350 Rigby Mauser, but Hamisi carried the .450/.500 Holland and Holland, and now I changed weapons with the gun-bearer. The rhinoceros was too quickly upon me for any hope of hitting it in a vital spot with a bullet from the light rifle; that chance had been sacrificed by my reluctance to kill one of the species in a prohibited area.

The bull reached the loads scattered on the veld, braked down on its lumbering gallop, and slid to a halt in order to investigate this peculiar collection of litter. I fired a glancing shot at its rump, after changing rifles again with Hamisi, in the hope that this might induce the beast to seek pastures new. The prospect of my personal effects being converted into playthings for a rhinoceros, and seriously damaged in the process, made no sort of appeal. Still I wished for its room and not company, and had no desire to be forced into killing the animal. The flesh wound seemed to make the beast more determined to wreck everything handy, and it proceeded to do this in a thorough and methodical manner.

Each time that I went forward to drive the beast away from my property, it swung around upon Hamisi and myself with a definite threat of charging home. We were compelled to retire. Sometimes we had to run fast for cover behind a tree; and once there, the rhinoceros halted midway between the loads and ourselves. A moment or two later it went back to its playthings. Judging by the yells and loud laughter of the porters in nearby trees, our undignified retreats were affording them immense entertainment. We were being held up to ridicule by this fool beast, and both deeply resented the fact.

As all well-intentioned efforts to scare away this animal had failed I shot at its neck from behind a tree and brought it down. Another bullet from closer range ended its vicious life. But I wished that the killing of this pugnacious creature had not been a necessity. The trophy must be surrendered to the Game Department because it was secured in a prohibited area; but a plea of self-defence was accepted when all the circumstances had been explained.

It required some time to reassemble the grinning porters, gather up the widely scattered remnants of their loads, and resume our interrupted march Nairobi-wards. The damage done by this idiotic and malicious beast had been considerable. My valise of bedding and its contents were badly torn, ridge-pole of my tent fractured in three places, and chop-boxes of foodstuff spilled about the veld. Seeing that I was on duty and had been made to surrender the trophy, I submitted a claim for compensation to the Government. This was bluntly disallowed.

During the Sotik Punitive Expedition in 1905 I was out on patrol with an officer of the 3rd battalion of the King's African Rifles and a small body of troops. He was recently arrived in East Africa and had no experience at all of big-game hunting. Each carried a rifle. We were together at some distance ahead of the troops. Without any warning a rhinoceros charged us viciously over the crest of a low ridge. Neither of us had seen nor heard it until it burst into sight as it breasted the ridge at a distance of roughly thirty yards. The instant my sights came on I shot, and down went the beast on knees and stomach. We stood still, waiting for it to rise and resume the charge. But the bull was dead.

My companion was hugely elated, though the trophy belonged to me. The animal had fallen in such a position that there was offered a realistic picture of a rhinoceros actually charging over the crest of the ridge. He begged me to take a photograph of him when recording a close-up picture of a "charging rhinoceros", as he wanted to send a print to his fiancée in London. I agreed to become a party to this deception. The resulting negative proved a lifelike record of exactly what was most desired by him; and, no doubt, the girl marvelled at his courage in facing a charging rhinoceros, when armed only with a camera. Human nature is ever frail! In this case a fake photograph harmed no one.

Not long after my arrival in East Africa I joined a friend on a shooting *safari* over the Uasin Gishu Plateau. Much against my will, I was compelled to kill a family group of rhinoceros—sire, dam and three-quarters grown son. For some inexplicable reason they persisted in disputing the line of march of our *safari*. It is possible that they had winded us, but I am doubtful about this being the correct explanation of what transpired. They approached suddenly over a slight rise, and we had not the least suspicion of their nearby presence until they showed themselves. All three halted upon the crest of the ridge for several minutes, staring speculatively at the porters as the *safari* trailed in single file before their grandstand. I hoped their intentions were to leave us severely alone and make off elsewhere. On our part, at any rate, we proposed to ignore them completely—this not being due to snobbishness, but because the year's quota of this species on our game licences had been secured. No more could be shot without incurring the penalty imposed under the game laws in current force. The horns of the bull were worthy ones. Since that day I often wished that this family had behaved more reasonably, for I much disliked having to kill the trio.

Their inherent curiosity gained the upper hand. It induced them to advance and investigate the *safari* at close quarters. I held the rifle ready for action, but was loth to take the initiative; and all we wanted was to proceed in peace and not to have unwelcome visitors forced upon us. Yet when they had come unpleasantly close and still displayed no inclination to sheer off, I asked my companion to shoot into the ground in advance of the three beasts in the hope that this would send them off at speed. But it failed.

The trio charged full tilt at the porters. I have no great objection to the unwanted and unsolicited attentions of a single rhinoceros, but three of them charging in line abreast does make an uncomfortable crowd. I fired across their bows, but this served only to accelerate the charge. They were as obstinate as mules. Obviously their minds had been made up to wreck our *safari*; and, as this was more than prepared to suffer, we felt forced to adopt offensive tactics. I killed the bull with the first bullet, and trusted that this might have the effect of making his widow and heir beat a hasty retreat. That was expecting too much, of course, of the poor intelligence of this species. The cow and big lout of a son charged the porters, who promptly dropped their loads and fled to a place of comparative security.

My companion shot at the cow, hitting her but not halting the charge. Then the mechanism of his rifle jammed, and the balance of the fight was up to me as he had no second weapon to fall back upon. Hamisi stood stolidly at my elbow with the .450/.500 rifle held ready for rapid exchange for the .350 Rigby Mauser. Seeing that they intended serious business, I killed the cow as she tossed a roll of bedding skywards. Her foolish offspring had got well home upon a chop-box filled with imported delicacies in tins; and wrecked this, as also three other boxes of food, my tent, and a case of whisky which I was taking to the District Commissioner at Baringo at his urgent request.

The youngster was old enough to have known better, but obviously lacking in grey-matter. All this damage had been per- petrated before I was able to get an unobstructed aim at a vital spot in the lout's body. Then it ambled up close to the dead cow in quest of more toys to smash up. A bullet into the heart ended permanently its mischievous career.

I had used every known device to scare this family of rhinoceros away from the *safari* before shooting to kill, but everything had failed in its purpose. The beasts had been their own worst enemies. Such a nonsensical display of ill-manners and destruc- tiveness had not only to be checked but also severely punished. Stupid, stupid animals not to have accepted a broad hint to go away!

From all this it should be possible to appreciate that the black rhinoceros can frequently behave in an unpleasantly objection- able manner. The species is not every man's friend. But I have never been able to rate it high on my list of the "dangerous" beasts in Africa.

20

Near-Tragedies with Elephants

I shall remember while the light yet lives,
And in the night time I shall not forget.

SWINBURNE: *Erosion*

IT IS inevitable that there should occur some experiences in the career of a persistent elephant-hunter which can never be

forgotten by the man involved in them. Mishaps, near-disasters
or tragedies cannot be eliminated entirely. Survival is often a
matter of sheer good luck, or else can be attributed only to the
courageous conduct of a faithful gun-bearer. The tally of the
latter instances is not inconsiderable.

Hamisi bin Baraka, my stout-hearted gun-bearer for six years,
was a Swahili from the coast region of Kenya Colony (then the
British East Africa Protectorate) and an African of the very best
type. Once, as related previously, he suffered some fractured ribs,
severe bruising and shock when coming bravely to my rescue while
faced with grievous danger from a bull elephant which I had
wounded but not killed outright.

The second episode, with which I am now concerned, was staged
on the west bank of the Nile and in the then Belgian Lado Enclave
(now West Nile district of Uganda). Although it happened half a
century ago, yet every single detail of the incident is still remembered vividly. Indeed, it would be difficult to forget that particular
day's events.

If an ivory hunter goes on too long after elephant in Africa, the
chances are strong that disaster will eventually overtake him.
Suddenly, at a critical moment his nerve fails. He stands helplessly
to face a charge. He is either killed outright or grievously injured.
I know of three such tragedies occurring to very experienced
hunters, who were either friends or acquaintances of mine. Con-
sidering the number of my contemporaries who had the misfortune
either to be killed or maimed by an elephant hunted by them, I
regard myself as extremely fortunate in having escaped a similar
fate. There is a French proverb applicable: "The pitcher goes so
often to the well that at length it breaks."

I had been hunting for ivory in the Lugwari country of the Lado
Enclave for several months, without a licence because it was next
to impossible to procure one from the Belgian authorities there
or in Brussels. In doing so, I was in good company. A small band
of hardy adventurers was based along the east bank in Uganda,
from where they were making hunting safaris into the region on
the west bank. They found it extremely rewarding and profitable.
That epic period in the history of East-Central Africa, from 1902
to 1912, can never again be repeated. It is of the distant past.

We all travelled light and lived rough. We were hunting in a
fiendishly bad climate, and amongst savage tribes who recognized
neither law nor order, and who sometimes proved treacherous or
unreliable. Moreover, there existed an ever-present danger of
being captured by an armed patrol of Belgian askaris (soldiers)
and the consequent punishment meted out to a transgressor could
be extremely severe. But the tribes hated the Belgian officials,

suffered much from the oppressive acts of their *askari* and, generally speaking, were ready to warn a hunter of the nearness of any Belgian patrol searching for him.

Now with a *safari* of African followers and a very large collection of heavy tusks, I was headed back to the Nile in order to contact a fleet of canoes at an agreed rendezvous. They would transport us across the river to my base camp at Wadelai in Uganda. I had been warned by Chief Issa of the Lugwari that a strong patrol of Belgian *askari* under a European officer was pursuing us, but still about two days' march in rear. We had travelled fast, making about 25 to 30 miles a day. There remained only forty-five miles to be covered in order to gain the rendezvous with the canoes. I intended to arrive there in two more days' forced marching.

We bivouacked for the night. I had issued instructions for the *safari* to march forward at three hours next morning, and all must be in readiness to take the road not later than that time. During the evening and night I constantly heard the loud trumpeting of a herd of elephants near our bivouac. The temptation to go after this herd at dawn in case one or more heavy-tusked bulls could be killed was not to be resisted. I knew this to be taking an unwarranted risk of capture by the pursuing patrol. My haul of ivory did not warrant any show of greed to add other tusks to it; but the decision was made to hunt that herd before crossing over the Nile into Uganda. Frequently, I had covered on foot forty miles in a day; and now reckoned that just the one day's hunting would suffice.

The *niapara* (headman) of the *safari* was despatched on his way at the appointed hour with the personal servants, main body of porters, all the ivory and our other loads. His instructions were to travel fast to the canoes, embark and cross over the Nile to Wadelai, and then send back two canoes to await my arrival at the rendezvous. Having seen them clear of the bivouac site, I started back just before dawn to search for the herd of elephants. Hamisi (the gun-bearer), and two expert Zande trackers, and eight of the best of the Wanyamwezi porters accompanied me. The intention was to travel light and live rough.

For two hours or more we progressed through high and rank grass, towering above our heads, and where the air was suffocatingly hot. It felt like being in the hot-room of a Turkish bath. At times, we were threading our way through dense patches of thorn-scrub and grass about waist-high. Then the sun, having risen well into the brazen dome of blue sky overhead, blazed down upon us pitilessly and made me extremely thirsty though the African companions seemed not to be similarly afflicted.

The Zande trackers were performing a difficult and intricate spooring of this herd. The tracks were abundant. They wandered hither and thither. The spoor was also liberally criss-crossed by many similar tracks: some ancient but others recent. The trackers disentangled the maze of huge footprints and heaped droppings with an amazing degree of dexterity, leading us unerringly over the correct spoor. Such expert spooring was quite beyond the capacity of Hamisi or myself.

Next they located the spoor of a large and solitary bull, and the size of its padmark indicated that this beast might well be carrying a pair of heavy tusks. But this does not always prove the case. Several times I had been deceived. On closing with the quarry I perceived that it was a huge bull but endowed only with unrewarding ivory. This bull was keeping a course close to, and more or less parallel with, the spoor of the main herd. I decided to go after the lone bull and, after dropping it, then follow up the herd in the hope of killing any other good tuskers. Obviously, we were not far in rear of this bull and steadily reducing the gap between us. It was travelling fast, at about six miles an hour, and luckily up-wind. We kept at a jog-trot in its wake.

Presently we began to traverse a wide and swampy valley, flanked by low and timbered ridges. The going proved rough and tough. The trackers advanced at an effortless trot over the spoor, never once being at a loss. An hour later I glimpsed the slate-grey bulk of our quarry, now standing immobile and broadside on in a patch of shoulder-high grass and scattered acacia thorn-trees. It was about 200 yards distant. We halted immediately, tested the wind direction, and found it favourable; and then, with Hamisi shouldering up, I crept forward to get within about thirty paces from the bull before taking the brain shot from a side. The tusks looked like 100lb or more each. Indeed, a worthy prize to collect!

Suddenly and inexplicably, the beast wheeled about and headed away from us at right angles. We trotted after it. The bull moved fast through high grass, but gradually we closed up. Now and again, a glimpse of its massive posterior ahead of us proved reassuring. At the far extremity of the valley the quarry turned off to the right and began to follow an old elephant-path, which was worn deep and badly rutted by the passage of generations of huge feet.

The path twisted about a lot. Advancing cautiously around an abrupt turn to the right, I suddenly came face to face with the bull, which inexplicably was now retracing its steps. The huge ears were fully extended and tip of trunk curled inwards to the fore-knees—a positive indication that a lethal charge was imminent. I shot between the eyes for the brain, but the bullet hit a trifle too high or low of the vital spot. It failed to kill the beast. The frontal brain shot was never my *forte*, having been bungled far more times than meeting with success. I disliked being forced to rely upon it, but there was no option. With a scream of fury, the bull charged. I fired again into the chest, as the trunk was now extended to grab hold of me, which deflected it off course; and then the bull whipped around to make off at speed back along the path. We ran fast after the bull.

For about thirty minutes we kept relentlessly in its wake over most unpleasant ground to run upon, and I began to despair of being able to deliver a merciful despatch. We were running through a tunnel of fifteen-foot-high elephant grass. Round a bend I was suddenly confronted by a bull endowed with tusks of good weight; but knew instinctively that this animal was not the one which I had wounded twice. The risk of losing the original quarry by shooting this bull had to be accepted in the circumstances. Once more I attempted the only shot possible, the frontal brain one, and again muffed it. The bull checked in its charge, which afforded me time to leap aside into the high grass and from there fire a bullet into the beast's brain as it stood broadside on. The bull went down on head and fore-knees, as if pole-axed, and then rolled over on to a flank. The bullet had killed instantly. Later, it was found that the pair of tusks weighed 85 and 82 lb. respectively.

Positively, this was not my original quarry. I had yet to locate, and kill if possible, the wounded bull—the unwritten law of big-game hunting. Half of the porters were left behind to hack out the tusks from the carcase, and also wait at the spot until we rejoined them. Then, with Hamisi and one Zande tracker, I ran onwards in quest of the other bull. We found it waiting for us about half a mile further on; and the bull immediately charged from a distance of about forty yards. There still seemed a great deal of life in the animal.

It was impracticable to withdraw or get in a fatal brain shot from a side; scarcely even time to bring rifle to shoulder before its bulk towered above me. I shot into the chest, hoping to take lungs and heart or at least divert its course. Then I threw myself back into the high grass beside the path. Hamisi, carrying my .350 Rigby Mauser, did likewise at the same moment; and the enraged bull braked in front of me. I felt myself seized about the waist by its trunk, then being brandished violently from side to side several times. I dropped the .256 Mannlicher-Schoenauer and strove to cling on to the tusks. The next instant I was flung hard on the ground. The bull knelt to stab at my body with the tusks, but luckily failed in its purpose. Grasping a foreleg with both arms, I managed to drag myself under its chest; and, as the bull came erect again, clutched desperately at a hindleg. The bull reached round with its trunk, seized an ankle, and forcibly plucked me from this hold. Once more I was swung on high, head hanging downwards, and then flung with considerable violence upon the ground.

Somehow I managed to grasp the tusks and drew my body up until it was clear of the ground; and thus swung like a pendulum while clinging with all my waning strength. Every instant I expected to be my last. High above the shrill screaming of the infuriated elephant I heard the sharp report of a rifle discharged from close quarters. The bull stood still, swayed drunkenly, took a step or two forward, crumbled on head and fore-knees, and then rolled over sideways. As it fell, I succeeded in swinging myself clear of that six tons of bone and flesh. But it was a mighty near tragedy!

The next thing remembered is that I was lying beside the dead beast and head pillowed against Hamisi's shoulder. I drank greedily from the water-bottle of cold tea, milkless and sugarless, held by him to my parched lips. I heard him say casually: "The bull is dead, *Bwana mkubwa* (Great master)!"

After a short rest I recovered sufficiently to stand erect. Miraculously, no bones had been fractured; but my body was severely bruised and my muscles badly strained. Except for Hamisi's gallant action, my hunting career would surely have been ended that day. Indeed, it was a marvel that I had not been killed. Hamisi was rewarded subsequently with half the proceeds of the sale of this pair of tusks, and that only his just due. The tusks of this animal weighed 105 and 99 lb. respectively, being sold later to a Greek trader at Nimule in Uganda for £130; while the first pair collected realized £105. All things being considered, that was a remunerative day's hunting for ivory! The Government collected 25 per cent. customs dues on all ivory brought for sale into Uganda from the Lado Enclave by any of these hardy elephant-hunters; even so, they found their enterprise financially rewarding.

The other Africans had bolted. But Hamisi, true to his character, stood fast to render me such help as lay in his power. He could always be trusted to face up courageously to any kind of desperate situation confronting us. Now he made me sit down and rest while searching for the errant African followers, who were soon collected by him and given the task of hacking out the tusks.

That prolonged tramp back to the previous night's bivouac was a ghastly business for me, and had to be tackled at a slow pace. Hour after hour, I plodded onwards while enduring excruciating pain; and it was sundown when our destination came in sight. Awaiting us we found a messenger from Chief Issa to warn me that the Belgian patrol was now only a day's march away. There remained only one thing to do, and that continue our journey to the Nile through the night and all next day. Fortunately, I was in good physical trim and tough. We covered that forty-five miles and gained the canoes during the second night. We immediately embarked, and were paddled quickly across the river to the landing-stage below my base-camp at Wadelai. The pursuing Belgian patrol had been left far in rear.

For the next three days Hamisi expertly massaged me until body and muscles were in good shape again. On the early morning of the fourth day the *safari* headed along the east bank to the Uganda *boma* at Nimule, where my large stock of heavy tusks was sold to a Greek trader at a gratifying price. A week later, having rested and refitted, we were back at Wadelai, crossed over the Nile, and again hunting for ivory in the Lugwari country for a month. It proved equally as rewarding financially, while nothing occurred to mar the pleasures of pitting my wits against those of herds of wild elephants; and, moreover, we suffered no interference by any Belgian patrols.

It may be surprising that so many elephants carrying a pair of tusks weighing about 100 lb. or over could be found at that time in the Lado Enclave. Herds were of an immense size and likewise the total elephant population enormous; they had not been persecuted overmuch; and many bulls had been allowed to attain a great age with a consequent growth of large tusks of good weight. It needs, possibly, a hundred years for a bull to grow teeth of 100 lb. or more. These animals have little chance of survival for any length of time because, as soon as their whereabouts becomes known, all hunters are avid to get such prizes in "the bag".

At the present time, indeed, any elephant shot which carries tusks of 100 lb. or better can rightly be deemed a "rare bird".

21

Rogue Elephant Tragedy

THE last elephant I personally killed was in the Akuma (now Zoka) Forest of Uganda, situated about midway between Nimule and Gondokoro on the east bank of the Nile. The incident ended in a ghastly tragedy. I vowed then never again to hunt for ivory or shoot an elephant except in self-defence, and that has been honoured scrupulously throughout the past half century. I then substituted a camera for a rifle. The reason for this reversal of policy in regard to personal relations with this grand creature will be understood, I think, after reading what happened that day close to the mighty Nile.

The encounter was utterly unanticipated. Neither my loyal and courageous gun-bearer, Hamisi bin Baraka, nor I had any cause to suspect a "rogue" elephant bull was around. Had it been otherwise, that day would have concluded differently and less disastrously. For what occurred neither he nor I could be blamed, only the elephant. It was punished suitably.

We were spooring a splendid buffalo bull, advancing silently over an old rhinoceros path through dense forest. Hamisi walked close upon my heels, carrying the .350 Rigby Mauser; and I was armed with my trusty .256 Mannlicher-Schoenauer, which I preferred to all other weapons, even for elephants. No sound shattered the intense stillness of that grim forest, save only our soft-footed tread and the warbling notes of birds in the treetops. I was deeply conscious of the intense hush. We trod virgin forest, seldom touched by the feet or hands of man: an age-old habitat of wild beasts. If we had wandered fifty yards off the game-path, as likely as not we should have regained it only by the merest chance. It was an eerie place—always in twilight, filled with queer smells and soft noises, and harbouring unfamiliar insects, reptiles, flitting small birds, and raucous-tongued creatures. Sudden death was all around us.

Life moved upon the face of its surface; also upon the treetops warmed by the sunshine and occasionally lashed by torrential tropical storms. But we saw it not. The creatures in this forest were free from mankind's idle curiosity, wanton persecution, and even reverent appreciation of their marvels. Over all brooded a mystic, almost menacing, silence which was so dense as to be unearthly. There came to our ears no sound save a rare bird's song from the gloomy depths, or an occasional crash as some wild beast, you knew not of what species, had heard our quiet movements through the dim aisles of giant tree-boles and bolted away.

Deserted it might seem. Yet nothing was more certain than that during every yard of our progress some forest-dwelling beast had its eyes fixed intently upon the intruders. However silently and stealthily we advanced, it was positive that they had heard or winded us. They had not waited for us to come to them. They had watched our approach, alert and ready for instant flight or bold attack. Then they vanished. We did not even hear their flight from the danger threatening them.

The scenery was wild and savage. So, too, were the beasts dwelling within this forest; and we walked over that game-path at our peril. We knew that well, too! Yet neither Hamisi nor I thought that we should be confronted with sudden death within the space of the next few minutes. Both were wholly unprepared.

I raised my eyes from the path after making a close scrutiny of the buffalo's spoor, and looked straight up at a huge elephant bull endowed with large and heavy tusks. Halting instantly, my rifle went automatically to the shoulder. The elephant had come silently and abruptly around a sharp bend in the path, not many yards ahead of us; and the instant it perceived two human beings the beast charged. There could be no possibility of doubting the deadly character of that vicious advance. It came at a fast pace, trunk hanging down to cover the chest and tip curled inwards; and a second more was in top-gear, screaming shrilly with hate, and trunk held straight out to seize one of us.

Standing my ground, I shot into the centre of the exposed chest from a range of less than fifty yards. It was futile to aim elsewhere. Indeed, no time was granted for being selective about the actual target taken. No bullet could have turned the bull in that narrow forest-walled pathway: certainly not one from a .256 Mannlicher. I knew myself to be up against the eternal law of the wilderness— either I killed this bull or it finished me, and possibly also Hamisi.

It staggered and dropped on the fore-knees to the shot; and, before able to rise erect, another bullet hit it between the eyes. I should much rather have fractured a knee, but this was not possible because the beast was upon both fore-knees. Before I was able to exchange the rifle for the .350 Rigby Mauser carried by Hamisi, the bull had regained its feet and was upon me. It could not have been more than ten yards distant, so I did the only thing possible. I fired blindly at it. The bullet did not have the slightest effect. I fully expected to hear Hamisi fire from my rear, but no shot came. The immense bulk of the bull towered over me, mouth open and screaming angrily, and tip of trunk questing for my body. The next moment I felt myself grabbed by the trunk around the waist, swung off the ground, and then hurled violently sky-wards. I landed with a nasty jolt in a nest of long and sharp-pointed thorns in the uppermost branches of a squat acacia tree.

As I was hurled out of the bull's way, I had dropped my rifle. I yelped at the excruciating pain caused by the sharp thorns, the size of a long toothpick, imbedded in my back, bottom and other portions of my body. Fortunately, no worse injury had befallen me. No bones were fractured. But the shirt had been ripped half off my chest, the skin grazed and bruised, and the rear portion of my body converted into a pin-cushion.

Regaining control of my wits, I struggled clear and dropped to the ground. I landed on hands and knees. At that same moment I heard an agonized scream from Hamisi. I do not know what actually happened, but think he must have about-turned to run for a safe refuge—most abnormal behaviour on his part. He was now some distance away. Scrambling erect, I saw Hamisi thrown to the ground and the elephant's massive bulk bestriding him; and then the bull began stabbing viciously with its long tusks, and trampling him savagely with the forefeet. Having recovered the dropped rifle and found its mechanism in perfect order, I hastily reloaded and ran to the aid of Hamisi. I had no clear idea of what to do for the best, but determined to save the life of my gallant gun-bearer if this was at all possible and drive away the "rogue" bull.

At almost point-blank range I shot under the root of the beast's tail, and followed this up with two more bullets into the same spot. This must have shaken the bull severely. I hoped one of the bullets might have raked the body to get the heart. It abandoned Hamisi, sped down the path, screaming shrilly, and tail well tucked in. That was the last I saw of the bull. Two days later, my trackers found its carcase and collected the pair of tusks—85 and 91 lb. of ivory. My loyal Hamisi had been avenged. Yet I experienced no pleasure from the acquisition of those two worthy tusks. Indeed, gladly would I have given them and a great deal more as well if thereby Hamisi could have been restored to me uninjured.

Immediately the bull had gone, I knelt down beside the gun-bearer to do all in my power for him. It needed only a glance at his terribly mangled and battered body to assure me that he was beyond all human help. The elephant had gored and crushed him almost out of any resemblance to a human body. The wicked tusks had disembowelled Hamisi; both legs and arms were fractured in several places; and the spot where he lay, scarcely breathing, had been converted into a blood-soaked shambles. Even the spare cartridges, carried in slots on his shirt-front, were bent and twisted almost double. Afterwards I found the Mauser rifle at some distance away and still in a perfectly sound working order. I fancy he must have dropped it when running away from the bull. How much I wished that the beast had picked upon the rifle instead of expending its violence of rage upon my incomparable gun-bearer.

But the angry beast had left behind not a human body, only a pulped mass of flesh and broken bones. I did everything possible to ease his passing. He died as I moistened his twitching lips with cold tea from my waterbottle. His eyes opened and stared into mine. A faint sigh, a light and convulsive shudder, and Hamisi had ended his last *safari* and six faithful years' service with me.

He had been an excellent gun-bearer, courageous and always

dependable. We had shared many especially tense moments; always stood shoulder to shoulder; and never once had he failed me or given less than of his best. I felt broken-hearted at his death. Although aware that nothing could have averted his inexorable fate, yet I wished that Hamisi's end could have been more kind and far less painful. I knew myself blameless for what had occurred, but this gave me no consolation.

As I stood over his horribly mutilated remains, I vowed that never again would elephants be hunted by me to kill them.

Night was closing in on the forest when we buried Hamisi near where he died and within the grim shadows cast by giant trees. The grave was not far distant from the life-giving waters of the mighty Nile. This sad task completed, we retraced our way back to camp. My thoughts were crushing. No more should I have this splendid African at my elbow; no more listen to, and heed, his sage advice when hunting big-game; and never again be able to enjoy his sturdy companionship and silent understanding. He could no longer share with me the bitter disappointments or heartening triumphs that are the lot of every hunter. His loss over- whelmed me. That night in camp my African followers, the majority of whom had served me continuously almost for as long a period as Hamisi, did not raise their voices in customary singing beside the log-fires; but all remained dumb and despondent, chattering only in low tones. Hamisi had been greatly admired and respected by them all. They, too, would miss him grievously.

In my recollections of the years of hunting big-game in Africa, with rifle or camera, the only regret of which I am conscious is the tragic death of my faithful gun-bearer, Hamisi bin Baraka. That will be understood by other hunters.

Whatever the modern-day standards of gun-bearers may be, this can be said in all truth of the gallant body of Africans who blazed the trail for the present generation—they were the unsung heroes of countless shooting *safaris*. In my younger years it was a common enough occurrence for an African gun-bearer courageously to risk his own life or a severe mauling by going immediately to the aid of an employer who was in grave peril. I do not think it has ceased to be true. Indeed, there have been recorded during comparatively recent times a number of cases of this heroic conduct on the part of gun-bearers. For instance, not long ago in Tanganyika two gun- bearers were each awarded the George Medal for saving their master's life when the latter was being badly mauled by a wounded lion. Those honours were richly deserved. One only regrets that others before them were not similarly decorated for their heroism.

Hamisi bin Baraka was one of that gallant breed of Africans. Indeed, he was one of the pioneers in his craft. Throughout his service with me as a gun-bearer he always proved an expert, efficient, and a supremely brave comrade in hunting. I rated him as highly capable and intelligent, and a past-master of his special craft. Always he stood staunchly at my elbow and ready for a quick exchange of rifles, no matter how nerve-racking might be the incident. That was his job, and for which employed by me; but I always felt that he earned far more than just his monthly wages. Anyhow, he won my wholehearted respect and liking.

Consider for a moment what an efficient gun-bearer is expected to do. For a hunter to go up to a wounded individual of any of the "dangerous" major species is a highly perilous business; and it always possesses elements of great uncertainty as to the ultimate outcome of the obligation to deliver a merciful despatch. As often as not, it also entails a grim fight to a finish of either the man or beast. The part which the gun-bearer is called upon to play must be little less than supremely nerve-racking for him. His duty is to stand up close to the elbow of the hunter, with the second rifle held ready for a rapid and expert exchange, and just look on while the encounter is in progress. He must depend for his own safety upon an employer shooting straight and in not losing his head. The gun-bearer must not shoot on his own initiative until it happens to become imperative to do so. In a great many cases, too, he could complete the task far more quickly and efficiently than the man employing him.

Should his master happen to bungle the encounter, always a thing liable to happen at times even with experts and about a fifty-fifty chance in the case of novices, the gun-bearer stands precisely the same danger of being mauled or killed as the hunter. Records have proved abundantly that it was often the courage of an African gun-bearer which saved a sportsman from a nasty situation and preserved his life. Too often this gallant conduct was not rewarded as it so richly deserved to be.

When you have discovered, as I did in Hamisi, a gun-bearer who will always face at your elbow, courageously and unflinchingly, a succession of perilous contingencies, then you cannot include such a type of man in the category of a hireling. I never did so. On the contrary, I always regarded and treated Hamisi as a friend, who was also a brave and trusty comrade in adventure. I honestly believed that he actually enjoyed sharing with me the worst sort of dangers; if he did not, then his true character was misjudged. I am quite positive that such a mistake was not made.

Such types of Africans are fully entitled to be treated as friends and not solely as hired men. That is how they regard you—as a friend more than as an employer. Indubitably, Hamisi and I were always intimate friends during the six years he devoted himself to my service; and I would have hated to think of him in any other way. He belonged to the old and fine types of Africans who, alas, seem now to have become very rare. You came genuinely to like, respect and admire Africans of his sterling calibre. I only wish it could be possible for me to say the same truthfully of the present generation of this race. I find difficulty in doing so.

In that respect, too, we genuine old-timers in Africa knew the best of services rendered by gun-bearers, personal servants, *niaparas* (headmen) and porters. As regards the African trackers, none among the modern generation, with very few exceptions, can measure up to the expertness and uncanny skill evinced by the old-time ones. I would make an exception of the members of the Wanderobo tribe, still primitive people and untouched by civilization, who hunt in exactly the same style as has been traditional to them throughout the ages. They still live by their hunting technique. Their craftsmanship continues unchanged and they are in every way as expert today as were their ancestors.

I have recorded scattered memories of hunting big-game as it was, not as it may be today. The modern generation does not hunt —that is, spoor and stalk a quarry—with no assistance except that forthcoming from gun-bearer or tracker. Hunters of my generation knew quite the best of it, and in that respect may well be envied. Yet in the main, hunting is unchanged in that it continues to follow the age-old law of the wilderness. Either you kill your quarry outright or you may suffer a mauling and possibly be killed yourself.

GLOSSARY

Names of African animals, birds and insects in Kiswahili

Animal, male	*Ndume*	Gazelle	*Paa*
(or meat)	*Nyama*	Goat	*Mbuzi*
Animals, wild	*Nyama za muritu*	Goose	*Bata ya Bukini*
Antelopes	*Nyama wakali (or Nyama)*	Guineafowl	*Kanga*
		Crested	*Kororo*
Bushbuck	*Bongo*	Hare	*Sangura*
Eland	*Mpofu (pl. Wapofu)*	Hawk (or Kite)	*Mwewe*
Hartebeest	*Kongoni*	Hippopotamus	*Kiboko (pl. Viboko)*
Waterbuck	*Mkulu*		
Wildebeest	*Nyumbo*	Hoof	*Ukwato (pl. Kwato or Kwata)*
Ants	*Chungu (or Tungu)*		
Driver	*Siafu*	Hornet	*Manyiga*
White	*Mchwa*	Horse	*Farasi*
Ape or Baboon	*Nyani*	Hyena	*Fisi (or Nyangau)*
Birds	*Ndege*	Spotted	*Kingubwa*
Buck	*Swara*	Insects	*Mdudu (pl. Wadudu)*
Buffalo	*Mbogo (or Nyati)*		
Calf	*Ndama*	Leech	*Mruba (pl. Miruba)*
Carcase	*Mzoga*		
Cat	*Paka*	Leopard	*Chui*
Civet	*Fungo*	Lion	*Simba*
Large Civet	*Ngawa*	Lizard	*Mjusi (pl. Wajusi)*
Crane	*Korongo*	Monitor	*Kenge*
Crocodile	*Mende*	Locust	*Nzige*
Crow	*Kunguru*	Louse	*Chawa (or Tawa)*
Dog	*Mbwa*	Maggot	*Funza*
Wild Hunting	*Bize*	Mole	*Fuko*
Donkey	*Punda*	Mongoose	*Mchiro (pl. Wachiro)*
Dove	*Hua*		
Green	*Ninga*	Monkey	*Kima (or Nyanya)*
Small	*Pugi*	Colobus	*Mbega (pl. Wabega)*
Turtle	*Hua*		
Duck	*Bata*	Mosquito	*Mbu (pl. Umbu)*
Eagle	*Koho*	Mouse	*Panya*
Elephant	*Tembo (or Ndovu)*	Mule	*Nyumbu*
Ivory	*Pembe*	Ostrich	*Mbuni*
Large Tusk	*Buri*	Owl	*Bundi*
Fish	*Samaki*	Pig, Wild	*Jivi*
Flea	*Kiroboto (pl. Viroboto)*	Pigeon	*Njiwa*
		Porcupine	*Nungu*
Fly	*Inzi (pl. Mainzi)*	Python	*Chatu*
Sand-	*Usubi*	Rat	*Panya*
Fox, Bat-eared	*Mbwaha*	Large	*Buku*
Francolin	*Kwale*	Rhinoceros	*Kifaru*
Red-legged	*Karing'ende*	Scorpion	*Nge*
Frog	*Chula*	Sheep	*Kondoro*
Game animals	*Mawindo*	Skin	*Ngozi*

Snake	Nyoka (pl. Majoka)	Turkey	Bata mzinga (or
Swallow	Barawi		Nguruguru)
Tail	Mkia	Turtle	Kasa
Tick	Papasi	Hawkshead	Ug'amba (or
Cattle	Kupe		Fgamba)
Tortoise	Kobe	Zebra	Punda milia
Track or Spoor	Nyayo		